REVIEWS

M000267353

"Jule Selbo's book is the new gold standard for aspiring and professional screenwriters. Her book demystifies the process of turning a good story into a great screenplay. It's a must-read."

Gale Anne Hurd, Producer of **THE TERMINATOR** *trilogy,*
ALIENS, ARMAGEDDON, THE WATERDANCE

"This is a clear, savvy and inspired guide that will teach you the craft and business of screenwriting while keeping your creativity intact. I'm keeping this one on my shelf."

Jane Anderson, screenwriter/director **NORMAL, BABY DANCE,**
THE PRIZEWINNER OF DEFIANCE OHIO

"Whether for the novice or the experienced screenwriter, Jule Selbo has come up with a precise, pithy and down-to-earth approach to writing successful screenplays. Her Eleven Step Story Structure is a great paradigm that makes structure, the bugaboo of most beginning writers, a much easier concept to grasp."

Dale Pollock, Producer **A MIDNIGHT CLEAR, BLAZE, SET IT OFF,** *and more.*
Dean of the School of Filmmaking, North Carolina School of the Arts

"Jule Selbo has, quite simply, written the definitive guide for screenwriting. Clear, concise, and above all practical, The Eleven Step Story Structure is not only essential for the beginner, but also a crucial refresher for the working screenwriter. From the first glimmering of an idea to the often intimidating task of structuring and writing a screenplay, this book guides you through every step of the process with creative expertise."

Rosalind Moore, screenwriter, **HOME IMPROVEMENT,**
EIGHT SIMPLE RULES, IN CASE OF EMERGENCY

"Of all of the books on screenwriting—and on writing in general—that I have read, this is both the most concise and the most complete, helpful guide that I have encountered. I wish I had it when I started writing."

John Schimmel, Producer and President, Ascendant Pictures

"Selbo's book is a gift to every writer committed to crafting a great screenplay."

Janet S. Blake, former Vice President,
Writer Development & Special Projects,
the Walt Disney Company

"The care, wisdom and practical approach to writing a story from character really sets this apart from other screenwriting books. The combination of her clear, engaging style, choice of existing flims to illustrate her points and exercises to get the writer going makes this an invaluable guide to focus, shape and create compelling fresh screenplays. Before you write your first... or next screenplay—read this book."

Irene Mecchi—Co-Screenwriter, **LION KING, HERCULES, HUNCHBACK OF NOTRE DAME, ABC'S ANNIE**

"*Screenplay: From Idea to Successful Script* is a masterfully written text on the possibilities and pragmatics of screenwriting. Jule Selbo presents the whole package; a fresh approach with her Eleven Step Structure that is concrete in concept yet avoids the trap of being a "cookie cutter" formula. Selbo's writing provides comprehensive graduate level content that is easily accessible to undergraduate students. *Screenplay: From Idea to Successful Script* is aptly characterized as a guide, as it provides the key elements without the dogmatic "rules" often connected to screenwriting texts. This is an excellent addition to the oeuvre of screenwriting texts; it will surely become a "standard" in the field."

Harold Casselton, Director of Film Studies,
Minnesota State University, Moorhead

"An invaluable guide for anyone who has ever dreamed of taking their idea for a movie and committing it to paper as a complete screenplay."

Marc Marcum, Producer,
Intellectual Properties Worldwide Entertainment

"This is the ultimate guide for anyone who wants to tell a story by writing a screenplay. Selbo's style and technique is easy to understand and her examples and research are perfect. This easy to understand book is required is reading for anyone who wants to master screenwriting."

Craig Anderson, Producer, Television's **ON GOLDEN POND, O PIONEERS, THE BALLAD OF LUCY WHIPPLE, FOR THE LOVE OF A CHILD** *and more*

"Jule Selbo is a masterful screenwriting teacher. Her Eleven Step Story Structure can empower you to write a multi-layered screenplay with unforgettable, complex characters, tension, twists, turns—and a message that will resonate with today's audiences."

Peter Buckingham, Historian and Screenwriter/Finalist
in UCLA Extension Screenplay Competition

"Insightful and helpful, Selbo's style and examples are so easy to "get" for a writer. *The Eleven Step Story Structure* has allowed me to glean new insights into my characters and let them take over the story. I wish I had this framework when I started."

Scott Gensch—Screenwriter and former student

GARDNER'S *guide to*

SCREENPLAY

From Idea to Successful Script

The Eleven-Step Story Structure

JULE SELBO

GARTH GARDNER COMPANY

GGC publishing

Washington DC, USA · London, UK

Cover Designer: Nic Banks
Layout Designer: Rachelle Painchaud-Nash
Editor: Chris Edwards
Publisher: Garth Gardner, Ph.D.

Editorial inquiries concerning this book should be mailed to:
The Editor, Garth Gardner Company, 5107 13th Street N.W.,
Washington DC 20011 or emailed to: info@ggcinc.com.
http://www.gogardner.com

Copyright © 2007, GGC, Inc. All rights reserved.

No part of this book may be reproduced, stored in a retrieval system, or
transmitted in any form or by any other means—electronic, mechanical,
photocopying, recording, or otherwise —except for citations of data for
scholarly or reference purposes, with full acknowledgment of title,
edition, and publisher, and written notification to GGC/Publishing prior
to such use.

GGC/Publishing is a department of Garth Gardner Company, Inc. and
Gardner's Guide is a registered trademark of Garth Gardner Company, Inc.

Library of Congress Cataloging-in-Publication Data
Selbo, Jule.
    Gardner's guide to screenplay : from idea to successful script / by
Jule Selbo.
    p. cm.
    1. Motion picture authorship. I. Title.
    PN1996.S3848 2007
    808.2'3--dc22   2006027863

Printed in China

ACKNOWLEDGEMENTS

A screenplay certainly doesn't find itself produced on the big screen without a lot of help from executives, a director, actors, a crew and lots of friends who encourage along the way. While writing this text, I have found books follow a similar path. I'd like to thank my students and clients for asking lots of questions and for making it necessary to organize my thoughts. Special thanks to Lisa Kettle, Lilliana Winkworth, Janet Blake, Susan Merson, Todd Parker, Lynne Gross, Philippe Perebinossoff, Diane Ambruso, Dee La Duke and Mark Winkworth, for their insight in the initial stages of the manuscript. Thanks to Chris Edwards for her supreme editing, to Anthony Mason for his patient detailing of the process, to Mary Beth Whelan at Globe Photos. My peers at California State University at Fullerton and UCLA Extension have been invaluable resources.

And, of course, thanks to the screenwriters who, since the beginning of the movies, have written fabulous stories.

FOREWORD

In *Gardner's Guide to Screenplay: From Idea to Successful Story,* Jule Selbo has put together an inspiring guide to screenwriting. Her *Eleven Step Structure* is practical and creative and allows for the writer's personal voice to shine. Are there other books out there on screenwriting? You bet there are. But how many of them are written by someone who is an accomplished screenwriter as well as an educator? Barely a handful.

Jule will inspire you to dig deep for the idea that will become a compelling story while she constantly provides practical (and ingenious) exercises that will challenge you to create your very best work.

What Jule does in *The Eleven Step Story Structure,* that no one else has done, is show how to understand storytelling structure through focusing on the events of the main character's journey. Her insight that character leads the writer to construct a compelling film is brilliant. Only truly gifted writers get that: the idea that when character comes first, structure will unfold. Synchronicity.

As a writer you want to have insight into people, events, the world. You write because you have things to say. Jule has the ability to share her insights on both the craft and the art of screenwriting, thus benefiting your screenplay by elevating it to a level far above the norm.

So as you read on, listen to Jule's voice. Let her guide you as you take your characters on their own amazing journeys. Let her help you discover your own distinctive ability to tell the stories you're longing to share. Let her inspire you to be the writer you were meant to be.

DIANE LAKE

Diane Lake, screenwriter of the Academy Award nominated **FRIDA**
has also written for Columbia Pictures, Miramax and Paramount Pictures.
She is also a Professor of Screenwriting, Emerson College

TABLE OF CONTENTS

INTRODUCTION

When I sat down to write my first screenplay nearly 20 years ago, I set out to write a fictional version of a traumatic personal experience. I strove to make it an outrageous comedy. Obviously, I knew the characters and I knew the beginning and middle and end of my story because I had lived it. Little did I know how important that was—knowing the beginning, middle, and end for my main character before I even sat down to write.

I got lucky; when I completed my first screenplay, it was optioned by a producer and that led me to landing assignments to write for Paramount Pictures, Warner Brothers, and Columbia pictures. The script served me well because the characters seemed real; there was a definite journey that the main character embarked on, and the consequences of taking this journey caused the character to change. I knew all the main characters in the story and **why** they did **what** they did **when** they did what they did.

As I continued working for major studios and independent producers and television networks, I found I was given many assignments that were more open-ended, story-wise, than others. I adapted a novel for Paramount Pictures that was basically an interior monologue; a character examining her life in a dream-like state. No real **story** there, I had to create one. The Disney studios hired me to write a bio-pic of a little known, but very interesting 1940s newspaperwoman. I had to cull through a large amount of research to decide which parts of the woman's life was the best **story** for a film. Other assignments already had actors attached; I was writing for a specific actor or actress so I understood how important it was to make sure they would want to **play the character** I was about to create for them. Over the years, on assignments, I found the most challenging part of every writing job was finding the great **character story** in the idea that had caught the producers' imaginations.

I knew I needed to create the characters that were real, empathetic and surprising, wonderful and maddening at the same time. I didn't have the luxury of taking well-known characters from my own life. In many cases, I needed to create a character and story from whole cloth; there was no "my life" template from which to draw.

I wanted somewhere to turn for help in working out my character-driven stories. I looked through countless books on screenwriting, I read magazine articles and talked to my screenwriting friends. I took seminars. All advice was good; there were helpful hints from many sources. But there was nothing that really struck me as a concrete tool that I could use to create a strong character story; one that would make sure that the story sailed on the main character's actions, emotions and personality.

Successful stories have a beginning, middle and end for the major characters —and much more. There needs to be obstacles, surprises, ups and downs, good times and bad times for the character. Once I started teaching, I found myself breaking down well-respected films to fully understand their structure—as it pertained to the main character's journey. Many of the films supported a method I had been working out for myself over the years. What came out of this study is the **Eleven Step Story Structure.** The Eleven Step Story Structure is designed for the writer to be able to hit all the great classic storytelling points by focusing on the events of the main character's journey. The Eleven Steps also help the writer in finding an original rhythm of storytelling. The Eleven Step Story Structure helps the writer focus on the inner and outer life of his main character, thus opening the door to exploring a theme and true character growth and change.

Being a screenwriter is one of the most exciting and wonderful careers in the film business. The screenwriter builds characters, builds story, inserts ideas and theme, and has the chance to put forth his or her own view of the world. It's not easy. Screenwriters can get bogged down in complicated plots, get distracted by supporting characters, and lose focus on what the story has set out to accomplish. Using the Eleven Steps can ground the writer, and at the same time, give him freedom to explore.

Audiences love stories. They love films. We need to make screen stories full, meaningful, challenging, new, with great characters that go on exciting emotional or physical journeys. It's up to the screenwriter to start the whole process. If this is a task you are ready to embark on, great. Go for it.

Happy writing!

Jule Selbo

Section One

BEFORE YOU START WRITING

Question: Who decides what films get made?

Answer: In the studio system, there is a very important job – Head of Production. This person oversees development and either decides or has the chance to lobby strongly (to the Head of the Studio) for the films that he or she wishes the studio to finance for production.

Development executives seek out and nurture new material to be put into this pipeline. Each development executive wants his or her projects to be chosen – it's a way to move up the ladder of power in Hollywood.

But where do you find these stories? First, you need an idea.

If ideas pop into your mind all the time, great—you're ahead of the game. But **ideas are only the beginning of the screenplay process.**

The **idea**, which is the initial seed of a story, is very important. But the idea needs to grow and blossom into a fully-realized **story** in order to engage and entrance an audience. Stories are multi-dimensional, stories explore, stories take characters on journeys of self-discovery and adventure. Stories have ups and downs, a strong point of view, strong themes.

You have to be committed to finding the story in the idea.

An idea, without the story structure behind it, is **not** something film development executives at studios want to take to their bosses.

Studio and independent producers and development executives have one main job: to find new properties that will make terrific films. Their job is to respond to scripts and pitches and ask: Is it right for their company? Would this property be something their bosses would be willing to invest money in to develop further? Development executives know that an idea, however exciting, is not enough. Their bosses will want to hear about characters, about plot points, about a crisis, about a climax. A story has to sustain interest for a film's 90 minutes to two-hour length.

The Difference Between an Idea and a Screen Story

There are a few distinct ways to determine the difference between an idea and a fully-realized story. Look for these elements:

A Beginning, Middle, and End
A Strong Character Arc
Plot Points that Increase Conflict
Presentation of Theme
A Point of View

How do you tell the difference between an **idea** and a **story**? Here's an example:

IDEA: *A crazy, eccentric family wins a trip to the Amazon and they have wild experiences in the jungle and adopt a lion and have to live with the natives and figure out how to survive.*

STORY: *A crazy, eccentric family finds itself in dire straits; the mortgage cannot be paid and they are about to be homeless. The father, Jack, a neon-*

competition and unless you commit to writing and finishing great material that can go into the marketplace, you will not be able to compete. It's up to you.

Expect to be challenged; by the process, by yourself. Expect frustration. There will be days when your writing and your thought processes spring from your mind with ease and there will be days when you feel you're pulling impacted wisdom teeth from tender gums just to get a sentence down on paper. Expect good days and bad days.

Sometimes the first thing you write will be the best. Trust that. Sometimes another thought will pop into your head and you'll see a character or story point in a new way. Trust that. Go with your gut. Don't write anything just because you think it's what someone else wants to read. Tell the story you want to tell.

Films come in all shapes and sizes. Screen stories need to be varied. Always keep in mind that **your** point of view, **your** ideas, **your** way of looking at the world is valid. It's the only way to be truly original—believe in yourself.

Know Your Medium

A writer who writes great film stories is a writer who cares about character. It's a writer who is interested in the human condition, a writer who believes that, down deep, it's the emotional stakes of character that are most important. It's a writer who is willing to dig deep and explore real human failings and feelings, a screenwriter who is ready to commit to examining the light and dark of her characters (and herself) and never shirk from putting her heart on the page.

A screenwriter needs to know films, the ones that are out in the marketplace now and the ones that have been successful in the past. Not only will this knowledge help and inspire you, but you'll be able to intelligently join in discussions in the film executive's office when you are asked questions like, "Do you see the tone of your movie being in the vein of THE GODFATHER or DUMB AND DUMBER?"

See as many films as you can. Read as many film scripts as you can. Have strong opinions. Create characters with strong points of view.

Studying the structure of successful films is a way to understand the art of screenwriting.

Here's a list of movies referred to in this book; if you haven't seen them, put them on your viewing list. Check the internet for online screenplays you can download and read the scripts. Learn from them and enjoy!

Excellent films to use as a companion to this book

IT HAPPENED ONE NIGHT (1934), written by Robert Riskin, based on story by Samuel Hopkins Adams

CASABLANCA (1942) written by Julius and Philip Epstein and Howard Koch, based on a play by Murray Burnett and Joan Alison

ALL ABOUT EVE (1950) written by Joseph Mankiewicz

VERTIGO (1958) written by Alec Coppel and Samuel A. Taylor, based on a novel by Boileau and Narcejac

THE APARTMENT (1960) written by Billy Wilder and I.A.L. Diamond

CHARADE (1963) written by Peter Stone based on a story by Marc Behm and Peter Stone

IN THE HEAT OF THE NIGHT (1967) written by Stirling Silliphant, based on a novel by John Ball

THE GRADUATE (1967) written by Buck Henry and Calder Willingham, based on the novel by Charles Webb

THE GODFATHER (1972) written by Mario Puzo and Francis Ford Coppola, based on the novel by Mario Puzo

THE STING (1973) written by David S. Ward

CHINATOWN (1974) written by Robert Towne

ONE FLEW OVER THE CUCKOO'S NEST (1975) written by Bo Goldman and Lawrence Hauben, based on novel by Ken Kesey

NETWORK (1976) written by Paddy Chayefsky

ANNIE HALL (1977) written by Woody Allen

KRAMER VS. KRAMER (1979) written by Robert Benton, based on novel by Avery Corman

RAIDERS OF THE LOST ARK (1981) written by Lawrence Kasdan, story by George Lucas and Philip Kaufman

SILKWOOD (1983) written by Alice Arlen and Nora Ephron

TOOTSIE (1982) written by Larry Gelbart and Murray Schisgal, story by Don McGuire and Larry Gelbart

OUT OF AFRICA (1985) written by Kurt Luedtke, based on memoirs of Isak Dinesen

WITNESS (1985) written by William Kelly and Earl W. Wallace, based on story by William Kelly, Earl W. Wallace and Pamela Wallace

RAIN MAN (1988) written by Barry Morrow and Ron Bass

BEAUTY AND THE BEAST (1991) written by Linda Woolverton and Roger Allers (plus ten people get story credit) based on an 18th century story by Jeanne-Marie Leprince de Beaumont

UNFORGIVEN (1992) written by David Webb Peoples

LION KING (1994) written by Irene Mecchi and Jonathan Roberts and Linda Woolverton

THE SHAWSHANK REDEMPTION (1994) written by Frank Darabont, based on a short story by Stephen King

TOY STORY (1995) written by Jon Lassetter, Pete Docter, Joss Whedon, Alex Sokolow, Joe Ranfft, Joel Cohen, Andrew Stanton

JERRY MCGUIRE (1996) written by Cameron Crowe

MEN IN BLACK (1997) written by Ed Solomon, based on graphic novel by Lowell Cunningham

THE WATERBOY (1998) written by Tim Herlihy and Adam Sandler

GLADIATOR (2000) written by David Fronzoni, John Logan and William Nicholson, story by David Fronzoni

TRAINING DAY (2001) written by David Ayer

SHREK (2001) written by Ted Elliot, Terry Rossio, John Stillman and R. Schulman

LEGALLY BLONDE (2001) written by Karen McCullah Lutz and Kirsten Smith, based on a novel by Amanda Brown

A BEAUTIFUL MIND (2001) written by Akiva Goldsman based on a book by Sylvia Nasar

SPIDERMAN (2002) written by David Koepp, based on a comic by Stan Lee and Steve Ditko

ADAPTATION (2002) written by Charlie Kaufman, inspired by **THE ORCHID THIEF** by Susan Orlean

NORMAL (2003) written by Jane Anderson

FINDING NEMO (2003) written by Andrew Stanton, Bob Peterson and David Reynolds

COLLATERAL (2004) written by Stuart Beattie

FINDING NEVERLAND (2004) written by David Magee, based on a play by Alan Knee

MILLION DOLLAR BABY (2004) written by Paul Haggis, based on stories by F.X. Toole

SIDEWAYS (2004) written by Alexander Payne and Jim Taylor, based on a novel by Rex Pickett

KICKING AND SCREAMING (2005) written by Leo Benvenuti and Steve Rudnick

BATMAN BEGINS (2005) written by David S. Goyer and Christopher Nolan, based on characters created by Bob Kane

THE SQUID AND THE WHALE (2005) written by Noah Baumbach

HUSTLE AND FLOW (2005) written by Craig Brewer

THUMBSUCKER (2005) written by Mike Mills based on a novel by Walter Kirn

CRASH (2005) written by Paul Haggis and Bobby Moresco

Chapter Summary

- Storytelling is a tradition that goes back to the early days of man.

- Film is a unique form of storytelling; visual and aural and is capable of working on many different levels.

- Film stories start with an idea and then must expand into a fully-realized story.

- A story has depth and dimension and focuses on character.

- A screenwriter should have a wide knowledge of film stories from the past and the present.

- Reading screenplays is as important as watching the films.

Chapter Two

WHERE DO IDEAS COME FROM?

Can a writer find ideas anywhere? Yes.

Can any idea be the base of a good film story?
Films come in all shapes and sizes.

Can a writer take an idea and put a personal stamp on it? Yes.

Where do your ideas come from? The short answer: Everywhere. Look outwardly: Newspapers, magazine articles, current events, opinion pieces, novels, non-fiction, short stories, music, paintings, photographs, graffiti, comic books, posters, want ads. Wander around a garage sale in your neighborhood or enter an antique store or thrift shop for inspiration; stories can come from objects that were once part of a stranger's life.

E x e r c i s e :

Choose a painting that focuses on one or more persons (go to a museum, find an art book at the library, browse galleries on the internet). Study the painting. Let your imagination go where it will. Imagine a story behind the painting. Who are the people portrayed? What do they want? What is their backstory? Write a paragraph or two about the main character you have created from this inspiration. Where did the character come from? What is his or her desire? Goal? Want? What heartache, what joys, what fears are part of this character's life?

Consider myths, legends, urban legends, fairytales. How would you update **HAMLET?** Can you find a fresh take on **HERCULES? THE RED SHOES? THE THREE LITTLE PIGS? FRANKENSTEIN?**

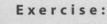

E x e r c i s e :

Choose a fairytale or folk tale. Set it in a new era (Caesar's Rome, the American Great Depression, far into the future, the 1970s, today, any era that inspires you…). Change elements of the story to make it work in its new time period. Example: A re-telling of LITTLE RED RIDING HOOD

> (A teenage girl inherits a car from her recently deceased parents and decides to drive cross country to California to visit her Grandmother. Along the way she meets a handsome but manipulative young man who covets her car and her inherited money and wants to "go to granny's house" with her—finding out that Grandmother is a famous ex-rock star who lives in a mansion in Malibu. The young girl, finally aware that he is a freeloader with a violent streak, manages to escape from him when they stop at a gas station—she quickly drives off. When she arrives, finally, in Malibu—she is amazed to find him at her Grandmother's house—and Grandmother is nowhere in sight...). How could this idea play out and grow into a story? Is it a horror film? A thriller?

Ideas can also come from biographies; historical and current. There are the great tales in history, the well-known stories (that can be re-visited) or the little known tales. There are war stories, great stories of courage and cowardice. There are inventors and destroyers. There are people who, over the years, sat back and let the world do to them and there are those who helped shape the world. There are the small stories within the big stories.

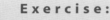

Exercise:

Choose a well known historical figure. Now explore the story of his or her spouse or child or assistant. How did fame or infamy affect a loved one's life? What new perspective on history can you present to an audience?

Consider Your Own Life

When trying to come up with an idea, don't forget to consider a very original source: You. What about stories that deal with your family or your personal experiences growing up, in school, in your career? What about your friends? Lovers. Enemies. What about your dreams? Your personal stories (just as they are or perhaps heightened) can be the stuff of great drama or comedy.

Exercise:

Ask someone to share a vivid memory. Take elements of that memory and build a story with a beginning, middle and end. Build one that goes beyond the memory itself or takes only components of the memory. Switch characters around, add news ones. Use the elements of the memory as a stepping stone to an original story.

Your imagination is also a well-spring of story possibilities. Every person sees the world in their own unique way. Imagine a setting, characters with needs or goals and characters who oppose them. Imagine events. Imagine emotions that play out on a grand or not-so-grand scale. Take a look at the world around you. Is your neighbor keeping strange hours? Imagine he has a dual personality and a dual life. What if she is a small town teacher by day and a high-rolling gambler by night? What if he is a nurse by day and Nurse Death by night?

Let the real world inspire you. Truth is often stranger than fiction. There are sites on the internet that gather strange stories, news events, weird happenings. Let yourself be inspired. Use your imagination to construct new elements. There are no limits. Storytellers must be able to see a story in everything.

Example: *There was a magazine article about an ambitious young woman who grew up in a middle-class home, met a man in college—and in a fairytale romance, married into a rich and powerful, political family. She reveled in her new social status—she dined with royalty, heads of state. She was asked everywhere; her photo was in newspapers and magazines. She raised a family, stood by her husband even when he was found guilty of illegal activity and received a very public slap-on-the wrist and huge financial fines. She supported him, entertained for him, was the dutiful daughter-in-law and in her mind, paid her dues big time. Twenty years later, her husband informs her he has fallen in love with a co-worker and wants a divorce. Suddenly, the woman is set adrift. The powerful, political family "drops" her, her financial standing falls, she is no longer invited to the best parties. Friends disappear. Her children are welcome at family gatherings, but she is no longer invited. Depression and anger set in. Does she lash out? Does she fight for her man? Can she reinvent a life for herself?*

The set-up for a story is here. The story can go many ways. Is it a drama?

Is it a horror film? A thriller? Does she seek revenge? Is it a woman-finding-herself movie? Is it a comedy; does she need to join the work-force and subsequently go on a comedic ride trying to find a well-paying job? Is it a crime story where she finds out some nefarious dealings of her ex-in-laws and exposes them? Is it a love story where she goes through humiliation and anger and depression but finds true love with a friend who always stood by her side?

Rights to Stories

Before you read a novel or magazine article or hear a story on the radio or get enamored of a real person's life and say, "That's it! That's the story I want to write!", be aware that there are legal issues involved.

Check out the "rights" issue. Do you have the *legal* right to use a true story without paying anyone for that right? Just as literary work is protected by copyright, people's life stories are also legally protected. Permissions, options, sale of material are all legal matters that need to be explored if your interests lie in this area. Every literary piece will have its own "strings attached" and should be checked into on an individual basis, this includes newspaper and magazine and internet articles. Do research into the availability of a literary work or personal story before committing your heart and soul to bringing that story to film.

As a rule-of-thumb, if the original publishing date of a literary work is 100 years old or more, chances are the piece does not have to be optioned or purchased and can be adapted by any and all. This is called "public domain."

Note: Check each literary piece's provenance. A writer *does not* want to spend his time adapting a story without knowing the screenplay will be able to be sold/produced some day. Even if a literary piece is more than a 100 years old, make sure it's in the public domain; there could be special circumstances. The internet is a source for lists of material in the public domain. You can also contact the publisher or find the agent or lawyer representing the existing material. Do your research.

A true life story? You need to contact the person whose life you want to explore. If that person is deceased, you may need to get the family's permission. If your subject is "famous" other rules apply. If you are interested in these type of stories, employ a lawyer to help you navigate the rights issues.

Protect your work, protect your time. Time is precious to a writer; you don't want to spend months or years on a screenplay that you cannot legally send out into the world for possible production.

If you can't get the rights to the material you're passionate about, ask: What are the elements of the piece that intrigues you the most? Is it a story of betrayal? Is it a story of great love conquering continents? Can you fashion an original piece that explores related themes or situations? Consider being "inspired" by someone or some book or some article and then let your imagination go and create an original piece that will be your own.

High Concept/ Low Concept Stories

In the film business, stories are often placed in one of two categories: HIGH CONCEPT and LOW CONCEPT. Both terms refer to well-respected and well-executed films, but there is a big difference in the *idea* behind each of them.

Every studio wants to buy a HIGH CONCEPT film. What is it? High Concept is a term used to describe a screen story that a person can easily understand after hearing just a few words—usually an exciting or mind-catching one-liner. 1997's **LIAR LIAR** is an example; the one-liner might've been *"A wild comedy about a cocky lawyer who has become a habitual liar in his business and personal life—suddenly, because of a wish made by his son, cannot help himself from telling the truth in every situation."* Comedic scenes, relationships and problems immediately spring to mind. **SPLASH** is another example—it might've been pitched like this; *"A man who has been searching for true love, finally finds it when a mermaid comes to find him in New York City."* Other High Concept examples are **MEN IN BLACK, ARMAGEDDON, THE GODFATHER, JAWS** (A man-eating shark attacks the summer crowds on Martha's Vineyard and a Sheriff, who is afraid of water, has to save the island...), **LEGALLY BLONDE** (A spoiled Bel Air, California sorority girl finds her way into Harvard Law School to snare her man...), **TITANIC, TOY STORY, TOOTSIE, VAN HELSING, TOP GUN, BONNIE AND CLYDE, RUNAWAY BRIDE, THE DAY AFTER TOMORROW, HOME ALONE, A BEAUTIFUL MIND, E.T., SCHINDLER'S LIST, TROY, LAWRENCE OF ARABIA, GLADIATOR, THE INCREDIBLES, EVER AFTER, 50 FIRST DATES, GROUNDHOG DAY, FINDING NEVERLAND, KICKING AND SCREAMING, SHREK, THE CORPSE BRIDE**... and many more are examples of High Concept ideas.

High Concept films generally need to appeal to a large audience (those under and over 25) and to males and females. High Concept films generally explore a theme that most audiences relate to: James Cameron's **TITANIC** is about love triumphing over disaster. **JAWS** is about overcoming fear and destroying the monster. Consider the family-related themes of **THE DAY AFTER TOMORROW, THE INCREDIBLES…** or the timeless romantic themes of love conquering all in **RUNAWAY BRIDE, 50 FIRST DATES, EVER AFTER….**

Simple definition? High Concept ideas are stories that can be easily grasped in just a title or short sentence description and also promises broad commercial appeal.

Low Concept refers to films that need more explanation than one sentence to set up the movie's story. Examples are **MYSTIC RIVER, REAL WOMEN HAVE CURVES, NORTH BY NORTHWEST, THE SEARCHERS, THE SHAWSHANK REDEMPTION, CHARADE, CASABLANCA, NURSE BETTY, THE GRADUATE, 21 GRAMS, THELMA AND LOUISE, AMERICAN BEAUTY, TRAFFIC, COLLATERAL, SIDEWAYS, CRASH, THE SQUID AND THE WHALE ….**

Low Concept stories may need more explanation for different reasons. Perhaps it's necessary to understand the character in order to understand actions that may not be predictable. Perhaps there are multiple stories. Perhaps subplots are complex. Perhaps an intense, complex backstory needs to be understood before the character's actions make sense.

HIGH CONCEPT movies can be good or bad. It all depends on the execution. LOW CONCEPT movies can be good or bad. All depends on the execution. It's easier to sell a High Concept film (especially on a pitch). But it's easy to see that both High and Low Concept movies are on the list of the most beloved films of all time.

Exercise:

Come up with a High Concept idea and a Low Concept idea. Remember, the High Concept idea needs to nurture an instant recognition and suggest story arcs immediately. Low Concept ideas will take more explanation of character and plot to understand why the story evolves as it does.

Know the Genres

Audiences, by and large, choose the film they want to see by its genre. There's the "date movie," which is usually a comedy/romance. There's the "action flick" that attracts the audience who loves roller coaster rides. There's the "teen flick" that is designed to bring in an audience of 12–17 year olds. Some people love Horror films. Others will avoid them at all costs. Know the audience your film will attract. Family? Teen? Men? Women? What age? Are you aiming for the lowest common denominator or the highest? Art house or mainstream? Knowing the audience you want to reach as well as the genre your idea falls into will help you construct a story that has a chance to make it to the marketplace.

Imagine the poster of your film. Will it feature romance, action, comedy? Producers and studio executives want to be able to "see the poster." They want to know they can attract audiences to your film. Knowing the traditions of each genre and paying homage to those traditions will move your project along.

List of the most common genres

Action

Adventure

Animation

Biography

Buddy

Comedy

Coming of Age

Crime

Disaster

Drama

Dumber than Dumb

Epic

Fantasy

Farce

Fish Out Of Water

Fantasy

Historical

Horror

Mock Documentary

Musical

Mystery

Romance

Romantic Comedy

Satire

Science Fiction

Sports

Thriller

War

Western

Remember that most movies are a combination of genres

CASABLANCA: Romance/Drama/War/ Historical

TOOTSIE: Comedy/Romance

MEN IN BLACK: Action/Comedy/Buddy/Science Fiction

BEAUTY AND THE BEAST: Animation/Fantasy/Romance

SHALLOW HAL: Dumber Than Dumb/Romance/ Comedy

TRAINING DAY: Buddy/Action/Crime/Drama

LEGALLY BLONDE: Coming of Age/ Comedy/Fish Out Of Water/Romance

SHREK: Comedy/Romance/Satire

TROY: Historical/Biography/ Adventure/War/Romance

MILLION DOLLAR BABY: Drama/Sports

THE AVIATOR: Biography/Romance/Historical

SIDEWAYS: Buddy/Comedy/Romance

BATMAN BEGINS: Action/ Coming of Age

BROKEBACK MOUNTAIN: Drama/Romance

CRASH: Drama/Crime

Know your overriding genre. If you are writing primarily an action movie, make sure there are car chases or horse chases or spaceship chases or whatever kind of chase fits with your story; make sure there's suspense, near-death experiences, intrigue is always good, make sure the pace is quick. If you are writing primarily a romance, make sure someone falls in love with someone else, make sure there are forces that keep them apart, work up to the first kiss or wedding or declaration of undying love, pay attention to the details that build romance.

A screenwriter should never dismiss or forget a very important and true fact: An audience has expectations. They want to be transported into a world for a few hours—one that they have enjoyed in the past and want to enjoy again. If they pay their money to see a horror film, scare them out of their wits. If the audiences pays money to see a historical epic—do your research and present history in a new and different way. If it's a comedy, make them laugh. If it's a heartfelt drama, make them cry. Make sure you give the audience the moments that they have paid for and anticipated, **and then more.**

Do it in your own way, but do not disappoint your audience.

Exercise:

Pick three very different genres from the list above. Write, in paragraph form, an opening scene for each of the genres. Make sure the genre is clear from the outset. Example: Action/Adventure/Period. Opening scene: Egyptian pyramids stand silent against a moonlit sky. Hundreds of SLAVES, wearing loincloths and tattered sandals trek towards a large pyramid featuring an open doorway. Six of the strongest slaves carry a golden sarcophagus. SLAVE MASTERS keep a watchful eye. A young KING, age 8, carried in a litter, surrounded by his ADVISORS and PROTECTORS, follows the sarcophagus. Suddenly, 12 masked BANDITS , on huge horses, burst out from behind sand dunes, their whistles and calls pierce the silence. The young King cowers. His protectors pull out swords and spears. Bandits swing leather bags in the air, GASEOUS FUMES pour out. Slaves stumble and fall to the earth, unconsciousness. Advisors choke, their eyes roll back in their heads as they fall to the ground. The King pulls his robes about him, tries to hide as the slaves carrying his litter fall to the ground. One strong Bandit sweeps in, grabs the King , ties him to his saddle. The King has lost consciousness, hangs limply. Other Bandits lift the sarcophagus. A chariot speeds out from behind the pyramid, the sarcophagus is loaded onto it—and as it speeds off, the Bandits follow. All that is left under the light of the moon are scattered bodies…. And it is silent once more.

Chapter Summary

+ Ideas can spring from any source—external or internal, true life or the writer's imagination.

+ A writer needs to be aware of the legal constraints on adaptation of literary work, true life stories and other existing material.

+ High Concept and Low Concept stories are both sources of fine films.

+ Each writer will approach a story in different ways. Embrace your original point of view.

+ A writer needs to know his genre, give the audience what it hopes for and more.

Chapter Three

THREE ACT STRUCTURE AND BEYOND

Does following a structure mean that screen stories will be predictable? No.

Does following a structure mean the writer is not being original? No.

Does following a structure inhibit the artist? No.

A fine artist or sculptor learns the basics of drawing; anatomy, light, shading, perspective. Once basics are learned, an artist can create with confidence. Part of an artist's work is craft, part is artistry. Writing is a craft and an art. Learn the basics of storytelling first; creating characters, plotting, exposition and more and *then* extrapolate, fine-tune, improvise on the art to create your masterpiece.

Knowing story structure helps the writer. It can help the writer make her story crystal clear. It can help the writer create a strong emotional component to his film. It can help the writer illuminate characters and theme. Knowing structure can help the writer create a satisfying, exciting, *surprising* screen story that will engage an audience.

Knowing structure will also help the writer get from beginning, through the middle, and to the end of his screenplay.

Using good structure does not mean you will create "cookie cutter" stories. Your work will always have an original stamp as long as you are exploring themes and characters that interest you. Your point of view will be original. Your individual voice will come through in dialogue. Your choice of visuals will be unique. If you stay true to your vision of the world, your screen story will always have "you" written all over it.

The Three Act Structure

Films, since their early infancy, have had a Three Act Structure. This comes from the live theatre tradition. Most theatrical plays were divided into three acts (two intermissions). It was only natural, when full-length screenplays were first written, to look at other forms of storytelling entertainment for inspiration and structure.

Some points of the Three Act Structure are basic good storytelling elements. However, films have morphed into a unique art form and the Three Act Structure is not adequate in and of itself. This book is designed to push you beyond thinking in the somewhat predictable Three Act Structure and urge you to consider different rhythms for your screenplay. You will explore ways of doing that in Chapter Four, the Eleven Step Story Structure.

But first things first. Everyone in the film business talks about "Three Act Structure." It's good to know the basics of that system so you can mingle at industry parties and bandy terms around. Also, film executives are schooled in this structure and they will invariably ask, "What act are we in now?" as you are pitching to them your fabulous screen story.

So let's make sure you understand the Three Act Structure before we go "beyond" it.

Screenplays, up until the mid-1990s, were expected to be about 120 pages worth of dialogue and action. (Rule of thumb is one minute of screen time per page equals 120 minutes, give or take.) Most studios now ask the writer to submit a first draft that is close to 100 pages. Their reasoning? Audiences, due to television, video games and fast-paced lives have shorter attention spans. The truth is, 100 pages is probably a good length for a first draft because, invariably, when you do subsequent drafts (after getting feedback from friends/agent, and/or from the studio or director) the screenplay will tend to grow in page count. When you're done with your final polish, if you're anywhere from 100–115, you're fine.

So, in the not-too-distant past, a 120 page screenplay was broken down into three parts. Pages 1–30 was the ACT ONE, pages 30–90 was the ACT TWO, and pages 90–120 was the ACT THREE.

You can do the math for the new 100 page count. 1–25 equals ACT ONE. 25–75 equals ACT TWO. 75–100 equals ACT THREE. There are certain story points and story elements expected to be reached in each of these acts. We will go "beyond" this structure (and specifically page count expectations) in Chapter Four, but first, let's explore the Three Act Structure.

Anyway you count it, you can see the bulge in the middle. The title, **Battle of the Bulge** could be apt, because once you're into Act Two you may be crying HELP! You may feel out of control, like your script is unbalanced, fat, like you're wallowing in quicksand, lost or definitely dying. For your own sanity, just cut that Act Two in half and think of pages 25–50 as Part One of the Act Two (at the end of which some big TURNING POINT should happen) and pages 50–75 as Part Two of the Act Two (at the end of which the CRISIS needs to take place). Check details in the chapter that addresses Act Two .

In most cases, as you will see in the chapter containing examples of film breakdowns, screen stories take a traditional shape. *Why? Because there are basic elements in the telling a good story.*

A joke that has no set up will not be funny. A monster without a victim we care about will not be as scary as you want it to be. A man desperate to win a million dollars is not interesting unless we know why. Basic storytelling elements must be used to help you set up your jokes. They must be used to lead your audience into caring about a character. They must be used to let your audience in on "why" your character is acting in a certain way. A writer must take the time to set the genre and tone, engage the audience, introduce characters and situations and conflicts before catapulting the protagonist into the deep complications of the story.

The classic Three Act Structure is designed to help the writer take his time. Yes, writers worry about boring the audience, they want to get to the exciting parts of the story, they want to twist and turn the story and keep the audience on edge. Keep in mind that all the car chases, funny scenes, romantic locations, battles or sword fights will mean nothing if the main character has not been illuminated sufficiently to engage the audience's interest.

What needs to be accomplished in Act One?

Act One

SET UP: *(pages 1–25) This includes many things. Genre/Tone. Where. When. The normal life. Protagonist's want/need/goal. Introduction of supporting characters. Story. Backstory. Inciting Incident. Conflict. Plot Point One.*

Set up genre and tone. Is it a comedy? Drama? Horror film? Drama with comedy? Adventure? Let us know the overriding genre, give us a clue whether to laugh or scream or hold onto our seats because it's going to be a bumpy ride.

Set up place and time. Where does the story take place? What time period? Present? Past? Future?

Set up the normal life. Who is the main character (the protagonist)? What is a normal day like? USE VISUALS. Film is a visual medium; the more you can tell visually, the less expository dialogue you will need (you don't want that clunky on-the-nose, lay-it-all-out dialogue that becomes awkward and boring).

LET ME REPEAT: First set up the *normal life.* In 1982's **TOOTSIE,** we don't start with Michael Dorsey (portrayed by Dustin Hoffman) in drag. We see Michael's *normal life;* his friends, his work as a waiter, how he deals with women, how he is serious about the craft of acting but can't get an acting job. In 1997's **MEN IN BLACK,** we see Agent K (portrayed by Tommy Lee Jones) in his day-to-day job of sniffing out aliens at the border. We see Agent J (portrayed by Will Smith) as a regular cop chasing down bad guys on the street. In 1985's **OUT OF AFRICA,** we see Karin (portrayed by Meryl Streep) in Denmark wanting desperately to marry. In 2002's **SPIDERMAN,** we see Peter Parker (portrayed by Toby McGuire) as a nerdy student in love with the most popular girl at school. In 1991's **BEAUTY AND THE BEAST,** we see the curse placed on the Beast, get the sense of him angrily roaming a lonely castle. We also see Belle's life in the village she has emotionally outgrown, with an eccentric, bumbling father she loves dearly. In 2005's **STARSKY AND HUTCH,** we get to know each character before they become unlikely partners.

Set up the protagonist's Overall Want. Think of both the immediate goal (to win the game, to get the girl, to become President, to solve the crime) and *more importantly,* the emotional overall want/need of your character. In **TOOTSIE,** Michael Dorsey wants respect and success—he thinks that will come with getting a good acting job; he learns that it comes with being truthful and respecting others. In **SPIDERMAN,** Peter Parker wants to impress the girl. He learns that fate has a larger task for him and that the ability to impress the girl comes at a high cost.

Create the Inciting Incident. What happens that changes the normal life of your character and sets her on a new journey? This term, "inciting incident" is a buzz word in screenwriting and film development circles. Put it into your vocabulary and use it when talking to industry types. It sounds important (and it is). The inciting incident is the event that brings about change in the protagonist's *normal* life. In **TOOTSIE,** it's Michael's learning that a role he wanted to audition for went to a daytime soap actor. When he complains, his agent tells him no one wants to hire Michael Dorsey because he's difficult and meaningless in the New York Theatre world. This is the incident that spurs Michael to take action. In **MEN IN BLACK,** Agent K realizes his elderly partner needs to retire and he has to erase his partner's memory. This causes Agent K to seek a new partner. In **OUT OF AFRICA,** the inciting incident is Karin asking the brother of her lover to marry her. This action changes her normal life forever. In **SPIDERMAN,** Peter gets bit by a spider and realizes he is forever changed.

Story Events. What are the results of the inciting incident? How is the immediate goal now the same or different? (The overall want must stay the same throughout the film story…more on that later.) What events will fill out the story? What supporting characters need to be introduced? How is the protagonist thwarted? (Most good film stories leave the protagonist unsatisfied, frustrated, unsuccessful for as long as possible.)

Create Plot Point One. The story takes a twist or turn and the character is forced onto his main journey, his new path. What event *pushes* your main character into the journey of the story? In **TOOTSIE,** Michael Dorsey auditions for the female role on the soap opera. In **MEN IN BLACK,** Agent K interviews for a new partner and chooses Agent J. In **OUT OF AFRICA,** Karin, who has moved to Africa to start a new life, finds out her new husband has changed their dairy farm plans and she will now be running a coffee plantation. In **SPIDERMAN,** Peter Parker's uncle is murdered and Peter's guilt drives him to use his new powers to seek revenge. In 2004's **FINDING NEVERLAND,** J. M. Barrie meets the boys in the park and finds a new audience for his stories. In 2004's **MILLION DOLLAR BABY,** Plot Point One is Frankie's agreement to coach Maggie.

"Tootsie" Sydney Pollack, Dustin Hoffman
photo supplied by IPOL/Globe Photos

Act Two

CONFRONTATION *(50–60 pages) Opening up or a change of the world. Increasing the stakes. Complications. New information. Midpoint. Obstacles and reversals and conflict culminating in Plot Point Two (Crisis)*

In Act Two there are forces (moral and physical) that work against your main character. There are hills and valleys of emotions. There are obstacles and reversals. The want/ need/ desire of your main character gets stronger and more complex.

That sounds simple, doesn't it? And in general terms, it is what you want to happen. But building the specifics in Act Two is traditionally the hardest row to hoe in your screenplay and we will get into that further in the next chapter.

In some film stories, the main character is literally propelled into a whole new world. The world of the film changes dramatically. Belle, in **BEAUTY AND THE BEAST,** is thrust into the enchanted world of the Beast's castle. Dorothy in **WIZARD OF OZ** finds herself in Munchkinland and faces the biggest nemesis (antagonist) of her life, the Wicked Witch of the West. In **TOOTSIE,** Michael Dorsey is now living most of his life as a woman. In **OUT OF AFRICA,** Karin finds herself living as a single woman in Africa, realizing her marriage of convenience is over. Think about 2004's **WHITE CHICKS;** in Act Two the African-American detectives disguise themselves as white women. In **DIE HARD,** McClane (portrayed by Bruce Willis) finds himself facing his antagonists in a tall building he is unfamiliar with where floors of offices are still under construction. In 1998's **ARMAGEDDON,** Act Two finds its main characters leaving their "normal worlds" to enter a space ship to go on a mission to save the world. In 2003's **FINDING NEMO,** Marlin leaves the safety of his community to search for his son and enters the deep, scary ocean. Think about **GLADIATOR, LORD OF THE RINGS, STAR WARS;** each of these films thrust the protagonist into a new world.

There are many stories that do not use a dramatic change of location or circumstance in Act Two. These stories use increased tension, problems, obstacles, varied circumstance, an introduction of a new character or a dramatic change in a character relationship to raise the stakes in Act Two.

Increase the stakes. Personal wants/needs of the protagonist should now affect a larger group. If the protagonist doesn't get what she wants, it's not just her personal life that is affected; now her family or her friends or her children or her community or global situations could suffer. Open up the world, affect a wider group. It could be as simple as "like" turns to "love" (and the stakes of a broken heart are introduced), or desire of getting into the dance company turns to getting the lead role in the ballet (to show all detractors that she has the heart of a champion). The protagonist's personal desire could move from rescuing one POW from prison to organizing a complete prison breakout. The protagonist's personal desire could move from investigating an odd burglary at an office building in Washington D.C. to discovering a huge political cover-up.

Obstacles and reversals. The main character experiences up and downs on his journey to reach his goal. Never let anything come easily. Just when things look good, pull the rug out. Just when things look so bad the protagonist will never be able to recover, let a little light shine in—then snuff that light out. The antagonist looks defeated, then he or she rises again—stronger and more evil. Remember, *the journey needs to be difficult.*

Midpoint. The middle of Act Two needs to introduce another twist or turn. New information, change in orders, change in relationship, new opportunity or new denial. Perhaps it's a high point where the protagonist feels success is within his reach—only to have it taken away again resulting in a change of plans. Perhaps it's a low point where the protagonist's frustration is roiling—and a fresh idea or bit of information comes to light. Perhaps the antagonist gets new power. Perhaps the antagonist looks like he's switching sides. Perhaps the protagonist sees the true stripes of a faux ally.

The midpoint of Act Two should introduce a new complication, a deepening of the conflict, perhaps a totally new path.

Plot Point Two. Crisis. This comes at the end of Act Two. The main character is in the deepest hell imaginable; in a situation where all seems lost and rescue chances are nil. This can be a physical hell or an emotional hell. Perhaps it looks like the antagonist will win. Perhaps it looks like dreams will never be realized. Does the character make the *decision* to give up on pursuing his or her goal? Give your main character a chance to quit, capitulate or switch sides. He has to make a *decision;* is he willing or capable of digging deep in order to continue on the pursuit of his goal? Who should she believe? Who should he trust? Is he willing to risk everything? The Crisis point should revolve around a *decision* the protagonist needs to make.

Act Two needs to KEEP BUILDING! FASTER, FUNNIER, CRAZIER, MORE DANGEROUS, whatever fits in your genre. Act Two propels the story into the climactic Act Three.

Act Three

CLIMAX, RESOLUTION AND SENSE OF FUTURE *(25 pages). The climax is the crazy or wonderful or scary or life-threatening race of your main character to reach the finish and accomplish an immediate goal that will lead to realizing his overall want. Emotional and physical challenges are at their peak. And then the Resolution; he wins or loses. Finally, the very important scene where the audience gets a Sense of Future (the new normal) for the main character.*

Climax. The climax could be a non-stop action sequence where the hero saves the world or the girl or the town. The climax could be a courtroom sequence where the fate of the main character is in huge jeopardy and he must use all his talents to affect the outcome. It could be a mad chase to make it to the church or courthouse before a great love marries someone else. Whatever form it takes, the climax is the highest point of your film. Your best stuff should be here. Stakes are never higher. This is the ultimate challenge. The protagonist comes face to face with the antagonist. The protagonist has to find extraordinary resources within himself to overcome the antagonist. Think of Luke Skywalker facing a galactic battle and then finding that his father is his greatest enemy and he has to battle him physically and emotionally (1977's **STAR WARS**). Think of Ferris getting back home without being discovered by the principal of his high school and his parents (1986's **FERRIS BUELLER'S DAY OFF**). Think of Bobby Boucher Jr. telling Mama he's going to live his own life and then joins his team to take on the toughest football team (1998's **THE WATERBOY**).Think of Michael Dorsey unmasking himself on live television and putting all his relationships in jeopardy (**TOOTSIE**). What about Frankie struggling with his decision whether or not to help Maggie end her life (**MILLION DOLLAR BABY**).

Resolution. The protagonist wins or loses and faces the consequences of his actions.

Sense of Future. A hint at the new normal life of the main character. Is he moving into an apartment with the love of his life? Is he facing a row of violent felons in prison? Is she leading an orchestra in Paris? Is she driving her car cross country, reveling in her freedom? Notice the book-end; start with *normal life* at beginning of the film, end with a sense of a *new normal*.

In some tragedies, this new normal is not part of the story. Tragedy, by definition, is a disastrous circumstance or story that relays no sense of hope. If you are writing a tragedy, consider how to convey that in the final moments of your story; will your main character live in shame or grief forever? Will the world be totally annihilated with no hope of renewal? Is there no way back to hope?

Exercise:

Take this idea and start to create a story with it: Joe Able has been in a cryogenic state for twenty years. Upon waking, he discovers that aliens, masquerading as humans, have taken over the national government and are out to destroy the world. Create an inciting incident that will heighten this dilemma even more and propel Joe on an emotional and physical journey.

Note: First thing to do is decide what drives Joe, who he is and what he wants. Does he want to find his family? Does he want power? Does he want to unmask the truth and bring the rightful rulers out of their cryogenic states? Is he a nerd with no military training? Or was he a military official? A surfer? Imagine a backstory for him.

"Ferris Bueller's Day Off" Alan Ruck, Matthew Broderick, Mira Sara
photo supplied by SMP/Globe Photos

Exercise:

Once your have determined your inciting incident, make a list of ten obstacles Joe will face in Act Two. They can be logical or arbitrary, let your list be a combination of both. Don't forget to create the antagonist that will be behind many of those obstacles.

Chapter Summary

+ Knowing story structure helps the screenwriter

+ The Three Act Structure is well-known in the industry and film executives will refer to it

+ Act One includes the set up of genre, tone, place and characters and the normal life that will be changed by the inciting incident

+ Act Two opens up the story and makes it more complex

+ Act Three includes the climax and the resolution of the story

+ The Eleven Step Story Breakdown can be used to further break down the film story. It focuses on the character's journey—and character is the most important aspect of a film story.

Chapter Four

ELEVEN STEP STORY STRUCTURE

Should a writer work out the story before starting script pages? Yes.

Should a writer explore events and character elements to enrich her story? Yes.

The Eleven Step Story Structure is designed to give you a stronger skeleton on which to hang your story. It will give your story solid bones and leave lots of room to add muscle and sinew. It will help you focus on character and help you determine plot points that will affect or be driven by your character.

No one wants films to be predictable. No one wants the structure to jump out at the audience. But audiences *do* want to be taken on a full and satisfying journey. They want highs and lows and twists and turns. They want to know *why* a character is on the journey, they want to invest in the outcome. So the screenwriters/storytellers' task is to provide good story elements and to handle them with a fresh point of view. This will make their film stories original.

I designed the Eleven Step Story Structure when I started teaching and doing script consultations. It evolved for me as I was learning and working on my craft. It's simple, and leaves lots of room for a character to advance on a long, arduous and complex story.

---

1. Character's Overall Want/Need and Why
2. Character Logically Goes For It
3. Character Is Denied
4. Character Gets Second Opportunity To Achieve Overall Want
5. Conflicts About Taking Advantage Of Second Opportunity
6. Character Decides To Go For It
7. All Goes Well
8. All Falls Apart

9. Crisis

10. Climax

11. Truth Comes Out To Make Things Right

Let's look at the classic Cinderella story to help explain the *Eleven Step Story Structure.*

Cinderella

1. CINDERELLA, who is kind, obedient and subservient, **WANTS** a new life. **WHY?** She is in an awful situation; her father has died and left her under the guardianship of a mean and selfish stepmother. Cinderella feels stifled. Lonely. Unhappy. Friendless. She is treated as a servant and she wants to escape this life. (See how I've stuck to the *emotional* want—yes, her IMMEDIATE GOAL of going to the Prince's Ball is a *plot point,* but the plot doesn't tell us anything about Cinderella. To get to know the character and why she will make the choices she makes, we must know her OVERALL EMOTIONAL WANT OR NEED.)

2. Cinderella **LOGICALLY** pursues her overall want by trying to take advantage of an invitation from the palace to go to the ball. The ball represents something that could change her life, get her out of her rut. So she does the *most* logical thing. She *asks* her stepmother. (Let the character do LOGICAL things to attain their overall want and immediate goals first, you will lose your audience if your protagonist makes too many illogical choices.) The stepmother says, yes, *if* you do the chores and make yourself a dress and help your stepsisters and clean the house, you can go to the ball. Cinderella *does* all these things—logically thinking that she will get her desire. This again reflects on character: Cinderella is a trusting and kind soul.

3. Cinderella is **DENIED.** Her hateful stepmother goes back on her word and denies Cinderella. Cinderella's dress is ruined; the stepmother and stepsisters leave without her. She is far out in the country; there is no way to get to the ball, even if her dress hadn't been ruined. This is a huge emotional setback; not only does she not reach her immediate goal, she is reminded in a devastating way that she is friendless, servile, unhappy and there is no one to turn to for help.

4. **SECOND OPPORTUNITY TO ATTAIN THE OVERALL WANT.** The Fairy Godmother arrives and offers Cinderella a chance to go to the ball. This is Cinderella's next chance to get that *new life* she desperately wants. The Fairy Godmother also represents friendship—an ally who cares about Cinderella.

5. Cinderella's **CONFLICTS ABOUT TAKING ADVANTAGE OF THE SECOND OPPORTUNITY.** This goes back to Cinderella's character. She's obedient. She's subservient. She feels conflicted about disobeying her stepmother. She worries about her stepmother and stepsisters reactions if she shows up at the ball. What if they make a scene? What if they toss her out? Cinderella also worries that she has nothing to wear. She is also concerned that she doesn't know how to act at a ball; after all, she's never been to one. She's never danced with a prince, what if she trips or falls? There's also a time limit placed on her—she has to be home by midnight. Conflicts are many, taking advantage of this second opportunity could bring about disaster.

6. **GOES FOR IT.** Cinderella decides to take advantage of the Fairy Godmother's offer. The opportunity is too wonderful to pass up and *Cinderella wants what she wants with all her heart.* The overall want has to be strong; unless your character's desire is strong, the audience will not connect with the story.

7. **ALL GOES WELL.** The Fairy Godmother provides Cinderella with a beautiful dress. She gets a cool carriage. She arrives at the ball. Her stepmother and stepsisters don't recognize her. Everyone thinks she's beautiful. She doesn't trip or make a fool of herself. And best of all: The prince falls in love with her.

8. **ALL FALLS APART.** Cinderella loses track of time, the clock strikes midnight and she has to race out without letting the prince know who she is; he can't call her, visit her, her identity is secret. Her dress turns to rags. Her carriage disintegrates. She loses a glass slipper. At home, when the stepmother and stepsisters arrive, they talk about the ball, the prince, and the mysterious, ravishing, charming girl. Cinderella can't admit she was there. They talk of how the Prince fell in love with this mysterious beauty. Cinderella cannot raise her hand and say "That was me!" Cinderella is back to being the "servant." Life is not looking good for Cinderella.

9. **CRISIS.** The Prince's emissary comes around with the glass slipper but Cinderella can't try it on unless she admits what she's done. Will Cinderella give up and keep her disobedience a secret? Will she deny herself happiness in order to not make waves? Is her flaw (subservience) going to get the best of her? How badly does she want to achieve her goal? She has *a decision to make.*

10. **CLIMAX.** Cinderella acts on her decision to continue pursuing her overall want; she faces the wrath of her stepmother, convinces the emissary she should try on the shoe—and it fits!

11. **TRUTH COMES OUT.** Cinderella has to *admit* that she disobeyed, that she was the mysterious girl at the ball. Only the truth will make it possible for her to attain her new life.

If the story is a tragedy, the final step is usually missing; things are *not* made right and the climax does not culminate in an emotional success for the protagonist. Consider **CHINATOWN, DOUBLE INDEMNITY, BODY HEAT, L.A. CONFIDENTIAL, GRAVEYARD OF THE FIREFLIES, REQUIEM FOR A DREAM.** These are tragedies where the protagonist suffers defeat, great loss or death.

So that's a quickie version of the ELEVEN STEP STORY STRUCTURE. Most film stories, whether independent or studio films, whether wild and out there or classic, follow this template.

The Eleven Steps Can Help Make Your Script Unique

What you will realize as you study the story structure of good films is that they all hit each of the Eleven Steps—but they do it at a different pace with different emphasis on each step. Some films spend time at Step #2, letting the protagonist struggle with the *LOGICAL ATTEMPTS* to achieve her goal. Many mysteries and investigative stories spend time in this area. Some films spend more time in Step #3, building up the *DENIAL STAGE* so that the protagonist's back is up against the wall in every part of his life. A large number of films spend time in Step #8, building a series of *ALL FALLS APART* events that make the circumstances of the protagonist more and more dire. Consider disaster films, relationship dramas or comedies that turn on misunderstandings. Step #10, the *CLIMAX* is also an area that invariably gets attention and time on the screen.

Wherever you spend the time in your story is up to you. In the chapter with sample story breakdowns, you will see how some of the best films spend a bulk of their screen time in various areas. But all the films will touch on each of the Eleven Steps. It's part of good storytelling.

Let's go into more detail:

1. Character's OVERALL WANT/NEED and WHY

Your main character needs to *want* something and the more he/she wants it, the better. It's got to be important. It has to be major in his or her life. It has to be consuming. The satisfaction of this overall want will be pursued by setting a series of immediate goals. Immediate goals have to do with the plot: The protagonist wants to win the game, get the girl, steal the diamonds, become a superstar, be elected President, find the kidnapper, get revenge… the list is endless. Immediate goals can change and morph as the story progresses; a boxer wants to win his first neighborhood bout, then he wants to get the girl, then he wants to win a more prestigious title, then he wants to be elected mayor—all goals that could work towards an overall want of gaining respect.

Immediate goals deal with plot, overall want deals with character.

There has to be a good and, most times, emotional *reason* for this overall want. You want to be specific: A mother *wants* to find her kidnapped daughter. But why? Because of an overall want of *love*? Or because she feels her daughter is something to be owned and she needs to feel the *power* of ownership? A man *wants* to be President of his country. Why? Is his overall want to have *power* (for good or bad reasons) or does his overall want have to do with a desire for *respect*? A teen *wants* money to get his homeless family off the street because his overall want is a sense of *security.* **SHREK** wants *love and acceptance.* Why? Because he has no friends. Jake Gittes in **CHINATOWN** wants *respect.* Why? He wants to cleanse himself of guilt due to past experiences in Chinatown. Benjamin in **THE GRADUATE** wants *purpose* in his life. Why? He feels rudder-less, he's confused about what to do now in his life. In **CASABLANCA**, Rick wants *connection* in his life. Why? He is uncomfortable with the disconnection he's embraced after being jilted by the woman he loved. William Wallace, in **BRAVEHEART,** wants *justice.* Why? To avenge the death of his love and bring an end to the threat to his people. In **SHAKESPEARE IN LOVE,** Shakespeare wants a *muse.* Why? His whole sense of self and success is wrapped up in writing a good play. In **MILLION DOLLAR BABY,** Frankie wants to *understand* right and wrong, he wants to know what is the right thing to do. Why? He can't find peace in his life and he desperately needs to do right by someone to feel that peace.

Ask yourself: What happens to your character if he does not get what he wants? Will his life be empty? Will he die lonely and miserable? Will she never know peace? Will the family be destitute? Will a criminal go free and kill again? Will a life be meaningless? Will great love never be realized? Will a son never find peace in a relationship with his father? Make the stakes and consequences high—your story will benefit.

2. *Character LOGICALLY goes about trying to fulfill his Overall Want*

Your main character needs to pursue his Overall Want in a logical fashion first. These logical steps are the first immediate goals of your character. If you don't have this step, the audience will be asking, "If she wanted the job, why didn't she apply for it? Or just ask?" Or just pick up the phone and call? Or enter the race so as to win it? Go to the cops/lawyer/judge to get justice? Date? Enroll in college? Go on job interviews? Finish writing the book? Try to talk peace with the mob boss? If a character wants to find a loving, long-term relationship, is it the logical thing to pick up dangerous-looking hitchhikers in a bad part of town? No. Logically she might ask her friends to set her up, she could try internet dating, she could join a club. Only when all practical, logical options are used up and she's feeling desperately alone will she be ready to make a choice that could very well change her life forever.

Follow the *logic* of the story as well as the emotion of the story; that way you won't lose your audience. A character must pursue the *logical steps* before having to resort to an action that will force him into unknown or unfamiliar territory.

3. *Character is DENIED*

At this step of the story, the main character needs to hit a large enough roadblock so that he needs to find a new path or way to accomplish his overall want.

a.   Think of Michael Corleone in **THE GODFATHER.** His overall want is *respect.* He wants to live a "normal American life" outside the mob, which means outside his family. He's taken the *logical* steps; he's joined the military and become a decorated soldier, he has a WASP fiancé, he's got plans for a life outside the family business—he even has his

Gardner's Guide to Screenplay: From Idea to Successful Script father's blessing. But then his father is attacked and Michael has to step up to protect his family and their honor. He has been denied his immediate goal, his plan has hit a major roadblock. He is pulled into the family "business"—and is now on a whole new path (which will eventually lead him to his overall want; to gain respect).

b. Think of Maximus in **GLADIATOR.** He wants to go home to his family and his land. His overall want is *peace* (the peace of being with his family, the peaceful life of a farmer). Logically he's done what he thinks will get him what he wants; he fought well in the war, thus he knows the Emperor owes him. Maximus also *asks* the Emperor to grant his desire. But when the Emperor is murdered and the throne is taken over by evil Commodus, Maximus is marked for death because of his loyalty to Emperor Aurelius. Maximus manages to escape the first attack and he heads home to see his family, but they are dead. Maximus is taken into slavery. The DENIAL stage of this film is multi-layered (which is something to consider in your story) and sets Maximus on a whole new journey that will lead him, eventually, to the sense of peace and reunion with his family in the afterlife.

4. A SECOND OPPORTUNITY to achieve Overall Want presents itself

Just when all seems lost, or too difficult, or too unfair—there's an opportunity. A *new* way to achieve the overall want presents itself. It could be a Fairy Godmother, it could be a new job, it could be the annoying neighbor who moves in next door. It could be meeting Han Solo or winning the lottery or meeting someone who will ask the character to join a soccer team, (2002's **BEND IT LIKE BECKHAM**) or forced to become a gladiator against one's will (**GLADIATOR**).

a. Think of 1990's **PRETTY WOMAN.** Edward (portrayed by Richard Gere) takes advantage of the opportunity of using Vivian (portrayed by Julia Roberts) to help his business problem. What the character *needs* (but isn't aware of at the outset of film) is not business success, but personal life success—and Vivian will eventually help him find it (not without a struggle of course).

b. Think of 1985's **WITNESS.** John Book (portrayed by Harrison Ford) has a second opportunity to stay alive long enough to solve the crime: He is given the opportunity to live with the Amish while he finds the answers he needs.

c.   Think of Disney's **BEAUTY AND THE BEAST.** Belle's second opportunity to fulfill her dream of finding a more challenging life is being stuck in the castle with a Beast. This second opportunity doesn't necessarily look like a *good* thing, but it will be the opportunity she needs to fulfill her overall want.

d.   Think of **FINDING NEVERLAND.** J.M. Barrie (portrayed by Johnny Depp) has suffered failure with his latest play; his relationship with his wife has deteriorated and does not inspire him. His second opportunity to find a muse is meeting Sylvia and her sons in the park.

e.   Think of **MILLION DOLLAR BABY.** Frankie (portrayed by Clint Eastwood) has lost his latest boxer as a client, he is denied spiritual satisfaction from the priest, his daughter refuses to communicate with him. His second opportunity to understand life is taking on the coaching Maggie.

The second opportunity doesn't always have to seem like a good thing. Does **GLADIATOR'S** Maximus want to be a gladiator? Does Belle want to be a prisoner in the Beast's castle? Frankie, in **MILLION DOLLAR BABY,** initially orders Maggie out of his gym, does not want anything to do with her. Remember, your character is on a journey, possibly not one of his or her choosing. They don't know what the end of the journey will be, they don't know "what's needed" to get them to the desired end. The journey should be difficult, it should have unexpected twists and turns. *The more difficult and challenging, the better.*

5.   *CONFLICTS INVOLVED in taking advantage of second opportunity*

If it's too easy, it's not good. Good stories need *conflict* and not just between the protagonist and the antagonist. Let there be conflict in all relationships, even friendships. The really good film stories also deal with internal conflict as well as external conflict.

So what's at stake for your main character if he accepts the second opportunity you have designed? What's the moral conflict? Is she making a pact with the devil? Is there physical danger? Is there emotional conflict? Does he have to go behind his best friend's back to accomplish this goal? Does she have to lie? Cheat? Pretend to be something he's not?

a.   Think of 1942's **CASABLANCA.** Rick's second opportunity to connect again with his passions is Ilsa coming back into his life.

Conflicts here? You bet. First, it's clear Rick still loves Ilsa even though he hates what she did to him. He finds out she's married—and married to a hero in the Resistance. Conflicts and questions abound. Why should he risk his life by giving the woman who jilted him letters of transport? He has declared himself neutral, so why should he get involved in politics again? The Chief of Police notices Rick's interest in Ilsa, this puts Rick in danger. The Germans are tightening the border, focusing more of their interest on Rick's immigrant-friendly club, this puts Rick's livelihood and the lives of his employees at risk.

b.   Think of **TOOTSIE.** Michael's conflict? He has to pretend to be a woman. He's lying. He is physically challenged every day, in voice and appearance. He's a guy who likes to put the moves on women. He can't pursue women (as a man) while dressed as a woman. His roommate thinks he's crazy. He took the acting job his best female friend wanted and if she finds out, she will hate him. The conflicts pile up *and this is good.*

c.   Think of **GLADIATOR.** Maximus has conflicts about performing as a gladiator: He doesn't want to kill. He doesn't want to be "entertainment." He's a slave and this is not how he wants to live. He does not get along with the man who "owns" the gladiators. But Maximus comes to realize that if he does well as a gladiator he will eventually end up in the Roman Coliseum performing for the new Emperor Commodus. This is a path to garnering the revenge he desires to bring a feeling of peace back into his life.

Note: *Step #5 is an area that can and should be built up. The more conflicts, the more chances you'll have to explore character as your story progresses.*

6.   DECISION TO GO FOR IT

The main character decides that despite all the conflicts and/or advice against taking advantage of this second opportunity, she must take advantage of it and continue to pursue her *overall want.* That's really important. Don't switch overall want mid-stream. Yes, your story may go down various paths and *immediate goals* may change as the plot unfolds, but the strong emotional overall want should not change.

a.   In **TOOTSIE,** Michael's overall want is *respect* and that never changes—but within the film his immediate goals move forward—

he wants the job, he wants the love of Julie, he wants to get his friend's play produced, he wants to apologize to Julie's dad… All these immediate goals will help him attain his overall want: Respect.

b. In **CASABLANCA,** Rick's overall want is a *connection in his life.* Within the film his immediate goals change. He wants to hide the letters of transport, he wants the girl, he wants the cause to go forward, he wants the respect of Resistance leader, Lazlo. These immediate goals all relate to his overall want of connecting to life once again.

Often this Decision to Go For It is a "taken for granted" moment and there's no big scene that heralds the acceptance or decision. Sometimes if seems as if the character has no choice. But remember, character always has a choice; try to survive or face death? Join the team or run away? Grab the girl from the burning car or drive on? Try to explore the scene where the protagonist makes a decision to engage (or not). In 1994's **LION KING,** the moment for Simba is punctuated by a *hit on the head* from Zazu—duh! How can Simba *not* take the opportunity to go back and save his pride and become the leader he is meant to be?

7.   ALL GOES WELL (…usually for a very short time)

Give your character the smarts, wiles, charm, physical prowess, comedic goofiness (or whatever) to have a go at getting close to his overall want while taking advantage of this second opportunity. Cinderella got to the ball, she wasn't recognized, the Prince thought she was beautiful, she fell in love—before all hell broke loose.

Think of Rick in **CASABLANCA:** The woman he loves, Ilsa, comes to him, tells him she can't live without him, she will leave her husband for him. She asks Rick to tell her to decide the proper path for both of them. He has achieved his latest immediate goal—get the woman he loves back.… Things are going great? Snnnzzzz—- snore snore snore. If there is no conflict, the story will start to drag. In **CASABLANCA,** the love scene that surely followed Ilsa's declaration did not make it to the screen. The screenwriters and filmmakers cut to the next moment of *conflict.*

Note that while things are going well for Cinderella at the ball there is always the chance that she will be recognized, the clock is always ticking towards midnight.

Keep the conflicts going even as your protagonist has a taste of success.

Build tension; this happiness is not meant to last, the villain is approaching, there's guilt, subterfuge, other forces conspiring.

8. ALL FALLS APART

This is the part of your story where your character is severely tested. Physically and/or emotionally.

Build this area of the film. In most cases, it's not just one incident, it's a series of events. Elements of the main plot, subplots, and relationships you've set up take a nose dive. The protagonist gets misunderstood, gets beaten up, loses love, gets cheated on, has his boss come down on him, has his parents disown him, breaks a leg, loses a battle, loses a spaceship, is betrayed ... *everything* falls apart. People, promises, weaknesses become real and scary liabilities...

a. Consider the 1993 film, **FALLING DOWN,** written by Ebbe Roe Smith and starring Michael Douglas. Ninety percent of the film is spent in Step #9. Disaster films, by their nature, spend most of the time here, as do Horror films.

b. Consider 1995's **TOY STORY;** a large percentage of the film takes place while things are falling apart for Woody as he attempts to bring Buzz back home.

c. Consider 1967's **THE GRADUATE,** things start falling apart when Benjamin is forced into a date with the daughter of the woman with whom he is having an affair.

In romantic comedies there is the typical "boy gets girl, boy LOSES girl, boy HAS TO GET GIRL BACK" template. Most of the time is spent in the FAILURE TO GET GIRL BACK section. That's the part of the story that is the most interesting.

9. CRISIS

Will the main character be able to make the difficult decision and go forward in the pursuit of his goal? Will she put her own judgment above others? Will he give up? Will he decide that he hasn't the strength to climb the last mountain? Is the emotional pain of trying again too much? Will she let her boss get the better of her? Will she stand up for herself or not? Will he put himself on the line and declare love/ patriotism/whistle blow or not? Will the protagonist decide to succeed or fail? The *crisis point* is a *decision*. Will the protagonist give up or go forward? Does your hero have the stamina? Does she have a strong moral code? Does he believe in himself? Does she realize that life means nothing if she does not test herself? Is your hero ready to risk death for what he believes in?

a.   In **NETWORK** Max has to make a decision; will he leave his wife to live with his co-worker, Diana?

b.   In **ANNIE HALL,** Alvy has a choice to make. Should he go to Los Angeles and propose marriage to Annie?

c.   In **GLADIATOR** Maximus, injured, weak and having every excuse to give up his quest, has to choose to go into the gladiator ring one more time; this time against his arch-enemy.

d.   In **KRAMER VS KRAMER,** Ted has a decision to make. Everyone has told him he has no chance to get custody of his child. Everyone has told him to give up. Will he decide, on Christmas Eve, to go to all lengths to secure a job in order to make his custody case look a bit better or will he give up?

10.   CLIMAX

The main character digs deep into physical and emotional reservoirs. He goes that extra mile to defeat the antagonist and attain his goal. It could be a courtroom scene, it could be a fierce battle in space, it could be the championship basketball game, it could be a chess match, it could be racing against time to save the world, a race to stop a wedding, robbing a bank, a plan to show great love. The climax *needs* to be the most difficult test, physically and emotionally, of the protagonist in the entire story.

In action films, it's usually the final battle where the protagonist fights against the hugest odds.

In love stories, it's usually the most emotional evidence of love. In dramas, it's usually the most revelatory scenes in the film.

If the task ahead looks impossible, that's great. Nothing should be easy. Your hero must find the strength to deal with what's coming at him. Experiment with writing yourself into a corner, construct scenarios where there's no hope. See if you can find a way out for your protagonist. Defeat should be near, a real possibility.

11. THE TRUTH COMES OUT

After the final test (the climax) has ended and the bad guys have been bested (or not) there are the details to be considered. Cinderella has to admit she went to the ball against her stepmother's wishes in order to try on the shoe and get her prince. The truth has to come out; sometimes in order to make things right.

a. In **TOOTSIE,** Michael has to apologize to the man who gave him an engagement ring. He has to make up with his friends. He has to try get the girl he loves to talk to him again… he has to admit he was a better man as a woman than he ever was as a man.

b. **WITNESS:** John Book and Rachel realize that even though they may love each other, they cannot live in the same world. He cannot live with the Amish, she cannot live in the big city. The truth is evident as he drives back to Philadelphia and Rachel's Amish suitor approaches her farm.

c. **IT HAPPENED ONE NIGHT:** Peter goes to Ellie's father and reveals his love for her. Ellie runs out on her wedding to be with Peter, thus showing her true love for him. Peter and Ellie await the telegram that relays news of Ellie's annulment and when it arrives, the "Walls of Jericho" descend.

d. **FINDING NEVERLAND:** J.M. Barrie accepts partial guardianship of the boys after Sylvia's death, proving his true connection to them. The youngest boy finally connects with Barrie.

e. **MILLION DOLLAR BABY:** Frankie finally finds the perfect lemon meringue pie after making the decision to help Maggie end her life. The pie symbolizes the peace Frankie has found through these actions.

This Truth Comes Out step will allow you to show that there is a "*new normal life*" for your main character. The journey of the story has changed the protagonist. The overall want has been gained (perhaps not in the *way* that was expected, but satisfactorily nonetheless) and now life is leading the protagonist down a new path or perhaps he is simply changed—and how he lives his life will now be different.

Note: In tragedies or those stories whose ending is meant to leave the audience hanging, you may choose to end at the CRISIS or at the end of the CLIMAX. Consider CHINATOWN, the neo-noir film written by Robert Towne. The film comes to an abrupt ending at the end of the climax. There is no sense of future, there is no hint to what comes next for the characters.

Remember, leaving your audience hanging may not be the most commercial choice. Audiences get a satisfaction from knowing there's a satisfactory (or unsatisfactory) future for the character in whom they've become so invested. But stories come in all shapes and sizes and you, the writer, get to decide.

Why is the Eleven Step Story Structure more helpful than just using the tent poles of the Three Act template? The Eleven Steps focus on *character* and *character is the most important part of your screen story*. The Eleven Step Story Structure will help you make sure that the character is making the plot happen, that the plot is integral to a character's journey. Stories live and die on building multi-dimensional, interesting, flawed and wonderful characters.

The Eleven Step Story Structure will also help you figure out *what scenes* you need to write in order to make your character's journey include ups and downs, challenges and conflicts. It will help you build to an exciting crisis and climax. It will help you track where you are in your screen story.

Overlay of the Eleven Step Story Structure

Remember, specific page count suggestions of the classic Three Act Structure do no need to be used. Think of the character journey, construct events that support the steps of the story—and let the page count fall naturally.

- **ACT ONE:** Steps 1–3; Character's Overall Want and Why, Character Logically Goes for It and the Character is Denied. The writer takes the time to set up the protagonist and his overall want. The writer sets up the antagonist who will be trying to stop the protagonist from achieving his Overall Want. The writer sets up the supporting cast. Tone, genre and place are set up. The protagonist logically goes for it, tries to accomplish his immediate goals that will bring about satisfying his Overall Want. Obstacles and reversals abound and finally there is a denial that is so large that he is forced to change course or find new methods to achieve his overall want. If you break down successful films, a high percentage of them will have the big denial on or near page 25 to 30. But there are exceptions. See the chapter on film breakdowns for examples.

- **ACT TWO:** Steps 4–9, Character's Second Opportunity to Achieve Overall Want, Conflicts About Taking Advantage of the Second Opportunity, Decision to Go for It, All Goes Well, All Falls Apart and finally, the Crisis. Your protagonist has gotten a second opportunity to achieve her overall want. It may (or may not) be the easiest or most logical path to follow, and there are many strings (conflicts) attached in taking advantage of the Second Opportunity. All may go well for a time, but then things fall apart, take a turn for the worse and great difficulties arise. Relationships sour, plots thicken, battles ensue, words are misunderstood.... whatever furthers the story on its downward spiral. Finally, the hero has a choice (crisis), should she give up or go forward? Should she go into the dark alley to face death or turn her back and live as a coward? Should she believe in love or not? Should she trust or not? Again, a high percentage of films will put the Crisis at about page 75 to 80, but it's not necessary to hit an exact page count.

- **ACT THREE:** Steps 10–11, Climax and Truth Comes Out To Make Things Right. In the *climax,* the protagonist digs deeper than he has ever dug, calls on resources he didn't even know he had, battles to the near death (emotionally or physically or both) and comes out triumphant (or not). Hopefully he has learned something new about himself. There should be a change in the protagonist; he should end the screen story a different person than he was at the beginning. After the intense or crazy or difficult climax, the *truth* is revealed. She did really love him. He did believe the world could be saved. She could win the race. He could think beyond himself and take care of his parent. She could escape the prison and find peace in the wilderness. There is a resolution of important supporting stories and a sense of the new normal life for the protagonist.. Traditionally, the Steps #10 and #11 will cover about 25 pages, but again, there are exceptions and it is not necessary.

Remember: If you make sure all Eleven Story Steps are represented and explored, your story will work whether or not you hit traditional page count. Let your film have a rhythm all its own.

Question: I have been asked in many of my classes; can one overlay the Three Act template onto the Eleven Step Story Structure?

Answer: Answer: There are two responses you should take into consideration:

#1. Yes, one can overlay the Eleven Step Story Structure on the Three Act template. Act One ends at the Denial (Step #3). Act Two ends at the Crisis (Step #9). Act Three ends when the Truth Comes out (Step #11). A high percentage of movies including **THE STING, BEAUTY AND THE BEAST, GLADIATOR, LION KING, MILLION DOLLAR BABY, SPIDERMAN** and many other successful films, follow an Eleven Step Story Structure that fits even to expected page count. But—

#2. It's not necessary to use the page count demands of the Three Act template. If you follow the Eleven Steps, you will have every story element you need in your screen story. You can choose to spend more time in one area or another, on whatever you think are the most compelling elements. Your Denial (Step #3) could be on page 5 or page 30. Things could start Falling Apart (Step #8) in a major way very quickly. The Climax could be short or long. You decide the rhythm of your story.

The Eleven Step Story Structure Has Its Own Rhythm

No one wants all screen stories to follow predictable rhythms. Films need to be varied, original and tell stories in new ways. You don't want the audience to get ahead of you. You want to satisfy their desire for a strong story, but you want to give them something fresh and exciting.

Using the Eleven Step Story Structure frees the writer from trying to hit the *page count* attributed to the Three Act template and to tell the character's story in a fresh rhythm.

Stories may spend more time on one step of the ELEVEN STEP STRUCTURE than another. A film like **KRAMER VS KRAMER** has its Denial (Step #3) close to the top of the film; Ted Kramer (portrayed by Dustin Hoffman), wants the *perfect life.* He thinks he's set it up; good job with a promotion in sight, blonde beautiful wife, nice apartment, a son. He arrives home after work and his wife announces she's leaving him. He is *denied* this perfect life and the audience is propelled into his journey of new understanding.

A film like Hitchcock's **VERTIGO** spends half of the movie in the *Logically Goes For It* (Step #2). Scotty (portrayed by James Stewart) desires a *purpose in life.* His expectation of working his way up to the head of the police force is over—due to his vertigo. Scotty asks his best friend, Midge, her opinions, but that doesn't help. He allows himself to be talked into doing a favor for an old college friend. He agrees to tail his friend's wife to determine if she is losing her grasp on reality. He finds *purpose* in this task and more *purpose* when he falls in love with her. The unraveling of the mystery of Madeline is his logical attempt to add a purpose to his life; and in true Hitchcock fashion, this unraveling is odd, full of eerie tension and conflict. The *Denial (Step #3)* does not arrive till mid-film, when Madeline falls to her death from the bell tower.

A film like **SHAKESPEARE IN LOVE** spends most of its time in *Step # 7: All Goes Well.* The protagonist, Shakespeare, is getting what he wants (a muse) through his love affair with Viola. He is inspired, his writing is going well, his play is brilliant. But there is danger in all his actions; he and Viola's forbidden love may come to light. Viola's acting in his play (which is unlawful because she's a woman) may come to light. The theatre could be shut down. Shakespeare's debts may catch up with him. John Webster may spy Viola and Shakespeare together and spill the beans… if the writer chooses to spend time in *All Goes Well,* he must build in tension and conflict even while the main character is making positive strides at achieving his overall want.

Another example of a film that spends time in *All Goes Well (Step #7)* is **KRAMER VS KRAMER.** After getting to a very quick *Denial*, Ted, who has been selfishly working towards accomplishing his want—to have the perfect life (perfect idea of family, perfect idea of good job)—enters a new world; that of being a single dad. He goes on a journey to really get to know his son, learn what it means to be a parent and to see the world (specifically men and women's roles) through new eyes. Because there is so much *conflict* in the struggle, the *All Goes Well* step remains riveting. There's conflict with Ted and his son, conflict with Ted and his boss, conflict with Ted and the neighbor—all these conflicts make Ted grow as a person and re-evaluate what constitutes a "perfect life."

Think about 1988's **RAINMAN.** It, too, spends the bulk of its time in *Step #7, All Goes Well.* Charlie (portrayed by Tom Cruise) is selfish and ambitious. His overall want is to feel loved and validated and have a sense of family (he would never admit this and doesn't even consciously realize it). The film begins with his wealthy father's death. Charlie returns home in hopes that getting his inheritance will make him feel appreciated by his father. He is quickly *denied* when he learns the bulk of the estate (the money) goes to a brother he never knew he had. Charlie kidnaps his autistic brother, Raymond, from his safe institutional home to try to get his hands on the money (to get the money is one of Charlie's first immediate goals.) The brothers journey across country and Charlie finds that he is attaining his overall want (sense of family and knowledge that his father loved him), but the *conflict* in dealing with his autistic brother is intense. Phobias. Fears. Miscommunication. When a flawed character like Charlie is on a journey of self-discovery and is actually making progress before the rug is pulled out from under him—spending time in *All Goes Well, Step #7* is the structure that really works.

Many stories spend most of their time in *Step #8, All Falls Apart.* Examples are: **FALLING DOWN, DIE HARD, MY BEST FRIEND'S WEDDING, WALK THE LINE, RAIDERS OF THE LOST ARK, UNFORGIVEN, TOY STORY, TRAINING DAY, THE SQUID AND THE WHALE**... films of all genres. Audiences are interested in watching a character deal with adversity and obstacles. Will the protagonist find the strength to combat the forces that stand in the way of him realizing his overall want?

The Eleven Steps can be used to make sure your character has a *journey* from beginning to end, one that includes a change. It will help you construct good times and bad times. It will put the climax on your main character's shoulders because it will be his or her *decision* at the crisis point that brings on the climax. Following the Eleven Steps will force your character to face their deepest, darkest hell and battle to win or lose. The Eleven Steps will ensure that there is a new normal for the protagonist at the end of the screen story.

The most important thing to remember is that you, the writer, are in charge. You are the original voice. You hold the key to a story that reflects your view of the world. The way you tell your story is your choice—and there is no right or wrong choice. It all comes down to *what works*. And what usually works is a well-crafted, well-structured screenplay that leads the reader (and eventually the audience in the theatre) down an emotional and exciting journey.

Learn the components of good story structure because each element in your screenplay should be designed to further your main character's story.

Plot is important, but not as important as character.

Focus on your main character's journey. Character makes the plot happen; let character choices drive the plot. Once you rely on plot twists rather than exploration of character, you are in danger of losing your audience.

Concentrate on your characters. Therein lies the gold.

Exercise:

1. How can you pinpoint the overall want of a character? Ask yourself: Is he a musician who wants to make a record? Is she the President of the United States and she wants a peace treaty with a specific country? Does he want to get the girl of his dreams? Is she a teacher who wants her school to win a Disco Championship? Once you have chosen a character and a strong immediate goal, think about why this goal is so important. Does your character desire respect from others? What is it in his backstory that makes him feel that he doesn't have the respect he desires? Does she want to be loved? Why does she feel unloved? Does he want power? Security? Find the emotional need that is making your character strive for his immediate goals.

2. List *three logical actions* your character could take to try to secure his overall want. Explore different areas of his life. If a desire for respect drives him, how does he go about getting respect at home? At work? At school? Among his friends? Don't forget what actions your protagonist takes to achieve his first or foremost immediate goal.

3. Now, for each of those three logical actions, write down how these actions backfire or fail. By doing this, you are creating reversals and forcing your protagonist to deal with obstacles that will force him to dig deeper within himself to continue on his journey.

4. Then come up with a major *Denial* that will force him on a new path.

Example: My character's name is Ellie and she wants a promotion (her first immediate goal) at the Clothing Design firm where she works. She wants others to respect her (her Overall Want) because her parents told her she was not smart or talented enough to make it on her own, they wanted her to stay in the small town she grew up in and work at the family grocery business. In order to try to gain respect she:

Logical Step A: Ellie works all night on new designs and goes to present them to her boss. Reversal: Unfortunately, the main boss has been called to Paris. He has left his talent-less and mean-spirited daughter, Valerie, in charge of choosing candidates for the promotion. Valerie doesn't even bother looking at Ellie's drawings, thinking Ellie is too young and too lowly in the company to consider for the promotion. Ellie is certainly not getting respect.

Meanwhile, at the apartment she shares: her roommate has invited her boyfriend to move in without consulting Ellie (showing no respect). Ellie tries to talk to her about it, her roommate won't listen (again, no respect!).

Logical Step B: Ellie tries to stand out in the staff meeting but a fellow designer, Rick (who also wants the promotion), cuts her off before she can get a complete sentence out. Valerie finds Rick attractive and it's clear she lusts after him. Rick gets to take Valerie out to lunch and Ellie again has failed to get Valerie's attention or respect. Meanwhile, Ellie gets her lunch from the deli downstairs and even though she goes there every day and asks for the same sandwich from the deli owner, he gets her order wrong again and she bites into an undesired hot pepper and breaks out into a rash. (No respect from the deli owner.)

Logical Step C: At lunch, Ellie asks her mentor at the company to speak to Valerie on her behalf. The mentor agrees. Reversal: Unfortunately, the mentor breaks a leg when he slips on the icy streets as they walk back to the office. He is whisked off to the hospital in an ambulance. Ellie sees Rick and Valerie coming back from lunch, looking very chummy. Rick smirks at Ellie, clearly thinking he's winning—and showing her he does not respect her.

After you have built some logical attempts designed to attain the overall want of your main character, build a scenario where the rug is pulled out in a more major way—this will be your *Denial (Step #3)*. Perhaps, in this story, Ellie decides to sneak into the offices late at night and put her portfolio on the top of the pile–or to put a photograph of Rick and the office secretary kissing in the stairwell on Valerie's desk—or to fax her work to Paris to the real boss… and she gets caught by security. Whatever she is doing looks very suspicious and the next day she is FIRED. Now that's a larger and more major Denial that the previous reversals and this Denial forces Ellie onto a new path.

5. Keeping in mind your character's Overall Want, think of at least three different *Second Opportunities* that could present themselves. Remember it's the Overall Want that is the most important, and the Second Opportunity doesn't always have to seem like a good thing.

    Example: Using Ellie's story (from above) here are a few things that could be considered as a Second Opportunity to gain respect. After being fired, she could get a new job at a competing design house. That could work, it seems a bit easy. Perhaps she gets a job as a waitress because she's broke. Feeling defeated—and frustrated with the ugly uniforms, she designs new uniforms for herself and fellow waitresses and this leads to success… Perhaps she takes the last of her savings and flies to Paris in hopes of pleading her case with the boss. On the plane she is pick-pocketed and arrives in Paris with no money and at the hotel where the boss is staying, she finds out he's just checked out. Penniless, she has to build a new life in Paris…

    Ask yourself what is the most interesting *new world* that the *Second Opportunity (Step #4)* can open?

6. Continue through the Eleven Steps, asking yourself as you go along; is this the most exciting, dramatic, envelope-pushing choice you could make with your story? No need to decide on anything. No need to marry yourself to one choice or another right now. Just get your mind thinking in the broad strokes of your story—always keeping in mind that each step needs to relate to the main character trying to attain the *Overall Want*.

Chapter Summary

- The Eleven Step Story Structure is designed to help you chart your story, making sure it is focused on character.

- Films with a strong beginning, middle and end that point to character change are satisfying stories for an audience.

- The Overall Want of the protagonist is an emotional desire or need. This does not change throughout the film story.

- The Immediate Goals are the tasks and aspirations the characters strive to attain throughout the film story. They are plot-oriented and can change and morph as the story progresses.

- The Eleven Step Story Structure can work in tandem with the classic Three Act Structure.

- Specific page counts for each section of the script are not part of the Eleven Step Story Structure. Each story should have its own rhythm.

- Each screenwriter's voice and personal point of view is important. Film stories that reflect the world as the writer sees it always feel original.

Chapter Five

CHARACTER IS EVERYTHING

Do actors help get films made? Yes.

Do writers need to write characters that will attract fine actors? Yes.

Think of your all-time favorite film. What is it about that film you love? It's probably a character. **STAR WARS** is made memorable because of Han Solo, Darth Vader, Luke Skywalker and Princess Leia. **LETHAL WEAPON** (1987) is made memorable because of the chemistry between two detectives; one a conservative family man and one a wild-haired daredevil who flirts with a death wish. **THE HOURS** (2002) is all about character; three women in different eras and situations striving to find meaning in their lives. So is **A BEAUTIFUL MIND.** The summer sleeper hit of 2004, **NAPOLEON DYNAMITE,** is all about a wonderfully eccentric high school character. **TROY** (2004) is interesting because the cast of characters are well delineated by their overall wants; Achilles wants fame, Hector wants peace, Agamemnon wants power, Paris wants to believe that love can conquer all.

What do audiences respond to in the **DIRTY HARRY** films starring Clint Eastwood? The character, the character's point of view, the way he reacts to life. Consider **LEGALLY BLONDE, CLUELESS, BEING JULIA, ERIN BROCKOVICH, SCHOOL OF ROCK, CASABLANCA, TOOTSIE.** Do you remember all the plot points of the story or are the character moments more firmly embedded in your memory? It's probably the character moments. This is as it should be. The list of 100 Best Films Of All Time could also be a list of the 100 Best Film Characters Of All Time. Films are character-driven. Action films need great characters, romances need great characters, comedies need great characters…every film needs to be peopled with great characters. *Good characters are essential in good stories.*

Special effects are fun and fancy and can make our heads spin, but if all the tricks are at the expense of good characters and their growth through the story, then you end up with something like the disappointing 2004's **VAN HELSING,** where character arcs are forgotten while special effects fill the screen.

What makes a good character? Duality. Dewey Finn (portrayed by Jack Black) in **SCHOOL OF ROCK** (2003) is irresponsible and duplicitous and wild but he knows how to treat young students with kindness and empathy. He brings out the best in them. Elle in **LEGALLY BLONDE** is blonde, spoiled, into the elite social scene of Bel Air. She is also smart, determined, resourceful and a great friend. Duality refers to various sides of a character; sides that compliment and contradict one another. A successful screenwriter friend of mine likes to build his characters with contrasting adjectives; kind but selfish, violent but understanding, silly but smart. Find the duality of your characters—doing so will make them more three dimensional and interesting.

All Stories Are Journeys of Character

Shakespeare's Romeo, in **ROMEO AND JULIET,** is an unfocused young man who finds passion and purpose when he falls in love with Juliet. He begins the story not sure of what he wants or what he should be doing; he is at a loss as he struggles to understand the meaning of life. When he meets Juliet, everything changes. He has a purpose in his life now and that is to be in love with Juliet. Because Juliet is from a family that has a long-standing feud with Romeo's family, their love begins in secret. Passionate young Romeo learns, in the short time of their affair, that love is a reason for living… and dying.

Michael Corleone, in **THE GODFATHER** wants a life outside his Mafia family. He wants to be a solid, respected American, which to him means being successful within the confines of the law. He wants to marry a non-Italian wife and keep his father and brothers' business at arm's length. His journey of change begins when his father is attacked and near death. Michael viscerally reacts and strives to protect his father. This journey takes him deep inside his Mafia family where he makes hard choices. He comes to realize that blood ties are stronger than his "all- American vision of the future." When he commits murder to avenge the family, he knows this act will forever change his life. Picture Michael Corleone at the beginning of this story; fresh-faced and handsome in his military uniform. Now picture Michael at the end of the film: his face is hardened, older, scarred, sadder and wiser. He has accepted that the rest of his life will be lived as a major player within the Mafia community.

Rick, in **CASABLANCA,** is first seen as a man who will not take sides in the politics of the day. He seems to care for no one; he does not crave

"The Godfather" Al Pacino, Marlon Brando, James Caan, John Cazale
photo supplied by Globe Photos

friendships or alliances. When the woman he loves comes back into his life, feelings of passion, duty and honor are re-awakened.

Michael Dorsey, in **TOOTSIE,** wants to be a recognized and *working* actor. He's obsessed, self-centered, at a loss with the ladies because he's pig-headed, abrasive and pushy. He does not have a clue about how to drop the persona he's manufactured for himself. When he cross-dresses for an audition, and gets the part (they think he's a woman), he becomes "Dorothy Michaels ." This "cross-dressing" journey takes him down a path of self-discovery. By the end of the film he has lived as a *working* actor (actress?) and become a great star. He has achieved his immediate goal but realizes that without truth and love, it is not enough. He comes to realize that being an honest and empathetic person is valuable, honored and appreciated. When he says to Julie, the actress he has fallen in love with and been rejected by because of his lies and deceit; "I was a better man as a woman than I ever was as a man…," we realize the long, personal journey he has taken in this story.

Some films succeed without a strong character change for the protagonist but they are rare. One example: Maximus, in **GLADIATOR** begins his incredible journey from war hero to slave to gladiator to martyr as a brave and moral man who wants nothing more than to go home to his wife and son and live his life farming the land. His journey is not one of character change, it is more *a test of character.* Can he stay brave and moral against all odds? Will he falter when he is faced with death? Will he falter when all around him are killed and there seems to be no hope? Maximus ends up a brave and moral man (where he started) but the test he has endured is massive. Could this very good film have been absolutely great? Yes. What is missing from this film is *character growth and change*. We are impressed with Maximus' courage, but we never worry that he will falter. Audiences get involved when they worry, when human frailties threaten to keep the protagonist from reaching his full potential. Maximus could have been a more universal character if he had a flaw or two, one that could have put his moral superiority in question.

What Does Your Character Want?

Your protagonist should be the most three dimensional character in your screenplay. He or she needs to have a driving *overall want* or need. Sometimes your protagonist will know his *immediate goal* at the beginning of the film; but the immediate goal is different from overall want. The immediate goal is the specific: he wants to save the world, she wants to find her child, he wants to be a successful actor, she wants to be married, she wants to be the head of the corporation, he wants to live his life on the beach…

The overall want is an *emotional* character need. What drives the character to go for his immediate goal? What does the protagonist need to find satisfaction, peace or happiness on a deep level?

Since we're not all in tune with what we really *need* in life, we tend to focus on our specific immediate goals. Examples: "I want to sell a screenplay for a million dollars" or "I want to have a relationship with that person" or "I want to save up for a house" or "I want my parents off my back." Often we don't examine what the overall want is that propels us to want to fulfill our immediate goal. Does a person want to sell a screenplay because she wants *respect and validation*? Or because he requires money to pay for an operation for a child and in having enough money, he can fulfill a *need to control* the outcome of his loved one's life?

A protagonist's immediate goal can change and morph and accelerate during the film story. At some point the protagonist may reach that goal and find it is not really satisfying on a deep level. The emotional need still needs to be chased and won. Consider **RAIN MAN.** Charlie, portrayed by Tom Cruise, wants an inheritance from his father because he is in financial difficulty. When he is denied (by the will) a financial inheritance, he is hurt in a way that angers him and gets to the root of Charlie's real problem in life; never feeling totally approved of or loved by his father. He is convinced his father slighted him because of their difficult history; one with which Charlie cannot comes to terms. What Charlie realizes during the events of the film is that the money from the inheritance isn't what is most important to him. When he understands that his father did love him, he finally feels validated. Charlie gets that overall want fulfilled through his relationship with his brother, Raymond, the "Rain Man." Charlie's *immediate goals* during the film change; he starts out wanting money, then he wants to be able to kidnap his brother and convince him to give him a share of the inheritance, then he wants to live with his brother and create a family unit. His *overall want* doesn't change; he needs to emotionally connect with family on a deep, intimate level—to feel truly loved and to understand what it feels like to love in return.

Ask yourself: What will my protagonist lose if he does not attain his overall want? How will his life be forever unsatisfying?

The plot can be taken care of through the character achieving *immediate goals*. Sometimes the immediate goal can not be achieved until the protagonist goes through a character change and gets what he *needs* emotionally. How many romantic comedies are based on the protagonist learning that she can love or be loved or feel loved or accept love? Think about **PRETTY WOMAN, WHEN HARRY MET SALLY, BRIDGET**

"Rain Man" Dustin Hoffman, Tom Cruise
photo supplied by Rangefinders/Globe Photos

JONES' DIARY? How many stories are based on the protagonist learning that truth is the only thing that can set you free? Or that acceptance of others' frailties is life-affirming. Or acceptance of one's own frailties is life-affirming? Think about **MILLION DOLLAR BABY, OCEAN'S ELEVEN, WITNESS.** In these stories, the immediate goals cannot be achieved without the protagonist experiencing an epiphany or moment of self-realization. In some stories, the *plot* of the story will be completed, but the *personal* character journey needs to be completed before the story really feels as if it is over; Think about **SHAWSHANK REDEMPTION** (Andy escaped, but it is not until Red takes control of his life does the story really end), **THE STING** (Hooker and Henry pull off the con, but not until Hooker's plans for his future are clear does the film feel complete), **CASABLANCA** (Rick has sent Ilsa and her husband off, but it is not until we hear his commitment to continue to fight the Germans with Renault do we feel Rick's journey is over).

Character is Key

Finding your character is a constant discovery throughout the creating-the-story process. Make a list of your character's strong and weak points. Imagine a full backstory. Always leave room for the character to "come alive" as you write. Adjust, let the writing process inspire you to fully realize your characters.

Consistency is important. You want to build a character that will be true to himself. You don't want your character to act "out of character"; if she is competitive, don't let her suddenly run away from a challenge without proper motivation. If he is indecisive, don't let him suddenly be able to choose which shirt to buy in two seconds. Films that allow the character to change his true stripes just to make the plot work will fail. If your character acts "out of character," you will lose your audience.

The wonderful thing that happens when you set your character up properly: The audience will grow to understand how your character will react in certain situations. They will begin to look forward to seeing that character challenged. When Elle (portrayed by Reese Witherspoon) in **LEGALLY BLONDE** shows up California pink and perky at the tweedy Ivy League Law School, the audience, who already feels like they know her, looks forward to the fun of seeing her interaction with dour eggheads and cut-throat East Coast students. If she hadn't been set up properly, the comedy would not work. In **COLLATERAL,** when the two characters,

"The Waterboy" Adam Sandler, Henry Winkler

photo supplied by IPOL/Globe Photos

Vincent (portrayed by Tom Cruise) and Max (portrayed by Jamie Foxx) collide, we quickly get to know their belief systems; Vincent is a cold-blooded killer with a skewed code of ethics; he never got attention from his father. Max is a man who lies to himself and his mother about the true state of his life, but he has big dreams for his future and a strong moral code. If the writer hadn't spent the time to let the audience get to know the essence of each man's character, the film would have been a regular/violent/action drama. But because the characters are so well-drawn, this film stands out. Take **THE WATERBOY** as an example. The characters are built with exaggeration in mind; from Bobby Boucher Junior (portrayed by Adam Sandler) to Mrs. Boucher (portrayed by Kathy Bates) to Coach (portrayed by Henry Winkler). Imagine the film with "normal" characters (who didn't have donkeys living with them in the house or didn't have an obsession with water or didn't have a knack for "visualization"). The story would not have risen above the typical nerd-makes-good film. It's all in the characters. Make your characters unique and keep them uniquely consistent.

Character Arc: Your Main Character Must Change

Your main character needs to start in one place and end up in another. If there is no character change, most likely you don't have a satisfying story. If your main character begins the film and ends the film in the same emotional/physical/intellectual state, re-think your story.

- What's she like as a sexual being?

- What does he regret from his past?

- What is her fondest childhood memory?

- What is his relationships with his parents?

- How does he view the world? Optimist? Pessimist?

- What's most important to him? Love, power or money?

Your protagonist should not be perfect. Perfect people are not that interesting. You want your audience to *relate, worry, get angry at, feel joy with, want to kick, want to scream at, encourage and care about your character.* Is your protagonist a jackass with women? Does he work too hard, compete too completely? Is he afraid of snakes? Does she have a physical handicap? Does Kryptonite affect him? Is she too proud? Is she too generous? Can people walk all over her? Is she shy? Is he unable to accept he has only a few months to live? Is he a momma's boy at heart? Think of the characters Jack Nicholson loves to play: they are *flawed* protagonists; in **CHINATOWN** his character is arrogant and carries around a huge piece of guilt. In **AS GOOD AS IT GETS** his character is bigoted, prejudiced and selfish. In **SOMETHING'S GOTTA GIVE,** his character is a man who cannot commit to a relationship. In **TERMS OF ENDEARMENT,** his character is a rude, boozing ex-astronaut. In **ABOUT SCHMIDT,** his character is a man who has never given his daughter a sense of being loved.

If your protagonist doesn't have a flaw, the chance for great character growth is lessened. If your main character is always doing the right thing, the audience will have a hard time relating to him or her. If your main character is perfect—you may want to re-think the character.

Think of characters Julia Roberts likes to play; in **RUNAWAY BRIDE** she's a woman who can't commit. In **ERIN BROCKOVICH,** she's abrasive, aggressive and has a huge chip on her shoulder. In **NOTTING HILL,** she's an actress who doesn't trust. In **PRETTY WOMAN** she's a woman who has low self-esteem. In **MY BEST FRIEND'S WEDDING,** she's insecure and jealous and manipulative.

Don't let your characters be perfect. An audience wants to hope that people can change, learn, emerge and grow. If your character is perfect, they have no room for growth.

"My Best Friend's Wedding" Julia Roberts, Cameron Diaz
photo supplied by Globe Photos

> **Exercise:**
>
> Have a friend ask you questions about your characters. Talking, thinking, jotting ideas down on characters will help make them real. Be strong in your ideas, let friends be of help, but don't let them make your characters their characters.
>
> Once you have a good idea who your main characters are, set two or more characters together in a room. This doesn't have to be a scene in your screenplay. Just let the characters start talking. Let them argue. Let them get on each other's nerves. Build conflict between the two characters; this will help you get to know them even better.

Imagine that the writer of **WHEN HARRY MET SALLY** did a similar exercise and put Sally (portrayed by Meg Ryan) and Harry (portrayed by Billy Crystal) together in a diner—and let all her ticks, arrogance and flakiness jockey against his wit and caustic humor. Remember that incredible scene where they discuss whether or not women fake orgasms?

Imagine the exercise was to bring Tom (portrayed by Robert Duvall) in **THE GODFATHER** into Don Corleone's office to meet with the Don and his hot-headed sons. The tension is great because he, as a non-Italian and non-family member whose bargaining chip is his much-needed analytical mind, is both resented and respected by the various people in the room. His sense of pride and desire to belong knock against their tight family code.

Make sure the characters in your story aren't all the same. Make sure they have different strengths, ideas, weaknesses, points of view.

A Protagonist Needs a Difficult Journey

Take time to create your characters and give them a difficult and complex journey. Characters will be the heart of your story. A well-written character will attract stars. Stars get films made. For the good of your script and for the good of getting it produced, *remember: Nothing is more important than your characters.*

Examples: The conflicts that arise in **TOOTSIE** give Michael a difficult journey:

a.   He has to pretend to be a woman.

b.   He has to get up extra early and shave closely.

c.   He needs a new wardrobe fit for a female.

d.   He has to lie to a good female friend.

e.   His roommate thinks he's crazy.

f.   A fellow actor on the daytime drama lusts after him.

g.   He can't be honest about his feelings of love for his co-star.

h.   The director doesn't like him.

i.   The producer wonders about him.

j.   The father of the woman he loves is attracted to him as a woman.

All those *conflicts* give the writer a great number of scenes that need to be written in the film. So the writer gets the challenge of arranging *needed* scenes. He doesn't have to sit around and ask; what *could* happen? He knows what *needs* to happen. He has done the hard work of setting up all the possible conflicts and now has the luxury of knowing "what *needs* to happen next?"

In **KRAMER VS KRAMER,** the conflict areas that make things difficult for Ted Kramer:

a.   His career

b.   His relationship with the son

c.   His relationship with the neighbor

d.   His ex-wife

e.   His new relationships with women

These are all scenes that aid in the growth of Ted Kramer's character and give insights into how he will be propelled on his journey.

Remember: The dramatic protagonist, in most cases, succeeds by digging deep, using his best efforts and finding new strength and sense of purpose. The tragic protagonist fails despite using his best efforts. The comic protagonist succeeds using outrageous efforts that usually go badly but turn out all right in the end.

The Antagonist

The antagonist is the character who gets in the way of the protagonist, who actively tries to stop the protagonist because of conflicting goals. Sometimes the antagonist is called a nemesis, sometimes a "bad guy", sometimes the "evil force," sometimes the "villain."

Every good protagonist needs a nemesis. A protagonist is only as good as his antagonist. If the antagonist of your story is weak, your protagonist doesn't have to dig very deep to overcome all odds. Never solve story problems by making your antagonist stupid or not resourceful. Keep your antagonist strong and smart. Good films stories keep the tension of who will win out, who will be stronger, who will achieve their ends first—to the very end of the story.

Ask yourself:

1.   Are the protagonist and antagonist on opposite ends of the protagonist's goal? Don't make the mistake of keeping these important characters apart; they need to be united in screen time and also in

Answer: No. Find a person or being to fill the antagonist role. **CLEAR AND PRESENT DANGER, TWISTER** are films that could have benefited from a strong personification of the antagonist. Yes, it could be a creature—but a creature really is not enough (**JAWS** also featured the Mayor as the antagonist, the *person* standing in the Sheriff's way of doing all he can to kill the shark). **THE EDGE,** written by David Mamet, pits an wealthy and paranoid Charles Morse (portrayed by Anthony Hopkins) against a jealous and younger Robert Green (portrayed by Alec Baldwin) against each other—the bear out to destroy them is secondary to the personal struggle between the two men.

pursuing the same goal—(for various purposes perhaps, but the same or similar goal.)

a. In **TOOTSIE,** Michael Dorsey faces off with the director of the soap opera. Their lives intersect at work as they vie for power. They also are romantically interested in the same girl.

b. In **GLADIATOR,** Maximus and Commodus are in direct competition; who will be the guiding force for the future of Rome?

c. In **TRAINING DAY,** the dirty cop and the idealistic cop are thrown together; the dirty cop's job is to train this new detective.

2. What are their personal beliefs that keep the protagonist and antagonist at odds?

3. Where will the protagonist's path and antagonist's path cross?

4. Is their opposition to one another overt or covert?

5. What are their back stories? Is the difference in their back stories what makes for their personal objectives? If their back stories are similar, *why* do these two characters want different things?

6. Are the protagonist and antagonist comparable in strength? Cleverness? Are they worthy adversaries? Are they friends who turn foes? Or foes who turn friends?

The more interesting and complex you make your antagonist, the stronger your story. Think of the great ones: Hannibal Lechter in **SILENCE OF THE LAMBS.** Commodus in **THE GLADIATOR.** Eve in **ALL ABOUT EVE.** Mrs. Robinson in **THE GRADUATE.** Detective-Sergeant Alonzo in **TRAINING DAY.** Vince in **COLLATERAL.** Darth Vader in **STAR WARS.** Again, a protagonist is only as interesting as his antagonist. Why did 2005's **CINDERELLA MAN** fail to attract audiences? There was no strong antagonist. Why does 2000's **GLADIATOR** work so well? Protagonist Maximus and antagonist Commodus are equally strong and compelling.

Design a complex antagonist. Let the audience love to hate him, or just plain hate him or just plain disagree with him. Don't *forget the antagonist needs a flaw too.* That flaw can bring the antagonist down and cause him to fail in his attempt to reach his goal. It can be pride, ego, bad judgment or….

Audiences go to films to watch characters struggle, to deal with conflict. Antagonists provide conflict. This conflict doesn't have to be continual shouting matches or guns blasting or chases or blowing things up. Conflict is built emotionally as well as physically. Conflict comes from facing antagonists and obstacles that seem insurmountable. The antagonist can be an overprotective mother or a sadistic killer, they come in all shapes and sizes.

Build your story's world with people who, for whatever reason, have opposite beliefs, morals, codes of ethics and, most importantly, different desires.

Other Characters Can Help You Tell Your Story

Who can help you open up your story and at the same time focus on the journey of your main character?

Friends and Allies

These characters are the confidantes, the sounding boards. They are the persons to whom your character can tell the truth. They are characters who can give advice (to follow or not). They are characters who can call your protagonist (or antagonist) an idiot or a hero. Maybe it's a character who knows your protagonist from youth or prison or army days or college. Protagonists need to be able to make their points, to explain themselves. Friends and allies can present that opportunity. But *remember*, these scenes should still be designed for conflict—absolute agreement on every point, absolute mutual respect, absolute patience are not very interesting on screen. Disagreement among friends is totally acceptable and desired.

Mentors/Guides

Mentors and guides can fill the friend's slot. Guides can come in almost any guise, from children to aliens to any person who illuminates a new path. Many coaches in sports films fill this role. Mentors can be teachers or elders or wise persons; someone who knows aspects of the journey ahead and can impart some wisdom. Think about Obi-wan Kenobi in **STAR WARS**…

Rivals

These characters keep the tension and conflict in your story. In 1981's **CHARIOTS OF FIRE,** the two long distance runners are rivals. Not antagonists, but rivals. They spur each other on to reach goals. In **LETHAL WEAPON,** the two detectives are friends and rivals. They want to show off for each other, they want to protect each other. In **MY BEST FRIEND'S**

Question: Can the protagonist also be the antagonist?

Answer: No. It is a given that every protagonist (every person), at times, is their own worst enemy. That is why you build a protagonist with *flaws*. Stories need a real and strong antagonist. You want to be able to create *scenes of conflict*. If you are building a story that explores an inner antagonist, consider how 1999's **FIGHT CLUB** uses two characters to play different parts of the main character's psyche; the protagonist and antagonist. Consider how 2002's **ADAPTATION** uses one actor playing *two characters* to bring out the inner antagonist of the main character. Consider 2004's **SIDEWAYS**; Miles is fighting his inner demons but Jack, his friend, is wreaking havoc on Miles reaching his immediate goals.

Max's desire to save her at the end of the movie would not have seemed motivated.

Max's character is also illuminated in his relationship with his Mother.

When Vincent gets into the cab, he and Max talk. Questions are asked. There is a connection; the two characters are intrigued by one another. Vincent appreciates Max's mastery of Los Angeles streets. It's a good starting point for a conversation and it's important to the story, it gives Vince a reason to keep Max as his driver.

Questions are a good way to explore character. Strangers ask questions. Lovers ask questions ("Why are you acting like that?" "Don't you love me?") Never be satisfied with *easy* answers. Let your characters be eccentric, have deep original thoughts.

Where do these thoughts come from? You. Find the different sides of your own character. Explore the dualities in your own personality. You have a point of view. Your point of views and ideas are as valid as anyone else's. Put your ideas into your characters. Let other characters disagree with "your ideas." Let characters be as well-rounded and thoughtful as you are. Different characters can (and should) have varying points of view. Let characters disagree!

 E x e r c i s e :

Never stop asking yourself questions about the characters you create in your story. First ask these three questions:

1. What is the character's overall want?
2. What is the character's immediate goal?
3. What is the character's flaw?
4. What is the character missing in his life?

Then go on with these and fill in the backstory of your characters:

Age	Hopes
Gender	Dreams
Human/Alien/Animal or?	Desires
Job	Childhood memories
Education level	Upbringing
Place in society	Important relationships
Motivation	in his life
Fears	Lifestyle

Give Your Characters Secrets

What is something that your main character has in his past that he would rather no one know? What doesn't she want to admit? How can this secret affect your character's journey? Having a secret will increase tension—and creating emotional, physical, and story tension is essential.

What *secrets* do some of film's most beloved characters possess? Blanche DuBois, in **STREETCAR NAMED DESIRE** keeps her guilt about feeling responsible for her young husband's suicide a deep secret. Rick, in **CASABLANCA,** keeps his heartbreak a secret, causing everyone to wonder just why he is so cool and un-emotional. Maggie Fitzgerald in **MILLION DOLLAR BABY** has a secret; she has a family that does not value her. And of course, there's **SPIDERMAN, BATMAN, SUPERMAN, WONDER WOMAN** and most of the superheroes. Keeping a secret is part of the fun of their stories.

Note: When pitching your story to a film development executive, concentrate on characters first. Set up the characters, a bit of their backstories and their strong overall wants and immediate goals before jumping into plot. You will lose their interest if they are not invested in the reasons why the plot is happening to the characters.

Exercise:

Here are more questions you can ask yourself about your main characters. Answering them may give you insights, even give you ideas for scenes that you can construct to help us know more about your character.

Is he happy? Unhappy? Hopeful? Optimist or pessimist?

What sign of the zodiac is she?

What kind of clothes does he like to wear?

Which books are on his bookshelves?

When people are asked to describe him, what do they say?

Does he like most people? Is he social, a-social, anti-social?

Is he truthful?

Does he believe in love? Goodness? Evil?

If she had to say she was addicted to anything, what would it be? (Work, shopping, sex, alcohol, trying to get approval… or what?)

Is he a perfectionist?

Is he patient or impatient?

If he had to describe himself as an animal, which animal would he be?

What did he want to be when he "grew up"? Is he happy with his job now? Does he feel like he's lived up to his potential?

Does he like himself? Does he approve of himself?

Do others view him as uptight? Loose?

What's quirkiest about him?

What's saddest about her?

What secret has he never told anyone?

How does he deal with authority?

Has she ever known true love? Hate?

Does she like her parents?

What's his Achilles heel (major weakness)?

Is he the boss of himself? Is he easily swayed by others' opinions of him?

Does she believe in a higher power?

Does he believe in fate or does he feel he can control his destiny?

Does he have a favorite word?

Does he sleep well? Nightmares? Silly dreams?

Did he have an elementary school love?

Has he ever killed anyone? Really hurt anyone physically or emotionally?

Does she drive fast? Safe? Careful? Slow?

What is his favorite sport to play? Watch?

Overweight? Too skinny? Body-conscious?

Even tempered? Or is every day a new challenge to keep it together?

Has the world treated her fairly?

What would the reaction be to being left by oneself on a deserted island? How hard would the struggle be to survive?

Is her home messy or neat?

Can she cook? Is take-out his favorite thing? Fast food or gourmet? Germ-a-phobic?

Does she say things without thinking? Is he a person who thinks before he speaks?

How ambitious is he?

Will he ever be truly happy?

Start with these questions and continue with as many questions that come to mind. This is a good way to discover scenes that can enrich your screenplay and make your character more complex. *Don't forget to ask the same questions about YOUR ANTAGONIST.*

Exercise:

Write down the good and bad traits of a sibling or friend. What are his (or her) strong character points? What are his weaknesses? What makes him angry? What is her passion? Is he as successful as he can be? If not, what is stopping him? Does she take advice well? Is he easy-going or difficult? Is she an optimist or a pessimist? How does the opposite sex react to him? Write a scene where you find the necessity to challenge him on a course of action he has chosen (anything from getting married to eating the last muffin to choosing to quit his job or…). Does she stand up for herself? Can he find the words to express his feelings? Let the scene escalate and let memories of past hurts or mishaps or actions surface.

Plot is a Reflection of Character

The plot is important, but it's *how the character maneuvers through the plot* that is at the heart of your story. In **DIE HARD,** John McClane (portrayed by Bruce Willis) is a cop, a man of action. He's determined, smart, and wants his wife to come back to the life they had in New York. He maneuvers through the plot of that story in a much different way than a bumbling, non-athletic man would maneuver. Ellie, in **IT HAPPENED ONE NIGHT,** is spoiled and naïve about the "real world." If a young, illiterate, ass-kicking woman from Appalachia had run away from home and run into Clark Gable… the story would have unfolded in a totally different way.

If your character is addicted to anxiety pills, make sure this flaw is reflected in the actions she takes. If your main character is a vampire who has lived many lives, make sure his actions show that he has a special first-hand knowledge of history. If your main character has been living a lie and can no longer look at himself in the mirror, this character might have an amount of self-loathing that can be shown in his actions. If your main character's a young girl who is obsessed with her estranged father, make sure her actions are focused on getting his attention.

A Character's Actions Speak Louder Than Words

Your characters will be defined by their actions. Not so much by what they say, but by what they do. In other words, one way to reveal character is through action. A woman says (or thinks) she loves her fiancé but as soon as he leaves her apartment she finds an excuse to knock on her best-guy-friend-who-happens-to-be-her-neighbor's door. We see she really wants to spend more time with her best guy friend than her fiancé. Another example: A man accepts a promotion and makes it look as if he's gung-ho to lead his company into financial success but late at night he meets with a competitor and exchanges company secrets for money. We see he's greedy and lacks moral character. No words have to be said to that effect, the audience discerns all through his actions.

Often, as a writer, you want to set up actions that will lead the audience to think one thing—and then you reverse their perceptions. It's not playing tricks; it's understanding the human condition. It's a way of showing your characters in their true colors, moment to moment, rather than dealing with clunky exposition. Some characters are duplicitous and know exactly what they are doing. Some characters will be lead by their subconscious and won't have a clue that their actions are contradictory until they go through some kind of epiphany.

Use the Magic Word: "No"!

Never let anything come easily. If it's a romance, it's not easy to "get the girl." If it's a treasure hunt, it's not easy to find the treasure. If a character needs to learn to love, don't let it be easy. If a character needs to save the world, don't let it be easy. Learn to use the word, "No." Learn to use "Can't be done," Learn to use "Not in this lifetime." Frustrate your characters. In doing so you will find they will have to become more resourceful and dig deeper to get what they want.

Scenes where two characters *agree* on a method of action, or on an emotion or goal are not interesting. If you need a scene like this, get in and get out fast. The interesting scenes are between characters who do *not agree,* who have opposing goals or beliefs, morals, codes, interests.

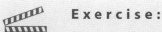

Exercise:

Write a scene: Put two characters in a scene discussing preparations for a funeral or wedding. Decide who the characters are and who is about to be buried or married. Let the characters disagree about how the event should be held, let them have varying opinions on what the event means, let them disagree about how much money should be spent and who should be the one spending it, let them disagree about everything from flowers to venue to time to the very philosophy of holding the event.

Exercise:

Write a two page scene: An employee is long overdue for a raise and sees that his boss has just bought a new fancy car. The employee strives to pursue his raise, the boss is determined not to give it, but he cannot afford to let this employee quit. What creative ways can each come up with to get their way?

Chapter Summary

- Well-drawn characters attract good actors. Actors can help get your film made.

- Creating a duality in your characters will make them more interesting. All good stories are journeys of character. The journey is best when it is difficult.

- Build a story where the protagonist goes through a change.

- Surround your main character with supporting characters who will help illuminate the story.

- Characters drive the plot.

Chapter Six

ENDING FIRST

Is it helpful for the writer to know the ending before she begins? Yes.

Is it necessary to have all the details of the story before one begins? No.

Once you have the bones of—or at least the idea for your story—and the character you want to take on this journey—ask yourself: *What do I want my main character to have accomplished by the end of the film? Where do I want her to be emotionally and physically? Will there be some sort of satisfaction for him or not? Will it be a happy or sad or tragic or ironic ending? What do I want the audience to walk out of the theatre thinking or feeling?*

Every good storyteller knows where he is headed. A storyteller knows how he is going to grab his audience's imagination, surprise them with twists, amuse them with a joke. A storyteller knows that she wants her audience to be with her every moment and to be always wondering what's coming next. A storyteller knows he can't let the audience down at the end, that he will lose their respect completely if he disappoints in the final moments. All jokes rely on a punch line. Mysteries are built to reveal a surprise ending. Romances are built for the lovers to finally unite after much travail at the end of the story.

It is much easier to build a story when you know the ending.

Screenwriters are storytellers. It's a craft that can be learned. Don't let yourself off the hook. You need to make a decision about the outcome of your story. If you don't, you risk not being able to write the scenes you need to write to advance the plot because you don't know the final outcome. *Where* will your protagonist be at the end of the story? Mexico? Top of Mount Everest? In bed with the one he loves? Prison? On the shoulders of a winning football team? Will your protagonist, following elements of true drama, understand the world in a better and wiser (happy or unhappy) way? Will he get the girl? Will she please the parents? Will he win the race? Will she fall in love with the vampire?

"I'll find the end as I write." "The character will let me know the ending."

"I like to discover as I go." These are words that strike fear into most seasoned writers' hearts. How many times have you found yourself in a situation where you have to listen to a friend (or stranger) tell a story or recount an event and find yourself wondering—*why* am I listening to this? Is there a point? Will this person get on with it? Perhaps the storyteller has wandered off onto a path that has nothing to do with the outcome of the story. Minutes, hours, days could go by and you may still be asking yourself, *why* am I listening to this story? A writer must focus the elements to they all contribute to the outcome of the story.

There are dangers in not knowing your ending. You are in danger of losing precious hours and days (perhaps months) as you write sequences that do not belong in your film. You will use up writing energy, which is also precious. You are in danger of incurring massive frustration that may cause you to throw your script into the deepest, darkest drawer in your desk, never to be looked at again.

Know where you are headed. Know your ending.

Once You Know the End, Shape the Beginning

Stories need a beginning, middle and an end. Once you know "the end," the construction of the beginning and middle will be easier.

At the end of your story, if you want your super-hero to be victorious and strong with a new sense of her power—then make sure at the beginning of the story that she's *not* strong and has little or no sense of her powers. That will give your protagonist a longer and more difficult journey full of discovery, danger, emotional and physical challenges. Think of **SPIDERMAN**. Peter Parker is not the hot guy in school, he doesn't have the girl of his dreams, he gets picked on, he has no sense of the powers that he will one day possess. He has a long journey ahead to become a man who will accept his super-human strengths and use them wisely. **SPIDERMAN 2** gets a little convoluted because at the beginning of the film he has super-human powers—he is a successful super-hero. The filmmakers decided to strip him of his powers at the beginning of the sequel and force the character to have to regenerate them in time of need. You can see why the writer went this route, a super-hero whose powers are always in tip-top shape is not a super-hero the audience worries about... *and you want your audience to worry.* Unfortunately, this **SPIDERMAN** sequel repeats many of the same ideas and story points as the original and the audiences of **SPIDERMAN 2** are not taken on a fresh and original character journey.

If, at the end of your story, you want your protagonist to realize that love is *not* dangerous, that it can be a safe and happy harbor in a difficult world, think about where you want to start your character. Backtrack. Perhaps at the beginning of your story, your character denies the importance of intimate relationships, or he uses sex/seduction as a game or form of exercise, or he has seen first hand that loving someone can be a trap and cripple a person's spirit. Show that this character will not commit to a healthy relationship; perhaps he lives alone and believes the world is unsafe and unpredictable and there's no reason to try to build a safe haven within it. The longer the character journey, the more significant the change, the stronger your story will be.

Think about **CITIZEN KANE.** Fame, fortune and possessions could not bring happiness—that is the point the writer is making in that film. So if the story ends with the character understanding that point, he has to believe the opposite at the beginning of the story. Build a character who believes having possessions and a fat wallet are important to attract attention and affection, a person who believes he can buy friends and love.

Consider these films:

CASABLANCA (1942) At the end of the film, Rick (portrayed by Humphrey Bogart) makes a politically active choice and understands that his personal happiness is not of utmost importance. He begins the film as a man who will not get involved in politics and as a man who has let personal heartache and anger cloud every decision.

NORMA RAE (1979) At the end of the film, Norma Rae (portrayed by Sally Field) leads her fellow workers in the formation of a Union at her local factory. At the beginning of the film Norma Rae is a person who does not stand up for herself, doesn't believe the struggle for good working conditions is worth the pain and danger to her family, does not believe she can make a difference.

BEAUTY AND THE BEAST (1991) At the end of the film, the Beast sacrifices his life for someone he loves. He begins the film as a vain and selfish man unable to consider others.

BRAVEHEART (1995) William Wallace (portrayed by Mel Gibson) ends the film willing to die so that his people can vanquish their oppressors. He begins the film refusing to get pulled into the politics of his people.

Question: In slice-of-life films, where the scope of the story and what is accomplished by the character seems small, how can the writer fashion a compelling tale?

Answer: Focus on a change in the character and how this change puts him on a new path or gives him a different view of life. In the film **SIDEWAYS**, the main character, in a matter of a few days, manages to face a few personal demons and decide to change. A story that is worth being told is a story that focuses on how a character deals with a small or large problem and makes an adjustment (small or large). A story where nothing happens, no one changes, no one makes an adjustment is not really a story. A story has a beginning, middle and end.

GLADIATOR (2000) At the end of the film, Maximus (portrayed by Russell Crowe) actively saves Rome from the evil rule of Commodus. He begins the film wanting to shun war and political involvement, wanting only to go back home to his wife and child and farm.

NORMAL (2003) At the end of the film, Irma (portrayed by Jessica Lange) realizes that love can transcend deep prejudices. At the beginning of the film she wants life to be safe, secure and is happy in her traditional family. When jolted from this comfort, she does not think love can withstand the problems and pain her husband's desire for a gender change operation brings upon her, her family and her community. By the end of the film, Irma has moved to a whole new level of understanding love.

SOMETHING'S GOTTA GIVE (2003) Harry Sanborn (portrayed by Jack Nicholson) ends up a very happy family man. He begins the film as a lothario who has never committed to one woman.

FINDING NEMO (2003) Marlin, Nemo's father, ends the film story knowing he has to let go of his son and trust that disaster will not befall him around every turn. Marlin begins the film as an over-the-top protective father who lives in fear of everything that swims in the sea.

SIDEWAYS (2004) Miles (portrayed by Paul Giamatti) ends the film able to move on with his life. He begins the film stuck; in his job, in his life, in his hopeless hope to get his ex-wife back, in a friendship where he doesn't stand up for himself.

KICKING AND SCREAMING (2005) Phil (portrayed by Will Ferrell), ends the film with an ability to stand up to his father, and at peace with himself about this parental relationship. He begins the film totally cowed and frustrated and unable to communicate successfully with his father.

The films that don't include strong character arcs do not stand the test of time. Spielberg's **THE TERMINAL** fails here. Viktor Navorski (portrayed by Tom Hanks) starts as a nice man who helps people; people slipping on the slick airport floor, someone who has trouble with her suitcase, lonely people, construction workers. He ends the film as a nice man who helps others. No moral crises. No change of heart. That's why the film is a series of episodes that add up to a not-very-compelling film.

You Don't Need to Know All the Details of the Ending

You don't have to have all the details of the final moments of your film; but if you know it's a big battle, who wins? And how? If your hero *doesn't* think she's clever but then rises above her own expectations at the end of the film to cleverly save the day—that's what you need to know. If your hero *doesn't* think he can physically handle the treacherous terrain of the enemy but then figures out how to make that happen by the end of the story—that's what you need to know. Not every detail, but the overall arc.

If your character is going to choose love above all else, you need to know this so you can give him other options (money, fame, sex, drugs or…) that the character decides *not* to choose. If your character is going to choose bravery and self-sacrifice above all else, you need to know this so you can give her other options to choose (becoming a hermit, walking away from conflict to a safe harbor or…).

Where do you want your protagonist to be emotionally at the end of the film? Where do you want your antagonist to be emotionally? Happy? Sad? Angry? Confused? Are you heading for a happy ending? Ironic? Tragic?

Always remember that a character must want something. In order to get it, he (or his life) has to change in some way. A character must struggle to accomplish that change. He is a different person by the end of the film. Track the change from beginning to end and make the journey a long and difficult one.

The ending will inform the beginning.

Make Your Screen Story Unpredictable

Audiences want to feel satisfied. Do not, just for the sake of being "unpredictable," be untrue to your character, genre or your story. An audience, paying money to see a romantic comedy, will not be satisfied if the characters suddenly and uncharacteristically overdose on drugs or are the victims of a drive-by shooting at the end of your film. An audience will not be satisfied if, in your gritty Western Drama, your gun-toting bounty hunter decides to become a tap dancer and lets the bad guys get away.

It's not the *end* of the movie that needs to be unpredictable—it's the *getting to the end of the movie that needs to be unpredictable.*

Consider how many films have this character arc: a guy starts out as a jerk and gradually, through the film, loses his jerkiness and ends up a good guy. Think of **SOMETHING'S GOTTA GIVE, BEAUTY AND THE BEAST, CASABLANCA, KRAMER VS KRAMER, TOOTSIE, RAIN MAN, WAR OF THE WORLDS.** What makes these stories different from one another? Genre, of course. But that aside, look how the main themes are similar: Without sacrifice, true love is never tested. So what makes these stories unique? Character. Character. Character. What are the character's immediate goals? What personality traits dictate how the story will play out? How do each of these characters view life? What is specific about each character's overall want?

Think about **JERRY MCGUIRE,** written by Cameron Crowe. Jerry (portrayed by Tom Cruise) is a sports agent and a jerk. What makes this story stand out is the *inciting incident* of the film, Jerry's realization that his life is a dishonest and selfish sham and that he no longer wants to be a jerk. We didn't have to wait for an hour and a half for him to realize that, the writer is exploring other areas of the "jerk to good guy" formula. The bulk of the film story is Jerry coming to grips with the fact that being a "good, honest, upfront guy" doesn't make life easier or more enjoyable. He has his initial epiphany very early in the film and as he tries to change things, he gets in trouble; with work, his girlfriend, his friends. He still struggles with jerkiness, he's *clueless* about how to change deep-seated fears. His struggle is true and real and has multiple layers. At the conclusion of the film the audience gets satisfaction from the romance but we know the struggle to understand himself will continue and (though we are not sure) we *hope* it will work out.

Think about **THE GRADUATE,** written by Buck Henry and Calder Willingham based on the novel by Charles Webb. What makes this film unpredictable? The protagonist's choices, his point of view, his unremitting commitment to "get the girl" that takes dark and twisting turns. At the end of the film is the audience sure this will be a "happy ever after" scenario? No. But there is satisfaction that a complete story has been told and that the protagonist (whose overall want is to commit to something in life, to find a purpose) has attained his want—he has committed to a path of action.

Know your ending. Commit to your tone. Commit to your genre. Yes, be creative, push the envelope. But do not sell out your story, theme, genre for a surprising twist ending if it is not true to all you have worked hard to set up. Be unpredictable in *getting to the end.* Be creative in action, location, character traits and quirks and points of view. A storyteller must satisfy his audience, but it does not have to be in the *expected way;* let your character lead us down *unexpected paths.*

The ending will inform the beginning.

Planning for a Sequel?

Even if you are thinking *sequels,* your story needs to be able to stand alone.

SPIDERMAN, BATMAN, SUPERMAN, the super-hero stories, manage to do this because they take one villain at a time. The fun of the story is the villain's plan, how he or she hopes to get the super-hero out of the way and how the super-hero has to overcome impossible odds to thwart evil.

The **INDIANA JONES** stories are constructed in the same way. One treasure, one villain at a time.

MEET THE FOCKERS, TOY STORY 2 are films that are sequels to money-making originals. The stories for these films are constructed to stand alone.

The original film has to be successful (financially) in order for a sequel to be made. Yes, **LORD OF THE RINGS** is an exception, but it was really designed as a six hour film, not as an original film and two sequels. The investment from the studio was huge and risky but there was an amazingly popular book at its base, and an A-list director. Advice? Focus on making *one* film the best it can be, don't worry about sequels. Satisfy the audience, create a convincing and titillating and surprising character arc. Complete one great story and *if* and *when* the studio wants to invest in a sequel—construct another great stand-alone film story that focuses on your great character.

> **E x e r c i s e :**
>
> Let's say that a main character ends the film realizing that happiness comes from working as a team. Decide who that character could be at the beginning of the film. What could be the inciting incident that forces him into a situation where he has to work with others? Does his attitude hinder him? What other obstacles could be put in his path? What could be the crisis moment of decision, what story elements could be in the climax. (You have decide what kind of team you are exploring—sports or business or politics…)

Chapter Summary

- Knowing the ending of your film story will help you shape the beginning of your character's journey.

- Track your character's emotional and/or physical change throughout the story.

- It's not the end of the story that needs to be unpredictable, it's the *getting to the end* that should be unpredictable.

- A satisfying ending does not necessarily mean that all loose ends need to be neatly tied.

- Sequels should be able to stand alone as good films.

Chapter Seven

ONCE YOU KNOW THE END
GO BACK TO THE BEGINNING

Does good planning make for easier scriptwriting? Yes.

Does a writer remain open to inspiration during the process? Yes.

After you know the ending of your story, go back to the beginning. Now you know your destination—you can plan the journey.

Build Your Characters' Normal Life

Who is the protagonist? What does she do? What kind of family? Job? House? Apartment? Friends? Enemies? What is a normal day like? Where does she live? Does he consort with queens and kings or does he live on the street and beg for food? Construct the one or two sequences that will clue your audience into your protagonist's normal life.

RAIDERS OF THE LOST ARK starts with a huge action/adventure treasure hunt scene and then takes the audience to the University where Indiana Jones' normal life as a professor is laid out. **DIE HARD** is an action movie that starts slowly, the audience gets to know the character and his immediate goal (get his wife back) and overall want (to know he is important) before all hell breaks loose. **SPLASH** is a comedy that begins with a set-up of Allan Bauer (portrayed by Tom Hanks) as a young boy and an event that changes his life. Cut to 20 years later and the audience is introduced to Allan's normal life as a hardworking vegetable purveyor who wonders if he will ever feel deep lasting love.

There are many films that start slowly, build a normal life, set up characters and place. In these instances, the inciting incident *means more* because the audience is invested in the protagonist's normal life and now can worry about how he will handle the challenges to come

How many times have you sat in the theatre and watched five minutes of special effects and battle footage at the beginning of a movie and itched to know the why and who and how? If you start with "a bang" make it short,

Question: Does the normal life have to come first? Can a writer build a nifty action sequence to wow the audience at the outset of the film and then go to the protagonist's normal life?

Answer: The writer can do anything he or she wants. Follow your gut. Tell the story the way you want to tell it. Own it. Many times writers will lead with a genre scene—to let the audience know they are embarking on a thriller or a horror or comedy or…Just remember to clarify the normal life before you move into the out of the ordinary journey of the story. You want the difference, you want to take your protagonist out of his comfort zone.

clue the audience into who the major character is, and help the audience connect with the story by letting them spend time with a character who desperately wants something. What should be part of a character's normal life? Place, time, life situation. Include what is missing from his life (love, self-esteem, peace, power, respect…)? Make it clear what he wants. What is his most ardent desire? What would make her life feel complete? Let your characters speak. In **BABE,** the main character (Babe) states his desire very close to the beginning of the film, "I want my mom." In **SPLASH,** Allan states his desire when he is drunk in the bar, very close to the beginning of the film; he wants to find true love. In the **GODFATHER,** Michael Corleone makes it clear he wants to be the one to avenge his father's death. In **FINDING NEVERLAND** and **SHAKESPEARE IN LOVE,** the two writers state their desire to write a play that will successfully move their audiences.

Know What Your Character Wants

Never lose sight of this. Your character has his immediate goal or goals. *And* your character has an overall want. The overall want is usually an emotional need that will help make the character feel good about himself or fill a deep-seated emptiness in his life.

Review the chapter on Character. Consider introducing this overall want as part of the introduction into the character's normal life. Your protagonist may work at a gas station and have a boyfriend and be supporting her sick mother, but her strong desire is making it as a successful country-western singer. The desire is part of her normal life and she's writing songs as she pumps gas. Ask yourself *why* does she want to be a country western singer? Does she want attention? Does she need to be creatively challenged? Does she want to prove to her parents (or someone) that she's worthy? How can you show the *why* in a scene?

Perhaps your protagonist is out of work, drifting, not sure who he is or wants to be, just hanging with friends and being a jokester. But he's got his eye on a girl who seems totally out of his social reach; it's his secret but the audience sees how he straightens up, how he lies about his life when he talks to her so he can impress, how he checks his armpits to make sure he doesn't smell sweaty when she walks by. His immediate goal is to get the girl's attention. Why? Does he need love? Does he need to feel worthy? Does he desire a sense of family?

Perhaps your protagonist is at home playing with his children, being super-daddy, preparing for the neighborhood BBQ that is to take place in his backyard. But he's wearing his phone's earpiece, his watch is set to beep at a certain time, his partner arrives; we see the partner is wearing a gun and talking to the Police Chief on his phone... what have you set up? That your main character is a family man, that he's a cop, that there's some big case in progress and timing is essential. You have also set up that your character wants to be successful, to do his job well. Why? Does he desire respect? Does he want to be part of making the world safe, does he want justice?

Round out your character's life. Home. Work. Love life. Want. Hobbies. Sports. Think of all areas of your character's life. It doesn't all have to be in the first five pages, in most cases you don't want it to be all front-loaded. But the overall want and immediate goal should be apparent early on—or the audience may not be able to connect with the character or story.

The All Important Inciting Incident

The inciting incident is a term that is thrown around a lot in screenwriting parlance. Studio executives know this term. And it's important. The inciting incident is the event or word or dream or visual—the something —that sends your main character on his new journey. The inciting incident will take him out of his normal circumstance and propel him into the journey of the story.

What takes your protagonist out of his *normal life?* What change occurs? What event happens? What words are said? What letter came in the mail? What did he see on TV? What did she hear from the psychic? Who got engaged? Did he lose his job? Did someone die? Who came back for the high school reunion? The list is endless... but the incident has to be there to jumpstart the story and pull the character out of his normal life. In 2005's **WAR OF THE WORLDS,** the inciting incident is the first attack of the aliens. This sends father and children on a journey to seek safety. This journey teaches the father about love, responsibility and his how his actions have direct affect on his children. In 2004's **FINDING NEVERLAND,** the inciting incident is J.M. Barrie's meeting of Sylvia and her sons in the park. This meeting sends J.M. Barrie on a journey to challenge his imagination, find his muse and understand what constitutes true love and bravery.

Question: What if I am going to tell my story in flashbacks?

Answer: Your story can be told in any order. But be careful of using flashbacks to reveal exposition and the normal life. The 2006 **DA VINCI CODE** fails in this area; its convenient flashbacks do not enhance the present day story, they merely provide static information. It's the present story of your protagonist that is of the most interest, consider showing his normal life in the body of the main story.

telling Peter he is failing? Is it Peter meeting the man who will turn out to be the villain? Is it Mary Jane saying she is going to get married? (That's *way* into the film). The film never really feels like it *starts*. One of the problems is that Peter Parker has no one to talk to (his secret life is secret) so it is unclear exactly what he wants when... At one point Peter decides he doesn't want to be Spiderman any longer but again—that's way into the film and he goes back on that decision very quickly. The lack of a clear inciting incident near the top of the film causes the film to meander and have a problem kicking into high gear.

Note: *Many film executives and studios will feel comfortable trying to recreate success from the same template when commissioning a sequel script. Why? They feel if the first film was successful, why change a good thing? Of course, if you are hired and agree to follow the formula, you must deliver. But spend some time trying to push the envelope, exploring new themes and new character arcs. Perhaps you can get the producers to push the envelope too and give the audience a more fulfilling event in the movie theatre.*

Ask yourself, *why* am I choosing to start my story when I do? Is it close to the inciting incident? Am I including only enough normal life to bring the audience up to speed? Is there a way to jump start my character's journey and also include enough information about the character so the audience can get invested?

Exercise:

Write a sequence that includes place, time, situation, a supporting scene or two to show your protagonist's normal life. Make it clear what the protagonist's overall want is (maybe even the first immediate goal). Make his or her state of mind clear. Be aware that every scene can (and should) contain some conflict. After you've written the scene or scenes that show his normal life, construct the inciting incident. What is your protagonist's reaction? Does the change this scene brings about seem like a good or bad thing?

Chapter Summary

- The opening pages of your film story need to grab the reader/audience.

- The genre should be clear in the beginning moments of the film.

- The protagonist's normal life and overall want should become evident near the top of the film.

- There should be a sense of conflict in every scene (overt or covert).

- Consider starting the film story as close to the inciting incident as possible.

- The inciting incident changes the normal life of your main character and sends her into the main story of the film.

Chapter Eight

PLOT

Will a plot feel more original if the characters are distinct? Yes.

Should the plot affect my characters and my characters affect the plot? Yes.

Plot is the development of events and actions that move a story along. A good screen story focuses on a character's journey. Therefore, *character arc and plot need to be totally inter-connected.*

Aristotle's Advice: Make the Story About One Thing

According to this Greek master storyteller around 340 BC, stories should be "the successful change from one status quo to another, to the emotional satisfaction of the audience."

The audience has a relatively short time to get to know a character, learn of his wants and desires, learn what physical and emotional obstacles are keeping him from accomplishing his goals, develop an interest in caring about whether he gets what he wants and emotionally connect with the outcome of the movie. Imagine a friendship where, after only two hours of knowing each other, you are viscerally attached to each other's life journey. Imagine a love affair, where after only two hours of knowing each other you are willing to die to make the other happy. That is the task of a screenwriter. You must connect with your audience; make them care about your characters. You must make them laugh, cry or cheer for someone they just met. If the story is about too many things or too many characters, the ability to connect will not be there.

ROCKY is about a man who feels life has passed him by and he doesn't want to face "being a nobody." All the elements in the story deal with this one thing: fear—his boxing, his love affair, his friendship. **FINDING NEVERLAND** is about a man who wants to transform his own and other people's worlds through imagination and theatre. All the storylines deal with this one desire; his wife's not understanding, his relationship with Sylvia and her sons that feeds this desire, Sylvia's mother who would crush creativity and joy, his theatre producer who questions but supports him.

Aristotle also encouraged simplicity and clarity. He taught his writing students to set up character and place. Make clear the main character's want or goal. Add "rising action"—in other words, let events and circumstances unfold. Add reversals, Complications, Obstacles. Force the protagonist into a recognition where he or she needs to make a choice about what path to pursue. He taught his writing students to move into the climax where the status quo is shifted and the main character's life is forever changed. He taught them to move the story into the "falling action" where loose ends are tied up. And finally, the denouement where the main character's new life is clearly stated.

How do Aristotle's teachings relate to the Eleven Step Story Structure? All of Aristotle's elements are reflected in the Eleven Steps, but again, the Eleven Step Structure breaks the story elements down even further and gives the writer even more signposts to use to map a story.

I believe the most important things to take from Aristotle: A good story is about *one thing*. Focus on one main character… commit to fully exploring *one person*. Let all elements of the story reflect on the protagonist's journey. What if you constructed a story about Jill, a successful advertising executive, divorcee and mother of three children who does not believe intense, all-consuming, passionate true love exists. She's cynical, she thinks her friends have married for security or companionship or social position. Her cynicism has left her a bit brittle and disappointed, but she was the kind of child who never believed in fairytales or happily-ever-after so she accepts her unhappiness. And then, one day, she meets a man who ignites in her feelings she never thought existed. She fights her feelings like a woman beating off a wild animal, refusing to make herself vulnerable. Depending on your genre, she finally accepts that true love is in her destiny—or she never accepts it and destroys that love. That's your main story. So what supporting stories and characters do you build to reflect on Jill's journey? What if one of her children is getting married? What if her best friend is getting a divorce? What if her boss is always hitting on her but she knows he just wants sex? What if her mother has decided to marry a rich, retired mogul for security and companionship? What if, in her business life, she is working on an account for Valentine's Day? Use supporting stories, elements, and characters to reflect on your protagonist's journey.

Your Protagonist's Overall Want Must be Paramount

A story is about a character's journey of change. This change is a result of the character's pursuit of an overall want or desire. This desire has to be *paramount*. This desire has to be *important* to your protagonist. Commit to this: If this desire does not get satisfied, your protagonist's life will never be happy or peaceful or, in the most drastic circumstances—worth living. If this desire is not satisfied, lives will be ruined. If this desire does not get satisfied, the world, as your protagonist knows it, will be meaningless or worse yet—destroyed.

Consider 2005's **CHARLIE AND THE CHOCOLATE FACTORY** as opposed to 1971's **WILLY WONKA.** Both films (based on the story by Roald Dahl) are visual feasts, but which film features a young Charlie who displays a greater want? The 1971 film fully commits to Charlie's tremendous desire to meet Willy Wonka and to change the lives of his family members. It is the most important thing in his life at the moment of the story, he can think of nothing else. His family is desperately poor, he wants to help them. Emotionally and physically Charlie is obsessed with finding a Golden Ticket that will gain him entry into Willy Wonka's world. And once he is inside the Chocolate Factory, the need to succeed is great; he wants to win to help his family. The 2005 remake loses that desperate need, thus the audience does not fully engage and the movie is not successful on all levels. The remake featured a Charlie who was a bit more passive, a family not in the direst circumstances, just "quirky." In the remake, once Charlie was inside the factory, he did not have a clear goal. He did not need to win the contest to help his family. He simply watched others self-destruct. Why did this remake lose its focus? It tried to do too many things and never did decide if it was Willie Wonka's story or Charlie's story. Whose story was it? Who changed the most? Who had the strongest desire/want? Who went on the most intense journey to satisfy their desire/want? The filmmakers never made their choice crystal clear, thus no clear protagonist fully emerged. Thus, emotionally, the film was unsuccessful.

Explore one character—all parts of her life (family, friends, work, loves…). Explore shades of her persona. Complicate one person's life. Let the story be about one person's crisis. Obviously, fill in the interesting people, things, events around this one character, but keep the focus. This is not as easy as it sounds. Ask yourself why your main character is not in every scene. Ask yourself why a scene is not about your main character even if

Question: What if my character doesn't care that much if he wins the game or the girl or gets the job?

Answer: Find something your protagonist *does* desire, in a massive way. He may not know it at the outset of the film story, but at some point he does realize it. He must commit to it or the story has a strong chance of not catching the audience's imagination.

Question: What if my story is about *not* wanting anything specific? What if my character has no clue what he wants?

Answer: Consider making the desire to find a purpose the most important thing to your main character. Take a look at **THE GRADUATE, VERTIGO.** Another way to approach it is to consider a character whose overall want is to *not* want anything. He strives *not* to connect, *not* to love, *not* care, *not* get invested. Take a look at **GOOD WILL HUNTING.**

she is absent. If your protagonist is not in at least 85% pf the scenes in your film, you may need to re-evaluate the focus of your story.

Give the Audience Time to Get to Know Your Characters

What are some of the elements that cause a film to fail in the first 20 minutes? Not enough character. Too much action. Too many plot points.

Time must be taken to introduce the main characters. Time must be taken to entice the audience to care about the characters, to be interested in them. The blockbuster, 2005's **HARRY POTTER AND THE GOBLET OF FIRE,** fails in this area. (The previous **HARRY POTTER** films were more successful). In **THE GOBLET OF FIRE,** Harry first has a bad dream about Voldemort. Then he's on an adventurous trip to the World Quidditch Match, Then he survives an attack by Death Eaters, then he arrives at school, sees a girl (Cho) he finds attractive. Then he meets One-Eyed Moody. Then he witnesses the arrival of potential contestants for the Goblet of Fire. Then he finds that he, despite his age, will be a contestant, causing his best friend to put a hold on their friendship. So much happens in the opening minutes of the film there is no time for the audience to get invested (or in the sequel world, re-invested) in the characters. What's missing? Character scenes. Where friendships can grow. Character scenes where Harry and friends wonder about the Death Eaters, wonder if they will target Harry. Character scenes of bumbling teen romance with Cho. Character scenes where Harry has to deal with an antagonist, not just with a series of physical tasks. *Character scenes where Harry actively pursues an emotional goal.* Harry's want is never stated in the movie, he is a pawn blown back and forth by plot. And the most important missing elements are scenes that allow the audience to connect with supporting characters that are going to be instrumental in the climax of the film. The end of the film brings about the death of a fellow student, Cedric, an event that should evoke an emotional response. Unfortunately, the audience never has the chance to really get to know Cedric, so the audience is not invested and cannot care whether he lives or dies. The audience does not see Harry in a relationship with Cedric (more than a few passing words), thus this character could have been interchangeable with any of the other students at Hogwarts. Thus, in the climax of the film, Cedric's death means little to the audience and they do not fully invest in its importance to Harry, the protagonist. This film is an example of how plot happens to the character and that is *not* what you want. Yes, the film made a lot of money, but it could have become a classic if the *character had made the plot happen.*

What is a good example of how you can start your film with lots of action and then take the time to get to know the protagonist? 1981's **RAIDERS OF THE LOST ARK.** Lots of action interlaced with character work in South America and then… the story slows down and the audience gets to spend time getting to know the protagonist, Indiana Jones, as he works as a professor in a college in New Jersey. There are character scenes throughout the film; ones with Marion, the love interest. Ones with his friend, Sallah. There are scenes where the protagonist and the antagonist face one another and reveal their different points of view. Yes, this is an action adventure film but note how many scenes spend time on character relationships.

Both **HARRY POTTER AND THE GOBLET OF FIRE** and **RAIDERS OF THE LOST ARK** are action adventure films. One manages to accomplish more than the other.

Question: Should a writer care if a film is not a satisfying, well-constructed story that tests character and illuminates a theme as long as it makes millions of dollars and the studios/producers are happy?

Answer: Yes. Care. The two can and should co-exist. Never settle.

Take the Time to Introduce Your Main Characters

If you want to start your screen story with a battle or a dream sequence or firing from a job or love scene or digging for buried treasure, of course, go ahead. Just know that when your action sequence is over, you must slow down and let the audience get to know the characters. Without knowing the characters, all the special effects and action sequences mean nothing. Remember, a good story is a character's journey. Without knowing the character, the audience cannot invest in the journey.

Consider Where You Begin Your Protagonist's Story

Make sure you don't start too early. Are you writing sequences, actions and events that really don't affect the plot of the story you have to tell? If your screenplay is about a female Senator running for the President of the United States, what will be the central story of your film? The struggle to get the nomination? The struggle to keep her moral center during the campaign? How the campaign affects her family? If it's one of these struggles, perhaps her time at Yale or in the Peace Corps or her third birthday party will not be events you want to include in your story. Choose the events that are going to move the story forward.

Make sure you don't start your story too late. Is there room for your protagonist to change, to have events in his life, for him to take action? Is there room for him to react to others' actions? If your story is about a shy,

Horror films must be scary. Explore the psychological fears as well as the physical fears.

Fish-out-of-water films must explore a character entering a new world. The character must struggle with strange-to-him rules, assumptions, ways of life, expectations. Is the language the same? Are the same things deemed attractive? Is evil honored and goodness despised? The plot points in this genre must explore the character's need to understand and to survive in a new world.

Fantasy films explore the world of the imagination, a world that is foreign to the world in which we live. A writer's task is to set the rules and logic of the new world he creates so the audience can know the limitations that will create obstacles for the characters.

Bio-pics, westerns, mysteries, comedies, family dramas... the list of genres goes on. No matter what the genre, remind yourself that the character and his journey of change is the most important part of the story.

When you build your story, acknowledge your genres (remember that most films contain elements of more than one genre). Consider using some of the *tried and true* plot points that are traditions of specific genres. Build on them, twist and turn them to find original moments—but always put character first.

Plotting the Passage of Time

Ask yourself: how much time passes in my story? Ten years? One year? One month? One day? Knowing the time passage will help you lay out the *events* that you need to tell your story. Will the story go from Christmas to Christmas? If so, what holidays are in-between? Valentine's Day, St. Patrick's Day, Thanksgiving, just to name a few. Any birthdays? Anniversaries of happy or sad times? Take note of the great number of movies that use holidays to subtly show the passage of time.

Events Are a Plot Must

Events are the things that happen in the story. An event can be anything; the first day at school, a birthday, a first kiss, an argument, a promotion, an interview, a love-at-first-sight meeting, a reunion, a divorce, a wedding, a trip to the beach, a sporting event, a contest, a bowling game, buying a present, going to the store or a bar or a restaurant, keeping an appointment at the dentist, making the call to start the next World War, walking the dog, killing the alien monster, adopting a child.... the list is endless. Some events in your story will loom large. You'll set up that they are on your protagonist's schedule and build anticipation or trepidation. Some events will be small. Build your tale from story-advancing-event to story-advancing event—this can help ensure you don't lose focus.

Concentrating on moving your protagonist from *event to event* will help give a sense of motion to your screen story. Events can illuminate character and plot.

Example:

The initial events for the protagonist in GLADIATOR set up character, plot, challenge.

1. Maximus asks the Emperor Marcus Aurelius for permission to go home to his family.

2. Emperor Marcus Aurelius is murdered by his son, Commodus.

3. Maximus is attacked, escapes.

4. Maximus finds his way home to see that his wife and child have been murdered.

5. Maximus is taken into slavery.

6. Maximus is forced to become a gladiator.

7. Commodus is now leader of Rome.

Those are the major events *for the protagonist* at the beginning of the film. These events affect the character—there are emotional reactions to each event. Without the emotional reactions, the events mean nothing. That is why the writer needs to focus on the events that affect his *main character*.

Simply having a series of events without the protagonist in the thick of them, will not advance character or story. Consider these random events—aliens arrive, kick butt, the town sheriff dies, all the animals are flash frozen, buildings disintegrate, cab drivers are the only ones saved and treated like gods, aliens discover ice cream and are suddenly weakened. Now add a main character that these events affect. John, our hero, is a maverick engineer at NASA. He accidentally opens a portal that allows violent aliens to enter the Earth's environment. They arrive and kick butt and John's father, the Sheriff, drunk and feeling belligerent, takes on the aliens single-handedly. He gets zapped and dies in John's arms, telling John that once

"The Gladiator" Russell Crowe
photo supplied by Globe Photos

again John's screwed up, that John's always creating problems. John, feeling guilty and determined to prove his father wrong, takes on the task of saving Earth. He seems to always be one step behind the aliens but then discovers they are sparing one small portion of the Earth's inhabitants; cab drivers. Why? Because one particular cab driver inadvertently introduced the head Alien to ice cream and the Alien is forever grateful. Who is this cab driver? The boyfriend of John's ex-girlfriend? A childhood chum? A brother? E*vents must be built that will directly affect the protagonist.*

Another Example:

Consider some of the most important events of **THE SHAWSHANK REDEMPTION.** Andy (portrayed by Tim Robbins) starts out as a man who cannot show emotion. He desires to be more effusive and demonstrative with his wife, he's not and she has started an affair. Here are some of the major *events* of the film.

1. Andy considers using a gun to confront his wife and her lover.

2. Wife and lover get shot and Andy claims innocence.

3. Andy stands trial for the crime, is found guilty.

4. Andy arrives at Shawshank prison.

5. Andy asks Red to smuggle in a rock hammer for him.

6. Andy is raped by inmates.

7. Andy overhears a guard complaining about paying taxes and gives advice.

8. Andy's advice is good; he's able to get beers for a few of his fellow inmates as they work.

9. The Warden asks Andy to do his taxes and oversee investments

10. Andy sets up library

11. Andy meets a new inmate who has information about the real killer of his wife.

12. The Warden will not let Andy pursue this new information, Andy is too valuable as the Warden's personal accountant.

13. Andy's constant letters finally get books and opera recordings delivered to enhance the library.

14. Andy plays opera over the P.A. system for the inmates.

15. Andy is put in solitary confinement

16. The inmate with the information to help free Andy is murdered by the Warden.

17. Andy gives Red information of how to find him if they should get out of prison.

18. Andy escapes.

Think of events that will be the tent poles of your character's journey. If you are "event-light," you may be in danger of working on a story that does not have a strong motor. You may be in danger of stretching out information and scenes.

When students in my class work on treatments or outlines for their screenplays, I suggest strongly that they experiment with building their story with events that affect the protagonist. This illuminates the character's journey, and opens up ideas and areas and new ways to tell the story.

Exercise:

What if your screen story will end with a wedding? What *events* could build up to the wedding day? Finding a place to hold the occasion? Deciding about food? Finding the wedding dress? Creating the guest list? Designing the wedding cake? Seating arrangements? Buying the rings? Finding a band for the reception (and the drummer hits on the bride-to-be)?? Wedding rehearsal? Saying final good-byes to past lovers? Bachelor party? Bachelorette party? Honeymoon plans? Arrival of in-laws? Moving into a new home?… keep the list going and you will get a good idea of all the possible *events* your protagonist might have to deal with in your screen story. Let the list be long, it's a luxury to be able to pick and choose.

Consider the Worst Things That Could Happen

Make a long list of possible events that can happen in your screen story. Plot needs to be pushed; stories can fail if events, circumstances, problems, relationships are not pushed far enough. Think big. Big emotions, big character arcs, big character reactions.

Think of the worst possible things that could face your protagonist. Most humiliating. Most dangerous. Most confusing. What will test her the most? What will push every emotional button? What is your protagonist's worst nightmare? Figure that out and see if you can make it come true.

Once you know your story, study every element. Explore each element to see how far you can push it to its extreme. If your protagonist is poor, illuminate what that means exactly. Can she only afford cereal and every serving is important to survival? Does a rat get into her cupboard and start to chew through the box? Does she have to face the rat that wants her food? Does she steal food from a store or from her family's house? If your protagonist has no social graces, illuminate what that means exactly by pushing the events you choose in order to show this. Does he ask a girl out while chewing on a hot dog and burps in her face? Does he get drunk at a debutante ball and make a fool of himself? Does he yell at his boss?

The first **DIE HARD** film is a story of man who wants to get his wife back; the plot begins when he arrives in Texas at his wife's office building to try to accomplish that goal. He meets with his wife, it's an unsatisfactory moment; she's busy with high-powered business guests, nothing he says comes out right. It's clear his ego has been sorely crushed, he wants to be the family's breadwinner and decision-maker. When he is denied his first immediate goal (Step # 3, the Denial), a Second Opportunity (Step #4) presents itself. What is it? Terrorists infiltrate the building. McClane is now "saving" his wife (and marriage) on a much bigger scale. How are elements of the *plot* pushed so tension will rise?

- It's a new building, very few floors are ready for inhabitants—thus there is a danger in just traversing the building. Also, this detail makes it clear that there are few inhabitants in the building, putting McClane even more on his own.

- The terrorists are technologically adept, fearless and strong.

- The protagonist is a fish out of water; he is not a part of the local police force. He has to win trust.

- There is a ticking clock.

So how do you push elements in a "small character-driven story"? You force yourself to think big. It's all relative. If it's a story of a young girl trying to get her absentee father to notice her—what are the big things she can do to accomplish this? What are her big emotions, what will she feel like the rest of her life if he rejects her? Let the audience feel that if this girl does not get her father to acknowledge her existence, she will grow to be a shell of a woman and never be able to have a satisfying relationship. Thus *any* attempt she makes is valid. Push her actions, exaggerate.

If it's a story of a boy in love with the girl next door, think big. What can he do to put himself in a good light? Who is his rival? What kind of showdown could there be with the rival? Choose events that will put your protagonist in awkward, difficult situations. Is he putting his life on the line just to get her attention? Think of the events in the story. Is there a dance? A sporting event? A picnic? An alien attack? A graduation? A TV Talent Show? A trip to Paris? How can each *event* be pushed to be as disastrous as possible?

Exercise:

Draw a straight line on a piece of paper. This will be your timeline. Make a decision as to how much time goes by in your screen story. Is it two days or three weeks? Two years? A decade? On a separate sheet of paper, make a list of the major events *you absolutely* need to tell your story. Now put them on your timeline, put them in calendar order. (Even if you plan to use flashback or want to tell your story out of order, put them in calendar order now.)

On your timeline make notes of other events that might work, turning points that you need. Study your timeline. When you see things are going well for a period of time, add an event that would be a reversal. When things are going bad for a period of time, add a reversal.

Conflict, Conflict, Conflict...You Gotta Have It

If there is no conflict rearing its head in your story, you may want to take another look at it. Your character must face obstacles. Physical obstacles. Emotional obstacles.

Use characters to create obstacles. Of course you have your antagonist. But explore other characters. Even friends can (and should) disagree and have falling-outs. Parents aren't always supportive. Teachers may have agendas that do not benefit students. Bosses can be nasty.

Use environment to create obstacles. Thick forests. Raging rapids. Quicksand. Insurmountable mountains. Creatures. Storms, rain, snow, hurricanes, tornadoes, earthquakes. Use intense sun. Use dark of night. Use all elements to make things more difficult for your protagonist.

Point of View

Whose point of view will you tell your story through? If **SHAKESPEARE IN LOVE** was told through the Nurse's point of view, the plot could be the same... but the way the story is told would be different. If **SIDEWAYS** had been told through the women's point of view, the plot points could have been similar, the way the story is told would have been different.

OMNISCIENT POINT OF VIEW: The writer allows the audience to move from character to character to fill in all the elements of the story. Examples: **IT HAPPENED ONE NIGHT, ALL ABOUT EVE, NETWORK, BEAUTY AND THE BEAST, SPIDERMAN.**

PROTAGONIST'S POINT OF VIEW: The writer allows the audience to know only what the protagonist knows. The story is seen primarily through the protagonist's eyes. Examples: **CASABLANCA, SUNSET BOULEVARD, CHINATOWN, OUT OF AFRICA, DIE HARD, LEGALLY BLONDE, ONE FLEW OVER THE CUCKOO'S NEST, THE GRADUATE, A BEAUTIFUL MIND, GOOD NIGHT AND GOOD LUCK.**

ANOTHER CHARACTER'S POINT OF VIEW: The writer allows the audience to see the story through an onlooker's point of view. This allows for a picking and choosing of the most relevant events of the story. Example: **THE SHAWSHANK REDEMPTION.**

Will you use flashbacks? Will you reveal plot points out of order? Once you know your story and your main character's journey, you can tell your story anyway that works. Take a look at **THE SHAWSHANK REDEMPTION.** There are flashbacks. There's a narrator. The stories of **MEMENTO** and **BETRAYAL** are told from the end to the beginning. **GOODFELLAS** starts at a present day crisis point, then flashbacks to 20-some years earlier and moves forwards from there. **OUT OF AFRICA** is a memory piece; the story begins as we watch an elderly woman write her memoirs—then the visuals dissolve to decades earlier. **ADAPTATION** moves backwards and forward in time.

Are there any rules that must be followed? The answer is no. There are no rules. There is just good storytelling. If the story works, if the audience is engaged, any method of storytelling is acceptable.

What About Subplots?

Subplots can be divided into "B" and "C" stories and runners. Read on.

Chapter Summary

- Aristotle's most important advice: A story needs to be about one thing.

- Character and his overall want drives the plot.

- Plot or action that does not affect character will not help the story.

- Where you start your character's story is important.

- Know how much time your story traverses.

- Events are a plot must.

- Stories can be told from various points of view.

- Stories can be told in many different ways.

for Belle's father to be taken to an insane asylum, telling her if she marries him he will arrange for her father's release. Gaston has few moral *conflicts* about his actions (he is the archetypal villain after all), but there are physical *conflicts:* Belle does not love him, his false actions could be discovered, the deal costs him money, his sidekick could blow the plan. *All goes well,* Gaston finds the asylum director who will sign the false papers. *All falls apart* when Belle spoils the plan. Gaston has a *crisis* of decision. He has been humiliated by Belle's disinterest in him and he will not walk away without vengeance. He decides to kill the Beast to prove to Belle he is the stronger, more powerful suitor. In the *climax,* Gaston, in a jealous, angry rage, battles his rival. The *truth* comes out, the Beast is the stronger and Gaston falls to his death. Note how the "B" story meets the "A" story near the crisis point, raises the stakes of the story and directly affects the climax.

GLADIATOR'S "A" Story Holds the Main Plot

The "A" story holds the main plot. The bones of the main plot can be, and in most cases, should be very simple. No need to overcomplicate it. Let the characters be complex, let the plot be simple.

GLADIATOR is a simple story. General Maximus *wants* a peaceful life, he wants to put war and killing behind him and go home to his quiet farm. He is in the Emperor's army and has performed well in the last campaign. He *logically* asks for his reward—permission to return home to his farm where his wife and son wait for him. Before Maximus can claim his reward, he is *denied* when the Emperor is killed by his own son, Commodus. To further his *denial,* Commodus has Maximus' family killed and Maximus is forced into slavery where he has to perform as a gladiator or die. What does he have to live for? Revenge. Justice. Maximus realizes his *second opportunity* to find peace of mind is to expose and de-throne Commodus. Maximus knows he can put himself in position to avenge his Emperor's murder and the murder of his family by becoming the best gladiator in Rome—this will ensure that he performs in front of Commodus. There are many *conflicts and dangers about taking advantage of the second opportunity,* but Maximus *goes for it.* Things *do go well,* he becomes a famous masked gladiator. *All falls apart* when his identity is revealed. Commodus has him strung up, weakens him with a severe knife wound. Maximus' *crisis* is a decision to stay alive long enough to battle Commodus in the gladiator ring. The *climax* is a battle between a strong and good protagonist and a strong and evil antagonist. The *truth* comes out at the end... we realize Maximus has found peace in death.

Note how various aspects of Maximus' life are explored; his prowess as a warrior, his friendship with the Emperor, his love for his family, his love of farming, his love of Rome. All these elements help make a complex character; and a complex character in a simple plot is something to strongly consider. These aspects of Maximus' life make up the various "B" stories.

What helps make the film interesting on many levels are the "B" stories. These "B" stories help reveal Maximus' character and help create the dangerous world in which he lives.

GLADIATOR'S "B" Stories

The "B" stories illuminate Maximus' character and raise the stakes in the final moments of the film. "B" stories include Commodus' sister, Lucilla; her relationship with Maximus as well as Commodus' lust for her. Another "B" story is the Senate's plan to de-throne Commodus, Maximus secretly joins forces with them. Another "B" story is Maximus' friendship with the other gladiators and his relationship with Proximus, the slave-gladiators owner. All these "B" stories are designed with simple Eleven Step arcs and all raise the stakes of the "A" story.

Consider the "B" story with the Senate. They *want* to bring down Commodus. They *logically* plot. They are *denied,* Commodus is too clever and strong. The Senate's *second opportunity* is Maximus' arrival in Rome as the celebrated masked gladiator. Maximus joins forces with the Senate, gives them new strength. *Conflicts* abound, if the plot is exposed there is great danger. *All goes well* for a short while, and then *falls apart* when Commodus has many of the Senators killed. The outcome of this "B" story focuses us again on Maximus. Now he is the *only one* left who can bring down Commodus. (Note: Most classic hero stories will be designed so that the hero, *alone,* has to bring about the final outcome.)

SIDEWAYS' "A" and "B" Stories

SIDEWAYS is a simple story about Miles, a man whose life is in shambles who comes to the decision to take the first steps to change his situation. The audience is introduced to two male friends, Miles and Jack, as they head to the wine country for a last weekend before Jack gets married. Miles is depressed and is having a hard time moving on with his life after his divorce. Miles resists Jack's attempts to knock Miles out of his depressive state. Miles resists Jack's attempt to set up a double date for them with two

"Sideways" Paul Giamatti, Thomas Haden Church
photo supplied by Globe Photos

women who live in the wine country. Finally Miles acquiesces and events conspire to force Miles to confront his depression and take action to change his life.

That's the story. Simple. It's the complex characters revealed in the "B" stories that raise this simple story to something special. The arc of the "B" story with Jack and bartender Stephanie affects Miles' state of mind. Jack *wants* to have a sex-filled weekend before his impending wedding. He *logically* tries to accomplish this by asking out the winery bartender, Stephanie, and arranging for her to bring a date (Maya) for Miles. Jack is *denied* when Miles is a downer on the double date and it looks as if Jack will not bed Stephanie. Jack gets a *second opportunity* to have sex when Stephanie suggests they extend the night at her house. *All goes well* for Jack, he and Stephanie have sex. *All falls apart* for Jack when Stephanie finds out Jack is about to married, she clobbers him with her motorcycle helmet. All the story points of Jack's "B" story directly affect Miles' growing relationship with Maya, Jack's actions could ruin Miles' chances of connecting with this woman who could be his soul mate.

"B" stories Must Directly Affect the "A" Story

In **CASABLANCA,** the "A" story follows Rick's re-awakening desire to commit to feeling and taking an interest in the world around him due to his long lost love, Ilsa, coming back into his life. A "B" story is Rick's relationship with Captain Renault (portrayed by Claude Rains). This

Question: Can a film story have more than one "B" story?

Answer: Yes.

Question: Do they all need to affect the "A "story?

Answer: Yes.

Question: If you spend too much time on your "B" story (stories) are you in danger of taking away from the "A "story and losing the focus on your story?

Answer: Perhaps (probably). "B" stories should remain *supporting* material no matter how exciting, funny, crazy the storyline becomes.

relationship includes following the whereabouts of the letters of transit. These letters directly affect Ilsa's relationship with Rick. As the "A" story of the tortured romance plays out, the "B" story motors on, constantly affecting the "A" story.

In 1960's **THE APARTMENT,** the "A" story follows Baxter's (portrayed by Jack Lemmon) desire to build a successful life, which includes gaining the love of Miss Kubliak (portrayed by Shirley McLaine). An important "B" story in **THE APARTMENT** is the troubled affair of Baxter's boss and Miss Kubliak. It has a beginning, middle, and end. (Beginning: Sheldrake and Miss Kubliak are having an affair; she believes he will leave his wife. Sheldrake arranges to use Baxter's apartment for their liaisons, not realizing that Baxter has a crush on Miss Kubliak. Middle: Miss Kubliak attempts suicide when she realizes Sheldrake does not intend to leave his wife. Sheldrake's jealous secretary spills news of the affair to Sheldrake's wife. End: Sheldrake's wife kicks him out; he wants to get back together with Miss Kubliak (whom Baxter now completely adores). Miss Kubliak is sure Sheldrake now plans to marry her, but when she realizes he does not really love her, she ends the affair—completing the "A" story because then she runs to join Baxter, knowing his love is true and she loves him in return.

How Can the "B" Story Help Reveal Theme?

The "B "story should support the theme of the "A" story. In **BEAUTY AND THE BEAST** the "B" story focusing on Gaston supports the theme, "Without the willingness to sacrifice for the one you love, there is no true love." The Gaston "B" story is *anti-theme;* meaning it explores the opposite belief, "It doesn't matter if you love me, my desires comes first." The Gaston story supports the "A" story by exploring the *opposite* of the theme. Gaston declares an empty love—shown by the fact he is not willing to sacrifice his desires for Belle's happiness.

The "B" story in **SIDEWAYS,** Jack's relationship with Stephanie, supports the film's theme, "Without honesty, there can be no real happiness." The main character, Miles, is not being honest with himself—he is holding onto a false hope that his ex-wife will come back to him, he is holding onto a false hope that the publication of his book will change his life, he is false with his mother (he even steals from her), he won't be honest with Jack about his feelings, about his dreams, about his life, about his need for sex/love. The dishonest relationship of Jack and Stephanie illuminates Miles' dilemma. (A later chapter goes more in depth on theme.)

Your "B" stories should reflect on the emotional journey of the protagonist. Let your "B" stories work for you to bring out more conflict. Let them raise the stakes of the "A" story.

What Makes a "C" story?

You may have a "C" story (stories). "C" stories take up less time and space than the "B" story, but they too should affect the "A" story. Their arcs can be much less significant, but they should have a shape—a simple nod to the Eleven Steps.

In Disney's **BEAUTY AND THE BEAST,** a "C" story is Belle's relationship with her father. One could argue it's worthy of being called a "B" story because it affects the "A" story so completely; but in this 1991 version of the story, the father doesn't have a complete arc because he doesn't have a change at the end. (Beginning: Maurice is a wacky but muddle-minded inventor and ends up in the Beast's castle by mistake. He's ill and Belle has to save him. Middle: Maurice lobbies the town to help save Belle from the Beast, no one believes him. He's tries to get back to his daughter, but gets lost and hurt in the woods; causing Belle to have to go to him once more. End: He (sort of) tries to protect Belle, but then pretty much disappears in the final climax.

In **THE APARTMENT,** the neighbor doctor/Baxter relationship has a small "C" story arc. (Beginning: Doctor thinks Baxter is a playboy—a man he would never want to befriend. Middle: Doctor admires Baxter's care of Miss Kubliak (even though he thinks Baxter's responsible, he sees Baxter as someone who will stay up all night and care for someone else). End: Doctor sees Baxter's good side and sympathizes with his sadness. He invites Baxter to a holiday dinner…). The "C" story supports the "A" story, but does not take a lot of time or focus.

In **SIDEWAYS,** a "C" story is Miles' desire to get his book published. At the beginning of the film, he is awaiting word from his agent about whether or not a publisher has accepted the book. This story is complicated by the fact that Jack lies to Maya, saying that Miles' book has already been accepted for publication. Miles has a crisis of conscience about living this lie. He eventually finds out the book has been rejected, which deepens his depression. He has to admit the lie to Maya, which furthers the complications caused by Jack's lie to Stephanie (not telling Stephanie that Jack's marriage is imminent).

Having "A," "B" and even "C" stories will allow you to cut from scene to scene, fill out the world of the piece, introduce characters that will live in your story and affect your protagonist. These subplots can have a life of their own until they intersect with the "A" story to add pressure to the main character in the final moments of his journey.

Think about your story. Sometimes a writer will try to get too much information into one scene; making it about more than one thing. Remember Aristotle's wise advice: *A story is about one thing*. Let the "A" story be about one thing. Your "B" story can explore a different aspect of your story. Likewise with the "C" story. If you divide your elements into A, B, C stories, then you can concentrate on getting each story rolling on its own merits. Slowly the stories will come together to affect the outcome of your main character's journey.

Runners

A runner is a series of repeated actions or words or visuals that comment on or enhance the story but have no plot arc in themselves. A runner can help show time passage, add comic relief, and remind the audience of the theme. A runner can be "repeated as needed" in a screenplay.

The runner in **SIDEWAYS:** Miles has a special bottle of wine. He's bought it for a special occasion. The unopened bottle symbolizes that no "special occasion" has come his way since he bought it. It symbolizes his refusal to take pleasure from the present. The bottle of wine becomes a symbol of his life; his life is on hold and that he cannot go forward. That bottle of wine is referred to throughout the film. At the end of the story, he drinks the wine, alone, from a paper cup in a fast food eatery—clearly not the typical "special occasion." But the drinking of the wine symbolizes that he has had an epiphany, he will no longer hold onto the past. He will move forward with his life.

Runners can be comedic or visual or dramatic and don't need an arc. Another example: The snakes in **RAIDERS OF THE LOST ARK.** The writer sets up Jones' fear of the snakes. He encounters one or two but not in a near-death circumstances. Finally, in the climax of the film, he's surrounded by thousands of them, they attack and he has to save himself and the girl he loves.

Another example: A runner in **THE APARTMENT** is the executives' constant pressure to get permission to use Baxter's apartment for their affairs. This is a constant *running* pressure. There's another runner in **THE APARTMENT** —the exchange of keys. The key to Baxter's apartment becomes a symbol for the choices Baxter makes in his life. When he finally chooses to be true to his own moral code, he keeps his apartment key for himself.

KRAMER VS KRAMER uses runners to good advantage. There are three breakfast scenes between new single father, Ted Kramer, and his son. The first is a disastrous attempt to make French toast. The second is a well-timed, silent breakfast of donuts. The third takes place right before Billy's mother comes to take him away from Ted's home. This runner shows time passing and a progression of the relationship.

Another runner in this movie is Ted's dropping Billy off at school. In the first scene, Ted doesn't even know what grade Billy is in, or who his teacher might be. In the second scene, Ted has the lunchbox, homework routine down. In the third scene, Ted drops Billy off and the audience sees Joanna, Billy's mother, watching from across the street. This runner shows progression of the relationship and introduces the Step #8 section of the film: All Falls Apart.

Using "B" and "C" stories and runners can open up your story. They can help the audience see your characters in various lights. They can help round out the characters' lives so they feel as if they exist in a real world. In most cases, no matter what crisis is happening in a person's life, everyday chores (work, grocery shopping, taking the kids to school, dealing with crazy neighbors, friends' problems...) still need to be handled. Use these subplots to reflect on your main character and enrich your story.

Question: How can you tell which is the "A" story of a film that has a strong "B" story?

Answer: There are many films designed to have a very prominent "B" story. The way to pinpoint which is the "A" story is simple. Ask yourself: What is the Central Question of the film?

Central Question

Will the detective find the criminal? Will the boy get the girl? Will the soldier make it behind enemy lines and save his unit? Will the stockbroker become rich and powerful? Will the has-been baseball player get another chance and redeem himself? Will the woman find her child and flush out the kidnapping ring? Will the candidate get elected?

The Central Question relates to the "A" story. It is the main question the audience will wonder about, worry about during the film. It is the main question presented near the beginning of the film.

In **WITNESS** the Central Question is: Will John Book catch the cop killer?

This is the question that is presented at the beginning of the film. The "B story" is the love story between John and Rachel because it affects the "A" story. Will John Book's love for Rachel cause him to stop looking for the cop killer?

In **THE GODFATHER** the Central Question is: Will Michael accept the challenge of keeping his family's position intact? The various "B" stories push him towards or pull him away from taking on the responsibility.

In **A BEAUTIFUL MIND** the Central Questions is: Will John Nash find success, fame and acceptance of himself?

In **RUNAWAY BRIDE** the Central Question is: Will the nervous bride ever find a love strong enough to erase her fears of commitment?

In **SIDEWAYS** the Central Question is: Will Miles be able to move forward with his life?

In **RAIDERS OF THE LOST ARK** the Central Question is: Will Indiana Jones find the Ark of the Covenant and ensure it's availability for archeological study?

In Disney' **BEAUTY AND THE BEAST** the Central Question is: Will the Beast be able to break the spell and become human again before the last petal falls off the rose?

In 2005's **GOOD NIGHT AND GOOD LUCK** the Central Question is: Will Edward R. Morrow's actions help bring down Joseph McCarthy?

Introducing Subplots

Remember that "B" stories are structured in the same way a primary "A" plot is structured. "B" stories should have an Eleven Step arc. They should have strong beginnings, middles and ends. They should affect the "A" story. Therefore, they too will take time to unravel, so don't wait too long to introduce them.

"B" stories are integral to the fabric of the film. **TOOTSIE** has a "B" story (relationship/friendship between Michael (portrayed by Dustin Hoffman) and Sandy (portrayed by Teri Garr) that is introduced in the first five minutes of the film. Another strong "B" story in that film is the relationship/love story between Michael and Julie (portrayed by Jessica Lange). That story kicks in just a few minutes later. A "C" story with Michael and the lecherous soap opera actor kicks in on Michael's first day of work on the set for the daytime drama.

Some subplots will be so integral to the main plot of the film that they will emerge naturally. In fact, the story will not be able to be fully told without the subplots taking stage almost immediately.

There are other times when you may look at your script or story and feel that it is too linear, too slim in its scope. This is a technical assessment of the state of your story and you may want to consider adding "B" stories or "C" stories. Where do you find them? Search the world of your protagonist. Is there a friend who has something going on in her life? A sibling who is a pain? A love interest? A work problem? A family conflict? Is there a bully in his world? Is there a desire to lose weight? Is there a desire to get in shape? Is there a hobby? An addiction? Is there a secret that needs to come out?

Consider 2005's **CAPOTE.** The "A" story is Capote's investigation and writing of the book *"In Cold Blood."* There are no strong "B" stories; they are begun but then fizzle out. The second half of the film lags because the "B" stories (his friendship with novelist Harper Lee, his relationship with his lover) are not explored fully and they do not *affect* the "A" story. Avoid the pitfall of your story becoming slimmer and less resonant as it progresses—use "B" stories to advantage. Subplots are fantastic story-telling tools. Use them.

Exercise:

Make a list of possible supporting stories that could reflect on your protagonist's journey. Example: If your protagonist is running for elected office and has an overall want to feel powerful, perhaps a supporting story has to do with an overbearing father who demands things to be done his way. If the father becomes ill and has to give up control as doctors try to save his life, what does the father learn—and what does the son learn in the process?

Chapter Summary

- The "A" story holds the protagonist's main journey.

- Subplots, or B" and "C" stories, support the "A" story which is the main journey of the protagonist in the film.

- "B" and "C" stories should have their own beginnings, middles and ends.

- Supporting stories should reflect theme.

- Supporting stories should ultimately affect the "A" story.

Chapter Ten

BEATS, SCENES, AND SEQUENCES

Does every element in a screenplay need to serve a purpose? Yes.

Does breaking the script down into its components make it clear what is working and what is extraneous? Yes.

A screenplay can be broken down into many components. It's good to know what they are so you can converse with other writers, producers, directors and film executives. Just as you would know the terminology in a legal or medical or other profession, as a screenwriter you are perfecting a craft. As you begin to create your screenplay, become familiar with these terms.

Beat

The term "beat" is over-used and often used incorrectly. In most cases, it means "pause." Some screenwriters who use this term will use it to instruct the actor to pause or take a breath before he or she responds to an event or piece of dialogue. This is *not* the correct usage of this term.

There is the problem with a screenwriter using "beat" in a screenplay.

It's *not* the writer's job to instruct the actor to pause at a certain point in the scene. It's not the writer's job to suggest when an actor should breathe. Or scratch her head. Or cough. Or brush the hair off his face. Or laugh or sigh. *It's the writer's job to tell the story.* That's it.

A screenwriter who indicates where an actor should take a beat before speaking or moving is wasting his time... and offending the actor, director and, sometimes, even the reader. A screenwriter who puts an excessive amount of actor-directives into his screenplay is clearly not trusting his own material. *If the screenwriter has made clear the intent of the scene, there is no need to write specific acting or directing instructions.* "Beat" should only be used to indicate a moment filled with tension or emotion or indecision... a moment in which dialogue or action will not suffice.

Question: What if a scene starts in the kitchen and moves to the living room without a break in dialogue? Is that two scenes?

Answer: Technically, yes. The writer (or more often it's the director) simply wants the actors on the move, doesn't want the scene to feel static. The content of the scenes may be serving one purpose, but technically, it's two scenes.

storytellers. The actors that the series attracted were of the highest caliber, they knew how to map their character's arcs. These artists were asked to commit to the writer's script and they did. The writer could relax (and not be rewritten by anyone else) and anticipate their work coming to life in the best way. Seeing the finished product made one realize that if all artists in the project are committed to telling *the story*, the end product can surpass the writer's initial vision.

There will always be projects that hit or miss. There will be great joys—there may be huge heartaches—when seeing your work done. Part of the creative process and the writer's task is to find the people who understand your sensibilities and the stories you want to tell. If everyone respects the other's contribution, films can be an enjoyable and artistic success.

Scenes are Components of Your Film Script

A scene is a piece of action that takes place in one location. When the writer changes location in the story, the scene is over.

A scene is introduced with a slug line that gives the scene's location. Examples: EXT. FARMHOUSE or INT. DINER or EXT. TOP OF EMPIRE STATE BUILDING or INT. DARK DUNGEON. When the story moves from INT. DARK DUNGEON to EXT. ENCHANTED WOODS, that indicates a new scene is beginning.

Scenes Build Sequences

If a scene is a man waking up in single bed—alone—that visual tells the audience that this man has no wife or lover. That visual lets us know about character. If, in the next scene, the man walks into the messy, dirty kitchen and searches for an old piece of toast, this scene tells us he has no interest in creating a pleasant home, perhaps has little self-respect and obviously no housekeeper. If, in the next scene, he takes a shower using dishwashing soap, this lets us know that he does not take care of himself well. If, in the next scene, he's wearing mismatched clothes and gets into an old, rusted car, we can surmise that he does not have a lot of money and has little interest in impressing others with possessions. If, in the next scene, he is hit by an errant driver on the freeway and his old car is wrecked and he reaches into the glove compartment and takes out a gun and goes on a rampage, killing strangers on the highway and then racing off to escape…

we have designed a SEQUENCE that shows a man who has nothing to lose, who has nothing in life that excites him, a man who is unstable and very dangerous. He is now on the run from the law…

Scenes are components of sequences.

Each Sequence Must Advance the Story

A sequence is a block of scenes that advance story. A sequence is a series of scenes that move the story forward in character and/or plot. 2005's **BATMAN BEGINS** has a sequence where Bruce Wayne travels to a Far East mountaintop to learn martial arts and spiritual lessons; he goes through villages, he goes through various weather fronts and terrains and finally reaches his destination. The series of scenes *that get him from point A to point B* is a sequence. A sequence accomplishes a certain action and advances the story.

Michael Dorsey's audition (as a woman) for the daytime soap opera in **TOOTSIE** is a series of scenes: He lines up with the other (much better-looking) auditionees and gets rejected because he is not attractive. He demands an audition. He interests the executive producer, he alienates the director. He finally gets his audition and gets the part. What does this sequence accomplish? It moves the story forward because now Michael has an acting job (his immediate goal). But he has gotten it while pretending to be a woman and this subterfuge will have to continue (conflict). This sequence also sets up the antagonist. This sequence could be titled: Michael Gets the Job.

A sequence should be designed to move the story forward. Consider **CHINATOWN.** The initial sequence is designed to set up Jake Gittes' character and job: Jake is in his office, it is clear he is a private detective. He deals with one client, expertly moves into meeting another client (the fake Mrs. Mulwray). When Jake attempts to deny Mrs. Mulwray's request that he follow her husband whom she suspects of having an affair, the audience learns Jake's point of view about infidelity. He believes if one loves another person, one should look the other way when confronted with an affair. He believes no one wins in contests of the heart. This element of the sequence lets the audience know Jake has principles and sympathy for human frailty. He takes the case when Mrs. Mulwray insists and offers a large sum of money. This shows that Jake is a businessman, and is not above being swayed by a big paycheck. What does this sequence accomplish? It sets up the *normal* life of the main character, elements of his personality and moral code and gets the main plot moving forward. This sequence could be titled: Introduce Jake.

The next sequence in **CHINATOWN** could be titled: Jake Finds Out About The Water Problem. Jake attends a pubic city council meeting because he is tailing Mr. Mulwray. At the meeting, a *"B" story* (the water problem in the Los Angeles area) is introduced. When Jake tails Mr. Mulwray to the dried-up land and then to ocean, Jake witnesses clues about the water problem. Jake is focused on his immediate case—proving adultery—but eventually these other clues will add up. This sequence sets up the motor— the reason—the *why* this story takes place.

Note: *Jake, the main character, is a first-hand witness to the clues in the Water Problem plot. This" B" story could have been revealed without Jake's presence, but it would not have been as interesting. The audience is seeing the elements of the story through Jake's eyes. This accomplishes a few things; the lead actor is onscreen, experiencing the story, thus making it more interesting. It also sets up the way of telling the story; the audience will know things as Jake knows things—thus the audience will be trying to solve the mystery as Jake does and thus remain an active participant.*

The next sequence in **CHINATOWN** could be titled: Jake Finds Out He's Duped. Jake and his employee track Mr. Mulwray to Echo Park Lake and take pictures of Mr. Mulwray boating with a beautiful young girl. Jake tails the pair and takes photos of a kiss. The photos, somehow, appear in the newspaper (we assume Jake's given the photos to his client by this time). Jake, feeling he's done an honest and good job, defends the honor of his job at the barbershop. When Jake returns to his office, he is confronted by the *real* Mrs. Mulwray and realizes he's been used and made to look like a fool. This sequence pushes the story and character forward in a major way; Jake's honor is at stake. He is determined to find out why he was set up.

Note: *Consider how the scenes in this sequence pump up Jake's ego. He takes great pride in doing his job well. He likes success, he desires respect. This sequence has a great arc because Jake is riding high, defending his job, feeling good about himself. And then the rug is pulled out from under him when he realizes he's been used.*

By the end of the first three sequences in **CHINATOWN,** most of the major characters are introduced, the audience knows what makes Jake tick, and the mystery is moving forward.

A sequence is a series of scenes that accomplish a goal and move the story forward. The scenes you choose to write for the sequence should all be targeted to accomplish a certain goal. A writer can give each sequence a title. This will help focus the story and give the writer clues as to what scenes she needs to write.

The Sequence Sheet

A sequence sheet is a list, scene by scene, of how your screen story will unfold. Title each sequence so you know what you want to accomplish in the section of your story.

No need to spend time building a sequence sheet full of "pretty prose." This is a tool for the writer to use to help focus his story and to make sure each scene helps accomplish the goal of the sequence.

For example: A sequence sheet for the opening of 2004's **HARRY POTTER AND THE PRISONER OF AZKABAN** could've read like this—

SEQUENCE #A: HARRY'S HOME LIFE IS MISERABLE. HE CAN'T STAY.

1. Harry Potter reads his wizard books under a bed sheet with a flashlight. His mean and petty Uncle checks in on him to make sure he is NOT reading and Harry pretends to be asleep. *(This scene shows that Harry is not free to be who he is at home.)*

2. Morning. The Uncle's obnoxious sister has come for a visit. She treats Harry terribly, casting aspersions on his mother and father. Harry loses his temper and causes the sister to blow up like a balloon and fly off into the sky. *(This scene reveals backstory and Harry's powers and—of course—gets him in big trouble.)*

3. Harry leaves his Uncle's house, knowing his punishment will be severe. He is positive he can no longer live there.

4. Harry gets picked up by the Knight bus and heads off to join his wizard fellows. *(This magical bus furthers the introduction of Harry's special world.)*

This initial sequence introduces the genre, the main character and Harry's normal life at home and puts Harry on the road to his next adventure.

Another example: **BOURNE IDENTITY**

SEQUENCE #A: SET UP GENRE AND BOURNE'S LOSS OF MEMORY

1. Bourne, near dead from bullet wounds, is rescued from the ocean. *(Note it's night, it's storming. This adds to the feelings of danger and drama.)*

2. Ship's Captain finds a code chip implanted under Bourne's skin. It has a number of a Swiss Bank account on it. *(This helps set genre; political thriller. Helps set up that Bourne is someone special.)*

3. Bourne attacks the Captain, showing his skills as a trained aggressor.

4. It becomes clear to Bourne that he has amnesia. *(This is the major element of the story, its set up is in the first few minutes of the film. The Dramatic Question is now clear, will Bourne discover who he is?)*

SEQUENCE #B: SET UP WHO IS OUT TO FIND BOURNE

1. Washington D.C. government officials are made aware that Bourne's assigned mission failed and Bourne has disappeared. *(The audience realizes the scope of the story; political intrigue that could ruin the careers of high government officials… a "B" story. It's clear to the audience that these two stories will go along a parallel path for awhile…they will eventually intersect.)*

SEQUENCE #C: BOURNE TRIES TO JOG HIS MEMORY

1. On the ship, Bourne works with the fishing crew. *(This sets up his character, he is a man willing to do his share of the labor and lets the audience like him).*

2. Bourne tries to jog his memory: He tries out different languages. He checks out scars on his body, hoping to remember how he got them. He studies maps in hopes in finding a familiar place.

SEQUENCE #D: BOURNE TRAVELS TO SEEK CLUES

1. Ship docks. The Captain gives Bourne a little money for travel to Switzerland. *(Remember: The only clue Bourne has is the number of the Swiss Bank account.)*

2. Bourne takes the train to Switzerland, always hoping something will jog his memory. His overall want continues—he wants to find out who he is.

3. Bourne arrives in Switzerland, sleeps in the park. When the police try to move him off, they ask to see his papers, Bourne attacks. He is able to disarm both officers, again showing him that he has talents that go beyond the ordinary. Bourne drops the gun, showing that he does not have a natural desire for a weapon of destruction. *(Note: Throughout the*

"Bourne Identity" Matt Damon
photo supplied by ES/Globe Photos

story, the audience wonders if Bourne is a "good guy" or "bad guy"… this adds to the mystery.)

4. Bourne arrives at the Swiss Bank. The number gains him entry. He enters the vault, finds a passport in his safety deposit box. Ah! He feels as if he's found his answer, he knows his identity.

SEQUENCE #E: BOURNE'S HOPES ARE DASHED, HAS TO CONTINUE

1. Bourne opens another compartment of the safety deposit box and sees more passports, all with his picture on them, all with various names, all from different countries. His momentary sense of success is taken away.

2. Bourne heads out of the Bank.

3. Washington D.C. officials are notified of his appearance at the Bank. *(Keeping "B" story alive.)*

4. Bourne makes a phone call to Paris, checks to see if a "Jason Bourne" still resides at the address given on one of the passports. He hears his own recorded voice on the phone machine. Now Bourne has a new immediate goal; to get to Paris. He needs to get there to keep accruing clues to his identity.

5. Bourne realizes he's being followed by police. He manages to get to the American Embassy… *(Here he meets the girl, his Second Opportunity, and the story (the chase) takes off in earnest.)*

apartment for a short tryst. Baxter hesitates, but the executive promises to put in a good word at the office and Baxter capitulates.

5. Baxter leaves apartment and falls asleep in cold park.

Note: Each sequence focuses on one thing at a time.

SEQUENCE D: SET UP OF BAXTER'S ROMANTIC DESIRE AND CONTINUE HIS LOGICAL ATTEMPTS TO ACHIEVE WANT.

1. Baxter, with head cold, interacts with Miss Kubliak, the cute elevator operator, in elevator.

2. Set up Miss Kubliak's character; she's fun, breezy, doesn't flirt.

3. Executive tells Baxter that men have tried to date her, but she's turned everyone down. Baxter respects her and is encouraged by that... maybe he has a chance.

SEQUENCE E: CLARIFICATION OF THE RULES OF APARTMENT USAGE AND RAISING THE STAKES

1. Baxter, who now has a cold because he slept all night in the park, tries to rearrange the use of his apartment so he can spend a night there getting well. Audience sees the extent and how far-reaching is the use of his apartment.

2. Introduction to the executive floor; how the executive workday is as opposed to the non-executive workday in the company.

3. Baxter gets call to go see Sheldrake, the personnel head. Baxter thinks it's about the promotion the executives promised him.

4. Sheldrake manipulates Baxter into thinking he's in trouble (for getting great recommendations from all these executives) but in reality, wants to use the apartment for his own affair.

5. Baxter witnesses Sheldrake lie to his wife on the phone. Baxter does not approve but at this point, he is not a man who follows his convictions or acts on moral principles. *(This sets up an area in Baxter's life that will change. Remember, if he does **act on principle at the end** of the film, make sure **he is not doing so at the top of the film**.)*

6. Baxter, to curry favor for promotion, gives up his apartment for that night to Sheldrake. He takes "Music Man" theatre tickets in exchange.

SEQUENCE F: ROMANTIC NEXT STEP/ TRIANGLE SET UP AND CONTINUATION OF BAXTER'S LOGICAL ATTEMPTS

1. Baxter asks Miss Kubliak to "Music Man." He's persistent. She agrees to meet him after her drink with the man with whom she *used* to have a relationship. (We get exposition that the relationship is over.) Baxter, excited she has agreed to the date with him, says he will meet her in front of the theatre.

2. A "B" STORY KICKS IN: Miss Kubliak and Sheldrake meet up, we realize Sheldrake is her "past relationship." Audience finds out they had a fling while his wife was out of town. It's clear Miss Kubliak still has feelings for Sheldrake, but it trying to make the right choice for her future. Sheldrake tells her he is going to get divorce. She is emotionally touched. She agrees to go to an apartment with him.

3. Sheldrake's secretary sees them together. It's obvious she's got feelings about the situation. *This is a "C" story kicking in.*

4. Baxter waits outside the theatre for Miss Kubliak and it's obvious she is not going to show for their date. *(Again, Baxter's lonely life is disappointing, unsatisfactory. There is need for change.)*

SEQUENCE G: RESULTS OF BAXTER'S DECISION TO LET SHELDRAKE USE HIS APARTMENT—LOGICAL ATTEMPTS CONTINUE

1. It's a week later. Baxter has his promotion. Executives come to congratulate him. We find out Sheldrake now has exclusive rights on the apartment and since he is the main boss, no one can do anything about it. But the executives resent Baxter.

2. Baxter gives Sheldrake a cracked compact that Sheldrake's "lady friend" left in Baxter's apartment. *(Baxter has no idea this lady friend is Miss K—this item will pay off later.)*

SEQUENCE H: CHRISTMAS PARTY AND PLOT. FINALLY BAXTER HITS HIS MAJOR DENIAL (Step #3)

1. Christmas party in progress. Baxter is happy, he is an executive, he's attained his goal. He is a little tipsy. He wants to share his joy—he goes to get Miss Kubliak from her job in the elevator to join party. He tells her he won't hold it against her that she stood him up at the theatre. It's clear Baxter still has feelings for Miss Kubliak.

2. Miss K finds out from Sheldrake's secretary that she is only one affair in a long line of affairs. That Sheldrake always promises divorce. Miss K is devastated.

3. Baxter, unaware, innocently shows Miss K a Christmas photo of Sheldrake and family.

4. Miss K takes out her compact to powder her nose. Baxter sees it's the cracked compact and realizes Miss K is Sheldrake's mistress. *(Baxter now sees how his ambition has contributed to his inability to get Miss K to consider him as a love interest.)*

5. Sheldrake calls to confirm apartment use—putting a dagger into Baxter's heart.

SEQUENCE I: BAXTER DROWNS SORROW/ MISS KUBLIAK IS PLUNGED INTO HER SORROW, DENIAL CONTINUES

1. Baxter is drunk in a bar and is joined by another lost soul; a comedic turn by a woman whose husband is in jail…

2. Miss K, at Baxter's apartment, gives Sheldrake a nice Christmas present, he gives her a hundred dollar bill. She is devastated, feels as if she is being paid for sex. She is fearful that all the secretary told her is true. When Sheldrake leaves her to get back to his family for Christmas festivities. Miss K is alone in apartment. She spies pills…

3. Baxter and woman at bar dance, Santa is drunk. No one has family/place to be. They decide to go back to Baxter's place (he thinks Sheldrake and Miss K will be gone).

SEQUENCE J: BAXTER SAVES MISS K—HIS SECOND OPPORTUNITY PRESENTS ITSELF (Step #4)

1. Baxter sees Miss K in his apartment and realizes she's overdosed on pills. Baxter kicks the woman he picked up out. He gets the neighbor doctor and they struggle to keep Miss K alive. *(This is Baxter's Second Opportunity to achieve his overall want—it doesn't look like a good thing but it will bring Baxter and Miss K together.)*

2. Baxter talks doctor into not reporting it.

3. Baxter sits vigil.

SEQUENCE K: AFTERMATH AND REPERCUSSIONS AND CONFLICTS ABOUT THE SECOND OPPORTUNITY AS THINGS START TO GO WELL (Step #5 and Step #6)

1. Landlady gives Baxter grief about the noise and having a lady in his apartment.

2. Baxter informs Sheldrake about Miss K via phone. Sheldrake is cool, tells Baxter to take care of it. Miss K overhears part of conversation, but Baxter covers for Sheldrake's coolness.

3. Baxter gets Miss K to stay until she is better, so that no one will suspect what she did. He gets her to play gin rummy with him.

4. They share secrets and emotional stories. They bond. Miss K asks why she can't ever fall in love with a nice guy like Baxter? Baxter's heart is on his sleeve but can't admit his feelings for her…

5. One of the executives shows up with a mistress, Baxter refuses him entry. Executive sees Miss K. Baxter does the "right thing" , he take responsibility for Miss K's presence. He is making a moral choice.

SEQUENCE L: FALLOUT AS THINGS FALL APART (Step #8)

1. Sheldrake fires his secretary.

2. Sheldrake's jealous and angry secretary finds out about Miss K's OD and calls to make an appointment with Mrs. Sheldrake for lunch.

3. Baxter admits to Miss K his own sorrow in his past love life—(and near suicide).

4. Miss K's brother-in-law finds out where Miss K is from executive at work and storms into Baxter's apartment and punches Baxter.

5. Baxter takes responsibility for Miss K's sorrow, covering for her and Sheldrake. This causes Miss K's brother and the doctor to disrespect him, but Miss K is grateful.

SEQUENCE M: REVERSALS AND TESTS AND THINGS KEEP FALLING APART

1. Baxter goes to Sheldrake to tell him that Baxter will take Miss K off Sheldrake's hand, that he loves her. Before he can, Sheldrake tells him his wife kicked him out and Sheldrake is now free to be with Miss K—but Sheldrake also makes it clear that Miss K will just be a "fun" thing, that he has no intention of marrying her…

2. Sheldrake gives Baxter another promotion. Baxter accepts promotion, he is not acting on principle, and he does not like the situation or himself.

3. Miss K thinks Sheldrake left his wife for her. But she now won't see Sheldrake until divorce is final to allay "talk." Miss K tells Baxter she wants to do things "right". Baxter makes a decision not to tell her the truth—he is conflicted but he does not want to destroy her happiness—and he has just take the promotion.

SEQUENCE N: BAXTER PUTS HIMSELF BEFORE HIS AMBITION—THE CRISIS, CLIMAX AND TRUTH COMES OUT(Step #9, #10, #11))

1. New Year's Eve. Sheldrake wants to use Baxter's place again. Baxter finally can't take it. He says no. Sheldrake threatens firing. Baxter finally acts on principle and quits. *(The opposite of how he started in the film story.)*

2. At Baxter's apartment, Baxter is packing up, telling the doctor he is changing jobs and changing apartments.

3. Miss K and Sheldrake at New Years Eve party: Sheldrake tells Miss K that Baxter won't let them use apartment anymore. Miss K "gets" that this means that Baxter loves her. She runs to his apartment.

4. Outside Baxter's apartment, Miss K hears champagne popping, thinks it's a gunshot. Worried that Baxter may have attempted suicide again, she rushes to him.

5. Baxter tells her he loves her. She clearly loves him back.

There is no need to go into great detail in a sequence sheet. Consider it a list of notes that will help create the bones of the screen story. As the writer thinks of other scenes or sequences that need to be included, she can add them (in their right place) to the sequence sheet. Some scenes or sequences may get moved around; some will get tossed in the garbage.

The sequence sheet is a tool to be used to keep the story on track.

Chapter Summary

- Scenes and sequences need to be designed to advance the story in a screenplay.

- Each scene and sequence must serve a purpose.

- Use the Eleven Step Story Structure to keep your sequence sheet on track.

- Building a story with the necessary sequences will help the writer ensure his story will advance and not get lost along the way.

Chapter Eleven

EXPOSITION

Are there ways to fill in pertinent backstory for character and situation? Yes.

Are these elements necessary to fully understand a story? Yes.

An audience needs certain information in order to hop on board the story train and enjoy the ride.

Exposition is the information the audience needs to know about the characters and their world to fully understand the stakes of the story. Audiences want to know who the main characters are; their personality quirks, aspirations, relationships, living situations. Audiences want to know the circumstances that are in place that make the story *need* to happen—and need to happen *now*.

Audiences need to know if a character is allergic to avocado or afraid of snakes or if she experienced rape sometime in her life or if there's a history of gambling or if the dam broke in town two years ago or if someone was lynched last week or if the mayor's daughter slept with the gardener or if the husband is a serial cheater or if the wife is a serial flirt…

Remember, as the writer, you understand the characters, stakes and situations, they make sense to you. You have the emotional baggage of each character in your head. It's your job to make sure the audience is clued into the important facts too.

Exposition Can Be Revealed Slowly

Not all exposition needs to be (or should be) loaded into the first pages of your script. Exposition can and, in most cases, *should* be metered out slowly over the film. But don't wait too long for the basics.

The audience wants to know *why* they should get invested in the characters and situation of the story and they, in most cases, want to know *why* in the first 5 to 10 minutes of the film. If you keep too much from the audience, give them nothing that grabs their interest at the top of the story, if they don't understand why a character is acting as he is; you may lose them.

person dresses, his accent, his home, his friends. Do we see her at the gym frantically working out and weighing herself? What's the size of the character's house? Is it full of French Impressionism or African art? Is there an electric car in the driveway?

The writer can bury the character exposition by creating people who reveal personality traits through actions: A track star loses his race and makes a show of *not* congratulating the winner. Or the novice newscaster sweats buckets of sweat when the cameras are turned on. Or a woman in the restaurant asks for "everything on the side" and grills the waiter about how much pulp is in the freshly squeezed orange juice.

Example: *A serial cheater, Hank, sits at the diner's counter. He sees a woman, Beth, get off the Greyhound through the diner's window. She enters, carrying a suitcase. She picks up a local newspaper and opens it to the Apartments to Let section. The man takes off his wedding ring, puts it in his shirt pocket. The waitress notices, rolls her eyes. Beth sits at the other end of the counter. Hank goes into his "Aw shucks I never did this before but you sure are pretty" act and asks if he can buy her a cup of coffee. Beth's falling for it, flattered. In walks Hank's latest mistress with a bag of underwear he's left at her place; she dumps it on the counter for all to see, telling him he can take it home for his wife to wash. The waitress laughs and Beth gathers her suitcase and quickly exits.*

A lot of character information and backstory is revealed in this scene; Hank is married. He wants to appear single, he takes off his ring. He has smooth lines that he has perfected over time. He already has at least one mistress. He still lives at home with his wife. We also know the waitress has seen Hank do this routine before. When she laughs at the end of the scene, we know she has no sympathy for Hank. We also find out about Beth. She is just moving to town. One suitcase means she didn't have much of a life. She took the bus, meaning her finances could be strapped. She accepts the flirtation at first, meaning she is open to a relationship. She leaves at the end, meaning she's not interested in getting into a messy relationship with a married man who fools around.

Another example: A young girl, Anjali, dressed in East Indian traditional dress, is dropped off by her father at the high school. Anjali heads towards the school's front door, but as soon as she knows the car has rounded the corner, she hurries to the high school's athletic field. She whips off her traditional dress and reveals a track uniform. On the field, we see the

Coach checking her watch, anxious. Coach glances at a row of college scouts in the bleachers. They look at their watches. Suddenly Coach sees Anjali racing towards her, waves her over. Anjali takes a lane in the 100 yard dash that is about to start. The starter pistol sounds, the race is on. Anjali runs like the wind, she beats everyone by a large margin.

What do we find out in that scene in an *active* way? Anjali comes from a strict, traditional home. She is lying to her parents. She loves to run, she's good at it. Her Coach believes in her and wants to help her. Anjali hopes to go to college on a track scholarship. The sequence gives a good amount of information about the girl's home life as well as her personal loves and drive.

No need to pile on all the exposition in the first scenes of the story. Some information can be used as plot points that shift the story as it moves along. This will make your story more complex.

There are many examples of films that are exposition-heavy in the initial five or ten minutes of the film. Sometimes it is well done and "buried." Sometimes it's not well done and the audience feels they are getting a laundry list of facts concerning situation and character. The writer's job is to let the exposition come out in a natural way, *when* it needs to be revealed.

How Much Exposition Do You Need?

Limit your exposition to what directly affects the story. No need to let the audience know that your protagonist lost his first baby tooth at age five unless it's important to the story.

Consider the **SHAWSHANK REDEMPTION,** written and directed by Frank Darabont, based on a Stephen King story. What information does the audience need to know about the protagonist, Andy (portrayed by Tim Robbins) so they can hop on the story train? The audience needs to know there was a crime. This information is relayed visually, not through dialogue. (His wife, while carrying on an affair with her lover, is shot.) The audience needs to know that Andy is accused of committing the crime (he is seen in the courtroom as the defendant). The audience needs to know Andy claims his innocence but is found guilty. The short trial scene takes place and we are quickly into the *heart* of the film; the Shawshank Prison. There was no need to show the protagonist in his bad marriage, no need to see him in the diner of his town talking to the locals or buying groceries or remembering his tenth birthday. The primary relationships in the film are in the prison so that's where the audience needs to be led in a succinct, emotional, active way.

Consider **MILLION DOLLAR BABY;** Clint Eastwood's character, Frankie, has to be well-drawn before Maggie comes into his life and asks him to train her so she can compete as a boxer. The audience needs to know that he's a good trainer, that he's a lonely man, that he is in crisis with his religion, that he's a tough negotiator in the fight business, that he would go the distance for a fighter he believes in, that he sees the world in its darkest terms and he doesn't appreciate women boxers. If the audience is not clued into his character in a solid way, his subsequent actions and growing emotional ties to Maggie will not resonate.

Consider **IT HAPPENED ONE NIGHT.** The audience knows Ellie is part of a wealthy family because she's on a yacht, her father calls the man she just eloped with a gold digger, and there are servants on call. The audience quickly comes to understand essential elements of stubborn, frustrated, over-protected Ellie before she dives off the yacht to find her freedom. In **THE APARTMENT,** we know that Baxter is a low level employee in a big corporation when we see him in a sea of desks with other workers, all doing the same task. We quickly get to know of his ambition, we totally understand, visually, what working conditions he wants to leave behind. **OUT OF AFRICA** opens in the snowy cold of Denmark, we meet Karin (portrayed by Meryl Streep) in an emotional state; she wants marriage and she feels it will never happen. Quickly she proposes to her friend, they agree to marry and we are transported to a country that is as opposite to snow and cold as possible; Africa. Because we have seen where Karin is coming from, we understand, without words, that she has a huge challenge ahead of her. We see that Africa is a huge expanse of countryside with few towns or centers of social interaction in an amazing visual of a train, carrying Karin. chugging through it. Denys Finchhatten, (portrayed by Robert Redford) is seen trekking through the expanse; he simply waves the train to a stop so he can load his ivory. This points out that Africa is not a world run by time-tables and rules. This action also tells us that this is a small social world, everyone seems to know everyone.

If You Are Revealing Exposition Verbally, Set It In an Active Situation

In **TOOTSIE,** Michael Dorsey tries to impress the women at his surprise birthday at the beginning of the film. No one at the party says "Michael doesn't have luck with women, he's so full of himself…" we *see* him trying to connect in a non-respectful and needy way and having no luck. While he is actively being his obnoxious self, we get to know the character.

In **KRAMER VS KRAMER,** Ted Kramer is spending extra time with his boss, working late, clearly putting work before family. The dialogue in the scenes does not "tell" the audience what is most important in Ted's life, it shows us his priorities. The audience puts together his character from the choices he makes.

In **THE GODFATHER** Michael Corleone is first seen in a military uniform. That's visual exposition. The dialogue between Michael and his fiancé (portrayed by Diane Keaton) fills us in on some of the rules and background of Michael's Mafia family. It also lets us know, in an active way, what Michael desires for his life.

In **NETWORK,** Max (portrayed by William Holden) tells his friend, Howard (portrayed by Peter Finch), about his favorite news reporting memory. This dialogue is meant to make his friend feel better about being fired, reminding him that being reporters of the news isn't what it used to be. It also serves as exposition because it lets the audience know Max's fear that his own best days could be over. This is a story that deals with a man's mid-life crisis… this scene accomplishes setting that up.

In **CHINATOWN,** one of the most climactic scenes takes place near the end of the film. It reveals exposition in a very active way; Jake Gittes is slapping Evelyn Mulwray while she tells him that the mysterious girl living with her is both her sister and her daughter. This is exposition that does not get revealed till the end of Act Two—when it *needs* to be revealed and affects Jake and the plans he has made.

Show, Don't Tell

Don't underestimate the power of the visual. If you tell the audience something visually, you don't have to say it verbally. If you make a habit of showing and telling, the audience will start to resent it; thinking you are spoon-feeding them. If you can *show* exposition it, no need to *tell* it.

Question: If a writer does use flashbacks, can he just use one? Or does he have to have a series of them?

Answer: There are no rules, your story needs to be told in the way you see as best. But be aware that the use of flashbacks is often a *style* choice and unless the style is balanced and consistent, the film story can be perceived as awkward.

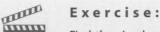

E x e r c i s e :
Find the visual way to show this exposition: Jack's birthday is today, he's just turned 30. He lives in Chicago and works at a department store. He's been in love with a co-worker, Kathy, for years but she is dating the store manager. Jack has worked late. No one has remembered his birthday. He lives alone in an apartment, his only companionship is the cat who hangs out on the fire escape outside his apartment.

Use Flashbacks

A story can be told in many ways. Any way that works is acceptable. Flashbacks can be used to fill in exposition, but keep in mind—each scene should help advance the story or character. This applies to flashbacks too. If the flashback is not advancing the character's story in the *present day* of the film… perhaps the flashback is not the way to get out the exposition in this story. Consider 2006's **DA VINCI CODE:** The use of flashbacks to reveal exposition is unnecessary. The flashbacks do *not* give the audience *new* information (the same information is in the dialogue). The flashbacks slow down the film and highlight an overly plot-driven story. Ask yourself: If the flashback is removed, does the story still work? If the answer is yes, cut the flashback.

Chapter Summary

- Bury the exposition while making the characters well-rounded and interesting.

- Fill in the backstory as needed in the script.

- Filling in the character and situation of the story should be buried in character actions and story advancement.

- A good writer will bury the exposition while he is making the characters well-rounded and interesting.

- A good writer will fill in backstory as he goes along, making sure the information comes out in an active, story advancing scene, at a time when the information is needed.

Chapter Twelve

DIALOGUE

Do you need dialogue in every scene? No.

Do characters have to use words to respond to a question? No.

*Do characters have to have something to say in response to
every comment or situation? No.*

Really good dialogue is wonderful to experience. Who doesn't enjoy funny, clever lines? Or blasting one-liners that cut a character down to size? Or heartfelt declarations of love or fidelity? What about those inspiring speeches in the locker room that coaches make? What about those cautionary morality tales told to steer a character along the right path? The great banter between two lovers or among good friends? The telling of a poignant memory? The stirring rally cries of soldiers?

Dialogue is very important in most film stories. But only use it when it's necessary; to reveal character and/or to advance story.

Remember, film is a visual medium. If the visual carries the moment, there is no need for dialogue.

You may "see" the scene in your head as you write it. Put those images down on paper. Does a character who is sitting, stand up suddenly when she hears of the murder? Or vomit? Or faint? Or punch someone? Does movement alone tell us enough about her state of mind that there is no need for dialogue? If so, cut the dialogue.

If a character witnesses her boyfriend out on a date in a restaurant with another girl, she could throw something through the restaurant window. Or she could cry. Or she could kick his car. Or she could rip the necklace he gave her off her neck, walk into the restaurant and drop it in his soup. Or she could go home and sit alone in the dark, staring at their high school prom photo. There is no need for dialogue in any of these scenarios because the character's actions make her state of mind obvious.

If the character's intent and emotional state can be conveyed visually, consider cutting any dialogue that only reiterates what is already deduced from the scene.

each other or familiar with the circumstances, dialogue is sketchier. The amount of words needed to understand a feeling or situation lessens with the closeness of the characters.

In most instances, keep dialogue short. One word is fine. Half a sentence is fine. If you have a character that is a bit more verbose, still be economical. In most cases, you don't want any character to drone on and on... if you need this element in your story, consider having another character break up the verbose character's monologues with questions or comments so that the scene will retain a sense of action.

Dialogue can reveal inner thoughts, obsessions. Dialogue can help make a person three dimensional; show interests, show depth or shallowness.

Exercise:

Sit down with one of your friends or a member of your family. Ask this person questions and write down their answers—word for word. Pay attention to speech patterns. Pay attention to words. Incomplete sentences? What makes their manner of speech unique? Do they look you in the eye? Are they sure of themselves? Do they want to please? Are they arrogant? Impatient? What words do they choose to reflect their attitude?

Who is Your Character Talking To?

A character may have different ways of speaking around different people. Imagine the difference between a character recounting her hot date to her conservative grandmother as opposed to her sex-crazed roommate. Or the difference between a character telling an uptight, judgmental boss he lost the business account or telling the details to the guys at the bar. Or the difference between a character telling his child that her mother has left home never to come back or telling a friend that his wife ran off with the plumber.

Exercise:

Nick, a high school honors student with definite nerd overtones, is trying to fit in with the cool, angry crowd. He's got a crush on Vickie, the multi-pierced, insolent and sarcastic leader of the cool crowd. Write two scenes; the first scene is Nick telling his best nerdy friend, Arnold, how he is scientifically approaching the idea of asking Vickie out for a date. Then write the scene where Nick, trying to fit into Vickie's world, finds the opportunity to ask Vickie for the date. Make sure you don't make Nick's task easy. Let him struggle, let him be creative as he finds the right words to explain himself in both situations.

Separate Rhythms For Each Character

Each character in the screenplay should have his own rhythm of talking. Each character should have his own vocabulary. Find a favorite phrase or a favorite word for each character. Some will speak quickly, some slowly. Some will use long sentences, some will use short sentences. Some characters will always use the wrong word. Some characters like big words. Some characters never speak with words beyond two syllables. Some characters are in your face, every word is aggressive. Some characters are more retiring and quiet and choose their words carefully.

Consider Annie Hall's favorite phrase, "la di da." This phrase helped reveal the character's self-effacing, insecure persona. Consider the characters Woody Allen creates for himself—full of self-examination and neurotic selfishness—fast thinking, fast talking and always defensive.

Michael Corleone, in the **GODFATHER,** has a measured way of speaking, he thinks before he talks. His brother, Sonny (portrayed by James Caan) has a more bombastic way of speaking, he lets his temper rule him, he talks before he thinks. The third brother, Fredo (portrayed by John Cazale) speaks quietly, mutters. He's insecure and his way of communicating makes that clear.

Think about the three main characters in 1975's **JAWS;** Matt Hooper (portrayed by Richard Dreyfus) never shuts up. Police Chief Brody (portrayed by Roy Schieder) doesn't share his personal thoughts or feelings, he's a quiet man. Quint (portrayed by Robert Shaw) is foul-mouthed and blustery and likes to make trouble. By making each character different and creating dialogue rhythms for each of them, the writers made this summer disaster film stand out from the rest.

Make sure each of your characters have their own voice, their own attitude about the world. Is one paranoid? Is one pessimistic? Is one insecure? Is one an egomaniac?

Exercise:

Pick a word for each of your main characters that refers to things going well. Does your character use "great" or "absolutely super" or "fantastic" or "fan-tab-ulous" or "rocking" to describe a good experience?

Pick a word for each of your main characters that refers to things going badly. Does your character use "that's unbelievably, intensely devastating" or "that sucks"?

Choose a *handle* for a few characters. Handles are words that come before or after the character actually says what they intend to say. Common examples; the "well" or "I don't know but " or "ahhhh" or "oh" or "don'tcha know" or "listen" or "darling" or "babe" or Annie Hall's "la di da." These are handles that have become habitual for the character. Sometimes the addition of a handle can help bring out a character. Sometimes it can make dialogue seem more natural. Caution: Don't overdo handles and don't have *every* character use them.

Exercise:

Write this scene: Five people of varying regional, educational and financial backgrounds wait in the lobby of a department store. Each has won a shopping spree, each has a half hour to grab desired items. Set up the situation (exposition) by letting each character fill in parts of the backstory in their own singular voices. Then add this conflict: the store manager enters and tells the shoppers that no one can choose the same item in the store. Reveal that three people desperately desire the latest video game. It's five minutes before the store's door are opened and tension is high. How will each of these three people try to achieve their goal? Will one attempt to bribe the others? Will one attempt to disable the others? Will one try to convince the others that his need for the video game surpasses the others' need? Make sure each character has a unique voice that reveals their background, age and social standing.

Good Dialogue Advances Story

2005's holiday film, **THE FAMILY STONE,** is a good example of "no wasted dialogue." It's an ensemble film so there are many characters to follow. Each person's story is clear, clean and emotional. The excellent dialogue helped make this happen.

"Training Day" Denzel Washington, Ethan Hawke
photo supplied by Globe Photos

Take a look at the script of 2001's **TRAINING DAY.** Every scene and every exchange of dialogue is designed to push Jack Hoyt (portrayed by Ethan Hawke) towards the moment when he is forced to make a moral choice about his future as a police officer.

Take a look at the script of 2004's **SIDEWAYS.** Every scene and every exchange of dialogue is designed to push Miles into making the choice to move on (or not) to the next chapter in his life.

Take Out All the "Niceties"

Unless "hello" has great meaning in the scene, cut it. Unless "how are you?" or "are you okay?" has great meaning in the scene, cut it. Unless "weather sure is nice" has great meaning in the scene, cut it. Yes, sometimes these simple, common words might be uttered to cover an awkward situation or to cover strong emotions… if so, great. That's subtext, which we will go into a bit later in this chapter.

Other dialogue that can be simply expunged from your script: Words that tell the audience what they are about to see. There is no need for a character to say, in a scene where he meets his brother at the family cabin in the woods, something like "Let's go to the lake at the bottom of the hill, that favorite place we always went to, first thing, when we arrived here every summer." All you need is the brothers' arrival at the cabin, a mad race through the woods, brothers peeling off clothes as they streak down the hill to jump into the lake. These visuals will clue the audience into the tradition and the love of the lake in the brothers' lives.

No need for a character to say "Let's go to the coffee shop…" when you can cut to him *at* the coffee shop. No need to *tell* the audience where your characters are going and then *show* the audience where the characters went. Of course, if going to the coffee shop is a *challenge* that is presented to a character to evoke a response… (perhaps the coffee shop is where the character's ex-wife works or where some emotional moment took place) then leave the dialogue in because there is *subtext* (deeper meaning under the simple line) in the exchange.

Another example of extraneous dialogue: A man asks a woman to marry him by offering her an engagement ring. She leaps up with happiness, kisses him, dances around the room, pulls him to the bed and proceeds to make love to him. The words "I am so happy I feel like dancing! Let me make love to you…" are extraneous to the scene. This may seem evident, but there are many scripts that appear in the marketplace that make this mistake.

If you can *show* it, don't *tell* it.

Good Dialogue Can Challenge, Amuse, and Evoke Emotion

Well-written dialogue can present strong arguments, new ideas, varied points of view. Dialogue can be fashioned to cause laughter or tears. Dialogue can be powerful. By finding the right words for the right character at the right time—the writer can cause an emotional response from the audience.

Paddy Chayefsky (**NETWORK, HOSPITAL**), Tony Kushner (**ANGELS IN AMERICA, MUNICH**), Wendy Wasserstein (**HEIDI CHRONICLES, THE AMERICAN DAUGHTER**), Steve Gaghan (**SYRIANA**) are among writers who create characters with strong political and sociological points of view. Their screenplays do not seem "preachy" because their characters are well-drawn *and* they present different sides of an argument or point of view. Consider letting all characters (even villains) have valid arguments and points of view that can be logically (or illogically) supported.

Think of the scene in **SHAKESPEARE IN LOVE** when Shakespeare happens to meet Marlowe, a fellow playwright, in the pub. Shakespeare is feeling insecure and envious of Marlowe's success. Shakespeare won't let on, he doesn't want to give Marlowe the upper hand. But he desperately desires Marlowe's help in figuring out a story problem in Shakespeare's latest play. Through their exchange we see these two men are competitive with each other. Both want to be considered "the top playwright" in London. Although no one comes right out and states their desires, the scene makes it very clear.

Those Spill-it-all, Heartfelt Moments

Is there a time when subtext is undesirable? Yes.

As a screenwriter, you get to express your point of view of the world; your personal view of relationships or illegal business practices or politics or… well, whatever you want to explore. Writing gives you the chance to express your feelings about the importance of love or evil or friendship or hope or…

When it's time to dig deep and h*ave the character say exactly what the character means, go for it.* When your character has gone through hell to achieve her goal, she's probably learned something. If you want her to voice what she has learned (as long as it is still pushing the scene forward and causing a reaction) go for it. No need to hide, be brazen.

The character may have realized that great love can exist. Or that violence is not the answer. Or that someone they trust is not worthy of trust. Or that friendship is the only thing that gives them a sense of security. Or that believing in oneself makes it possible for one to achieve a dream. Or that a goal that once seemed so important is not as important as seeing a child safe or being a good friend or…

Characters can voice emotional feelings and realizations. An audience can appreciate well-spoken truths. An audience longs for a character to stand up for himself. How to keep it from sounding too "on-the-nose"? Perhaps the character struggles to find the right words. Perhaps they use an analogy or metaphor. Perhaps they manipulate a situation that will speak for them. Perhaps their thoughts and words tumble out in one direction, then stumble on a *real* truth. Perhaps they admit their feelings through anger, sarcasm or attack. Somehow characters must find a way to express themselves.

There are times the writer can let the audience fill in the blanks and there are times when the writer wants to make sure the audience knows exactly what the character wants to say.

Chapter Summary

- Dialogue is an important part of most films.

- Good dialogue pushes the story forward.

- On-the-nose dialogue states the obvious.

- Subtext is dialogue that says one thing but means another.

- Each character should have an individual voice and rhythm of speaking.

Chapter Thirteen

ACTION, CONFLICT, AND OBSTACLES

Does there need to be a sense of action in every genre? Yes.

*Does a story risk losing its audience if things
are too easy for the protagonist? Yes.*

Action

Action is movement of story. Action is a sense of things happening to *character*.

Action is *more* than just physical events; the car chases, the battles, the dance contests, the big game, the attack by the wild animal….

Action is also something that happens in an emotional sense. There are galactic battles and then there are looks across the room that can change a world. Both imply action—or *movement of story.*

Your story should feel as if it is constantly moving forward. Every sequence should *actively* move the character arc while moving the plot towards its climactic end.

Make Sure Your Story Has Action

Elements to keep in mind:

1. *Character Arc.* Is your character moving from one emotion to another? Are the emotional stakes getting higher? Is your character going through highs and lows? If your character learning? Growing? Deepening?

2. *Is your character driving the plot?* Is he causing problems? Is she forcing an issue? Are his deeds, thoughts, questions making a difference in the details of the plot? In 2001's **OCEAN'S ELEVEN,** Danny Ocean (portrayed by George Clooney) is making the plot happen, driven because of his love for his ex-wife. In **CHINA-TOWN,** Jake Gittes is making the plot happen because he wants to find out why he was chosen to be made to look like a fool. In

LEGALLY BLONDE, Elle is making the plot turn at every juncture; she follows her ex-boyfriend, she works hard to get the internship, she finds a way, in court, to defend a fellow sorority girl.

3. *Characters will make your plot important.* A corporate takeover is not interesting drama unless one gets to know the characters involved. A mail-order bride scenario is not interesting unless you get to know the characters involved. A battle to take over the world is not interesting unless the characters attacking or being attacked are interesting and *changing.*

4. *Are there enough events in the story?* By going from event to event, the writer gives the feeling of time passing, things getting accomplished (or not).

Make Physical Movement Integral

Screenplays are written for *moving* pictures. What movies do best is tell a story visually, with *moving* pictures. First, there are the physical components of the scene; where should the scene take place? When you have a choice between: a) two people sitting across a table from one another discussing their relationship or b) two people discussing their relationship while playing handball or picking flowers or hanging from a thirty story building—go for the latter. Search out the *physical* arena where your scene can take place.

> **E x e r c i s e :**
> List ten of the oddest settings you can imagine for a scene. Then think of two characters; a boyfriend and a girlfriend. Write a scene where the girl breaks up with her boyfriend. Place that break-up scene in one of the odd locations and *use* the location in the scene. (Example: Location: A Bull Fighting Ring. A Girl in the stands tries to break up with her Spanish Boyfriend, he cannot understand English, she does not speak Spanish. In trying to make herself clear, she accidentally bumps against a rabid bullfight Fan. The Fan reacts with anger, tosses her Boyfriend into the ring, the Bull charges the Boyfriend. The Girl, who happens to be wearing a red dress, jumps into the bull ring to save her Boyfriend. As they run away from the Bull, she makes herself clear—she wants to break up and now! The Boyfriend, upset, decides to fight the Bull to the death to prove to his beloved that he is worthy of her.)

Don't Confuse Physical Movement With Story Action

Physical *movement* in the scene is just that—a car chase, a race against time in a bank robbery, dancing, playing a game… it's the movement that you have decided to use as you tell your story. Movement alone does not make for the action of the scene. (Consider the above example of the Bull Fight. If there was no emotional or story action going on, the fight with the bull would not be needed in the story, thus ultimately would slow the film down.) Movement can make the scene more interesting, tense and enjoyable only if it is relevant to the story.

The *true action* of the scene is the progression of the story and the progression of the protagonist's character arc.

Example: 2002's **BOURNE IDENTITY**. In the action sequence in the American Embassy, Jason Bourne realizes that even the Americans are after him and there is no safe haven. The sequence advances plot and advances the audience's knowledge of Jason's character. He is shown to have incredible knowledge of how to subdue attackers, perform physical feats, find escape routes. This sequence of escape makes it *necessary* for the next plot point to take place: Bourne asks for a ride to Paris with a young woman he does not know.

Random Action Sequences Can Stall Your Story

No matter how imaginative and well-executed, action sequences that do not advance character or plot do not enhance the film story. Huge wars in space. Sporting events. Dance performances. Battlefield skirmishes. Car chases. Busses careening out of control. A writer can write a stunning opening-of-the-film action sequence that involves near-death experiences or great failures or successes… and all his hard work will be for nothing *unless* the audience is invested in a character and story. Until the audience has hopped on board the story train, special effects and camera angles and daring physical movements will not be compelling. The audience will be *waiting* for the story to begin.

Why do most good films introduce the protagonist before thrusting him into a huge physical task that will test his skill, cleverness, determination to survive? Because then the sequences will have true action—character progression and story advancement. Consider **DIE HARD.** John McClane's character is first seen on a plane, nervous about seeing his wife. He arrives in Texas to confront her about their troubled marriage. The audience gets

"Die Hard" Bruce Willis
photo supplied by Globe Photos

invested in a man who cares about his family, about a man who is in love with his wife even though he is not dealing well with his wife's ambitions. The audience gets to know the man and empathize or sympathize before the building is attacked and McClane is forced into the position of action hero saving the day. 2005's **WAR OF THE WORLDS** introduces the protagonist, Ray (portrayed by Tom Cruise), as a man who will not help out others at work, as a failed husband and as a not-so-great dad. He also has a biting sense of humor and there's a "lost" quality about him that makes the audience sympathetic. Clearly this is a man who needs to take responsibility in life. He loves his kids but he hasn't committed to fully caring for them. We root for him to get it together *before the aliens attack.* 1995's **BRAVEHEART** introduces a protagonist, William Wallace (portrayed by Mel Gibson), who only wants to marry the girl he loves, lead a simple life. He will not join in the force to bring about change in an unacceptable world. When his wife is murdered, we feel for this man, we care about him *before the big battles take place.* Knowing the characters makes the action sequences work.

Create the *normal life* of your protagonist, let the audience *know* who is in the middle of a car chase or battle or competition…and *why* this sequence affects the character and the story.

Everything Should Have a Consequence

Just because you have a car chase or major gang warfare or a love scene does not mean that the action in your story is working. *Each sequence needs to have some consequence.* The 2005 **MR. AND MRS. SMITH** is an example of "a lotta bang for very little story." Lots of guns, fires, bombs, falling wine bottles… but very little real story or character progression. This film clearly stalled at the premise stage; no true *character-based story* ever evolved. (Check out Hitchcock's only comedy, **MR. AND MRS. SMITH** (1941) with Carole Lombard; a totally different premise—and there's a good story in that one.) Why did the 2005 **MR. AND MRS. SMITH** fail to make the grade as a good story? Lack of character exploration and lack of character growth. First of all, the audience never got to know anything about the two main characters. Why are they hired killers? Who do they work for? Who do they work against? Why are they doing what they were doing? Why did they fall in love? Why is this marriage important to save? What is the emotional impact of trying to kill your spouse? It doesn't matter that this film falls into some "one-ups-manship-comedy-action" genre; there needs to be stakes and there needs to be consequences that carry emotional baggage. (Yes, the movie made money because of its star power, but that still does not make it a good film.)

Some directors love to choreograph battle scenes and car chases and martial arts fights. That's a challenge that will interest them—and not the story. Some directors want to make a ninety-minute film a music video—quick cuts, sexy sound, emotional visual bites (think of 2005's **FRIDAY NIGHT LIGHTS**). Those directors are not storytellers. Find the director who will ask you, "Why is this fight happening? Does it advance the story? Will it change the characters in some way?" Or—"Why do we want to spend five minutes of film time on this high-speed motorcycle chicken fight here? Does it advance the story? Will it change the characters in some way?" The character's arc and good storytelling must always come first.

Create a Physical Progression For Your Protagonist

The emotional and physical stakes of a film story should escalate throughout your screenplay. Growth in a character's skill is satisfying to an audience. A boxer starts out taking on local gym bouts and works his way up to fight for the title of World Champion. A stock car racer goes from the hicksville circuit to racing on national television. A lowly trader in the stock market rises to head of a brokerage firm. A hotel maid uses her smarts and wiles to purchase a hotel chain and become one of the richest women in the world. You could go backwards of course; the richest man in the world loses it all and finds happiness in the sprouting of one vegetable in his garden. Or perhaps the most beautiful woman in the world experiences a tragic accident and finds peace when awarded a medal that celebrates her inner beauty (or in a tragic or horrific world, finds her outer form now fits the monster that has always been inside her as she spirals down a destructive path). Whatever the story is, consider making the beginning and end as far from one another as possible. You want a long, difficult journey for your character. The physical arc of the piece can help you explore the *true* action of the story.

Create a Strong Character Progression For Your Protagonist

Character action is the emotional arc and change in a character's belief system.

Let's say your protagonist is a woman who does not believe in love. She insists any intense feelings make her a weaker person. She meets a man in Act One, finds him annoying. Through Act Two she realizes her feelings are changing, he interests her. She fights the feelings. She realizes she is falling in love with him. She refuses to see him. She does everything she can to make him hate her. She tries to make herself despicable. By the end of Act Three, she has an epiphany and she knows her life will seem meaningless if she does not find a way to live it with this man. She finally admits to believing in love. She risks being vulnerable and finds that truly loving has made her *stronger*. She has changed from a love-a-phobic to a woman who will do anything to get the man that she desires because love gives her strength. That is character action.

The physical action and world of that love story could be in any area you want it to be: the woman could be on an archeological treasure hunt, she could be leading a corporate takeover, she could be in a NASCAR competition. The physical plot of the film will have its own components and its own arc, but the *character action* of the story will bring the emotional and empathetic resonance all good stories need.

In **THE APARTMENT,** C.C. Baxter thinks Miss Kubliak is cute and the best elevator operator in the building, but his main focus is on climbing the corporate ladder. That is what is most important to him. He is "selling his soul" for a promotion. However, as Baxter's feelings for Miss Kubliak grow (many events illuminate this growth; he asks her out, she stands him up, he tries to squash his feelings... she takes an overdose in his apartment, he nurses her, his feelings rise again and by the end of the film, we know he's heartbroken when he thinks his boss, Mr. Sheldrake, and Miss Kubliak are beginning their affair again. His heartbreak turns to anger when Mr. Sheldrake makes it clear that he has no intention of marrying Miss Kubliak. Baxter finally puts his career in grave jeopardy when he tells Sheldrake he can no longer use his apartment to meet Miss Kubliak...). Baxter's growing knowledge of the dishonest and immoral business world and his growing feelings for Miss Kubliak cause him to make choices he would have never made at the beginning of the film. Baxter makes physical choices based on his ever-changing emotional feelings; he has a strong and clear character arc. This is a clear example of Baxter *making the plot happen.*

2005's **MEMOIRS OF A GEISHA** fails in achieving a strong, clear and long character arc for its main character. The young girl, Chiyo, wants freedom at the beginning of the film story. She is led by another character to achieve her goal—she runs away from her slave status at the geisha house to find her sister. Things do not go well and she goes back to being a slave. When she matures, she is led by another to achieve her goal (freedom) by becoming a desirable geisha, in hopes of earning a certain kind of freedom by being in charge of the geisha house. Note that these events are not instigated by Chiyo; other characters devise the plans and Chiyo is pulled along, thus making her seem passive and ultimately, not very interesting. At a certain point in the film, Chiyo's want/desire changes, she falls in love with the Commander and wants only to be with him. (Note that when the main want/desire of a character changes mid-film, it is difficult for the audience to remain connected. The audience becomes a passive observer because they no longer trust that what they have grown to hope for the protagonist (in this case, freedom) is what the protagonist will strive to achieve. The audience disconnects because they no long trust the storyteller.) Even in Chiyo's new want/desire (love from the Commander,) she remains passive, a victim of her circumstances. She does not take action to achieve her goal. Is this the point of the film? That a geisha is trained to submit and thus cannot go to great lengths to achieve her own happiness? Does this point of information (if it is true) make for a good story?

A film story should not be constructed merely to make a point or simply to instruct. *A story needs to have a true emotional engine that allows a character to achieve (or not) a strong want; a story needs a beginning and middle and end that explores that one strong want that permeates a character's existence.* **MEMOIRS OF A GEISHA** is an example of plot pushing the characters to act in ways that solely service the plot. The character is used as an instrument to explore a tradition and a time in history. What about the freedom Chiyo desired at the top of the film story? Chiyo becomes the Commander's main mistress at the end of the film, she will be kept by him and supported financially. Is that freedom? When one looks at the film and its lack of clear, strong character arc, it's easy to see why the film did not catch the imagination of a wide audience.

Bring True Action Into Every Sequence

Each sequence should accomplish something; advance the character's arc or advance the plot (or both). A writer has a hundred pages, give or take, to tell a story that will transport, inform, entertain and challenge an audience. There is no time for sequences that do not enhance the story.

Because each sequence needs to advance the story and/or character, there is no time for sequences that repeat information (even if it's being told in a new and different way—it's still the same information). In **LEGALLY BLONDE,** Elle's boyfriend breaks up with her at the restaurant. The audience has that information. If Elle then goes back to the sorority house and *tells* her friends that she's just been dumped, that is *repeat* information. Note that the next time we see Elle, she is in bed, stuffing herself with chocolate, and her friends already know. Once Elle decides to pursue entrance into Harvard Law School and *tells* her friends her plan, note there are no repeat scenes about announcing that desire. The following scenes start in the middle—*after* Elle has (obviously) made her intentions clear: the scene where her parents try to talk her out of it, the scene where her college counselor tells her what she needs to accomplish an acceptance into the law school. Starting scenes "late" can help the writer avoid repeating information that will slow down the telling of the story.

Construct scenes in your screen story so the needed story/plot information is only given once. Let each scene move the story and character forward.

Conflict

All stories need conflict.

Michael Corleone and his non-Italian fiancé, Kay, arrive at the family estate for his sister's wedding in **THE GODFATHER.** How many elements of conflict are introduced? To name a few: Michael's fiancé doesn't understand how his family works and he can't tell her the truth. The new husband (Michael's brother-in-law) expects a full acceptance into the family business, no one trusts him. Neighbors and friends are lined up, anxious, to ask the Godfather for special favors. Sonny is connecting with a bridesmaid upstairs when he should be paying attention to his own family. There is a mention of plans of the other Mafia families to enter the drug trade and it is clearly a problem, but because of the special occasion, the Godfather will not deal with it. This film opens on a wedding and yet this "joyous" occasion is filled with conflict.

2005's **KICKING AND SCREAMING** is full of father-son conflict. Phil(portrayed by Will Ferrell), and his father, Buck(portrayed by Robert Duvall), are in constant competition. Buck and his neighbor, Mike Ditka, are in constant conflict. Ditka and his wife (even though she is off screen and never seen) are in constant conflict.

2005's **TRANSAMERICA** is full of conflict. Bree (portrayed by Felicity Huffman) is filled with personal, emotional conflict as she anticipates final transgender surgery; the surgery that will change her from man to woman. Her therapist refuses to sign the necessary papers until Bree investigates a strange phone call that leads her to believe she has a son (fathered when she was in college). When she bails her son out of jail, more conflict is introduced; he is into drugs, prostitution and is determined to go to California to meet his biological father. Against her best judgment, she decides to travel cross-country with her son (not telling him she is his biological father). Conflict grows when their car is stolen, her hormone pills along with it. More conflict is added when she has to go to her parents for help; her mother does not want to accept her son as a woman. The conflict continues to escalate—*nothing can be easy.*

All genres thrive on conflict.

All stories thrive on conflict.

Conflict gives a motor to the story. Conflict creates drama, it creates comedy, it creates adventure. Construct a story that is full of conflict.

Every Action Should Cause a Reaction and Create Conflict

Conflict can be generated by *not* giving your characters what they want; creating *obstacles*. (See, back to the *character want—in each sequence or scene the character must want something*.) It's the magic word "no" that can make a scene more interesting and push your character to dig deeper to achieve his goal. It could be something as simple as a character going to a grocery store to get milk—the store is out of milk and he is denied. The character reacts. His reaction affects the plot or reveals character. It could be something big—the President wants the missiles to arrive at a certain location in time for an invasion; the delivery is sabotaged. The President's reaction will be key. Alternate plans need to be made in a very short time—the stakes have been raised.

Use the magic word; "no." Don't give your characters what they want when they want it. Make them work hard to earn it. *Nothing can be easy.*

Another magic word screenwriters embrace: "but". Create conflict by implementing "but": It's good news for the hero that the Empire State Building is still standing *but*—the time travel machine is still out of control and he can't stop the bomb…

Or—it looks like the wedding plans are all set and the bride is ready to walk down the aisle *but*—mother won't be there because she won't face her ex-husband. Or…but the groom realizes he really loves the sister instead. Or… but space ship is about to land. Or…

It looks like she will get the promotion *but*—she has to sleep with the boss to seal the deal or she has to agree to employ a wacky secretary or she has to sell secrets to the competitor or….

Nothing can be easy. Everything should have strings attached. Use "no" and "but" to help you raise the conflict in your story. The more conflict the better. Explore how the protagonist deals with each obstacle put in front of him; these are the events that are going to make your character grow.

The Eleven Steps Can Help You Focus on Conflict

Use the ELEVEN STEP STORY STRUCTURE to help you create conflict. As the protagonist moves through Step #2 (Logically Goes For It) he obviously does not attain his goal (if he did, the story would be over.) He may try two or three (or ten) *logical ways* to attain his goal, but is stopped or fails at every attempt. Example: The protagonist (let's call him Ray) is a man who wants to feel more powerful in his life. Ray logically signs up for Kung Fu classes. Unfortunately he throws out his back and can't continue. Next he tries to tell his mother that she has to stop packing him a lunch for work, after all he is 45-years-old. His mother doesn't listen and, unfortunately, packs his favorite lasagna and hard boiled egg and brownie the next day— and he doesn't have the strength to *not* take the lunch. Next Ray finds out there's a promotion open at work, he sends in his application. Unfortunately, Ray overhears his boss laughing when he reads Ray's application and Ray sees the boss toss it in the trash can. All the logical things that Ray tries to do in order to feel powerful fail. Finally, there is a Denial (Step #3) that is a *bigger and more all encompassing slap in the face* that forces Ray on a new path to attain his goal. Perhaps he is fired from his job. Or perhaps his mother dies and he feels powerless to save her. Or perhaps the woman he thought would eventually marry him gets tired of waiting and marries another. Or perhaps aliens attack and instead of joining the fight, Ray hides and is too cowardly to assert himself.

The "no" should be used over and over in the ELEVEN STEP STRUCTURE.

Steps #4 through #9 are also built with "no" in mind. There is a Second Opportunity (Step #4) but Conflicts about Taking Advantage of the Second Opportunity (Step #5) is there to make sure nothing is easy. Things may Go Well (Step #7), but they soon Fall Apart (Step #8). Lots of "no." *Nothing can be easy.*

Whether your script is a story that involves huge physical set pieces or an intimate domestic drama, make sure each sequence has emotional and physical conflict.

Obstacles

Pile on obstacles. If there are no obstacles, the character's journey will come across as too easy. If a character's journey is too easy, perhaps this story does not deserve to be made into a major motion picture. Audiences respond to stories where the characters come up against great and dangerous odds. A character dealing with adversity is a main ingredient in stories. Exaggerate. Pile on the obstacles.

Obstacles create conflict. Conflict will enrich your story.

"Boy gets girl, boy *loses* girl, boy has to overcome all obstacles and conflicts to get the girl back." That's the tried and true format for a romantic comedy. Without the *loses* part, you have "Boy gets girl—and keeps her." Not a lot of ups and downs and struggle and emotional pratfalls. Basically: not interesting.

"Hero *resists* being pulled into the battle, hero is pulled into the battle, hero *risks* failure and almost dies in the battle, hero finds a way to triumph." That's the tried and true format for an action film. There's a lot of push and pull there. If your hero is just sitting around looking for a battle or a task; it's not as interesting as him *resisting the battle*. In 1995's **SEVEN,** Morgan Freeman's character is about to retire, but he is pulled into one more case. In **GLADIATOR,** Maximus wants to retire and go back to his farm but he is pulled into the fray when the Emperor is assassinated. In **BRAVEHEART,** William Wallace does not want to fight, but after his wife is killed, he leads the underdogs into battle. In **THE HEAT OF THE NIGHT,** Mr. Tibbs does not want to stay in the bigoted Southern town to solve the murder but circumstances make him stay. In **SHREK** the lead character does not want to help the other fairytale characters, but realizes it's the only way he can achieve his immediate goal—to be left alone. Shrek doesn't want a donkey as a helpmate, but he realizes fighting the Donkey's persistence is too much trouble. Shrek doesn't want to slay a dragon, but it's the only way to accomplish his task.

A character can be *tricked* into having to take action. A character can be *seduced or challenged or forced* into taking action. Put obstacles in the way of your character *staying away from taking action*. What's more interesting —a woman who wants to fall in love seeking a soul mate? Or a woman who doesn't want to believe in love and then meets her "dream guy" but still *resists* falling in love? What's more interesting: A man who wants to work his way up in the family business and then does goes up the ladder to be head of the company? Or a man who doesn't want to sell tires, who wants to follow his dream and *resists* entering the family business until circumstances give him no choice? Again: conflict.

The Audience Likes to Worry

If your protagonist is never in danger of **failing,** he can't show many heroic characteristics. If your hero has no obstacles to hurdle—he is not really a hero. If he doesn't have to fight, if he doesn't have to overcome all odds— he is not really a hero.

If the protagonist is immortal and can never die—a life or death struggle means nothing and the audience will not worry. Perhaps he is immortal, but his *heart* can break if the woman he loves is taken from him. Find the part of your character that your audience can *worry* about. Find the vulnerability in your characters.

If your protagonist is stronger than everyone else—the audience will not worry about him. Create weaknesses. Create flaws. Will he be able to reach his goal? Will she get what he wants and needs? Let your audience be on the edge of their seats; will he or she survive? Will your hero/heroine overcome their weaknesses and be victorious this time?

Think about your character's *flaw.* A character who is *not* perfect is more interesting than Mister or Miss Perfect. Let the obstacles he encounters relate to his flaw. What kind of obstacles would hit an impatient person extra hard? A person who has a violent temper will deal with obstacles in a different way than a too-timid person. A handicapped person's obstacles will be different and create special problems. A vain person will have to deal with obstacles that are aggravated by his ego. An intellectual who is not in touch with his physical body will have certain obstacles. What about a character with low self-esteem? A character's flaw can be physical, mental or emotional. Find the vulnerable part of your character and let the story *attack it.*

Obstacles will make the protagonist's journey more difficult; they could be scary, funny, dramatic, violent… whatever fits your story.

When characters are happy and content, the story can stall. Take your characters out of their comfort zones.

Think about **TOOTSIE** and all the obstacles Michael meets as he struggles to understand what it means to be a woman. Think about **A BEAUTIFUL MIND** and all the obstacles (mental, emotional) the protagonist encounters as he deals with his mental illness. Think about any of the **INDIANA JONES** films—they are all about obstacles. Think about 2003's **21 GRAMS;** one character has huge emotional obstacles that have to do with the death of husband and child, one character is dealing with a huge physical obstacle (a bad heart), another character is dealing with obstacles that manifest themselves while trying to live a good and moral life. Think about **WITNESS;** there are physical, emotional, cultural obstacles. Make a list of the obstacles that could present themselves to your main character in your story. Use them!

Overcoming obstacles is how your hero grows along his arc. Overcoming obstacles is how lessons are learned and new choices made. Facing obstacles will challenge and change a person.

Obstacles should grow in difficulty. The challenges should get more and more difficult as the film progresses. If, at the beginning of the film, your protagonist has to uproot the Empire State Building to save throngs of people—and then at the end the protagonist has to make a phone call to bring the climax of the film to its highest point... you might want to rethink the ending (or the beginning) unless you can make that phone call seem more difficult than uprooting the Empire State Building. Audiences want to be lifted up to the climax. Surprise them. Awe them.

In Act Three, at the climax of your film, the final obstacles are overcome (or not) and finally, after a grueling and emotional journey, the protagonist reaches his goal... or not.

Red Light/Green Light

How do you make sure your story doesn't follow a straight line, move at the same pace throughout? You want curves, you want stop signs, you want traffic lights, you want yield signs. Mix it up! You want to hit bumps in the road. You want mountains to climb and valleys to speed into (and maybe have your brakes go out as you descend...), you want a traffic jam, you want a crash or two... in other words, nothing should go smoothly. Your film should not be on cruise control. Your characters should not all be the best drivers. They may feel road rage. They may be nervous drivers. Some characters drive big rigs, some drive VW bugs. But most importantly—they all *stop* and *go* and *stop* and *go*...

In other words, think of your OBSTACLES and REVERSALS as *red lights and green lights.*

Take a look at the first ten minutes of 1981's **RAIDERS OF THE LOST ARK.** Lots of red light/green lights in the first moments. Indiana Jones enters a cave; there are <STOP> lots of traps set up. He gets through <GO>, moves in a few feet, <STOP> something stops him. He <GO> gets through. A few feet more and <STOP> one of his guides gets killed. He continues on <GO>. A few feet more, <STOP> the floor goes out from under him. He finally reaches the golden treasure,<GO> the greedy guide steals it and leaves Jones for dead <STOP>. Jones manages to get the treasure back <GO> and finally escapes the cave! He's got it! He's just gone through a series of action-packed, death defying elements, but he's got the treasure! He exits the cave to <STOP> come face to face with his *main rival,* the French archeologist, Belloq. Jones thinks he can overpower him <GO> and then sees his rival's back-up crew of cutthroats. Belloq takes the treasure <STOP>. Go, stop, go, stop, go a bit faster, stop and almost die, go at a breakneck speed, stop and feel great frustration and betrayal; all in the first few minutes of the story.

Where do you go from there? More series of action sequences? No, now it's time to *get to know the character.* Fill out and color in your protagonist's life. Let us know more about him, the different sides of his life. In **RAIDERS OF THE LOST ARK**, Indiana Jones goes from the wilds of archeological treasure hunting to his rather pedantic and frustrating teaching job at an University. He wants others to share his passion for archaeology; he's lecturing <GO> and hoping he's reaching his students. But what does he see? The girls in the classroom have painted love notes to him on their eyelids and are clearly not listening. <STOP>.

So where do you go from there? Broaden your protagonist's world even more. There's another <GO>. The government is considering hiring Jones to retrieve one of the most famous of missing artifacts, the Ark of the Covenant. He's excited; he wants the job. But it's not easy, <STOP>. The government has reservations about Jones' success record, about his ability to carry out the assignment. This is just an interview. The job is not handed to him. But late that night, when Jones is at home (again, showing us more about his character; his bachelor home), the head of the department at the University visits. He's got news; Jones has been chosen. And that's it; the <GO> that will propel Jones into the rest of the story. Look at all the red lights/green lights in the opening sequences of this film—this is good storytelling.

And, of course, this film is filled with red lights/green lights that never stop. At every step there's another obstacle; in Jones' relationships (friends and

Chapter Summary

- Action is movement of story, a sense that things are happening to character.

- Physical movement alone does not constitute true action.

- All actions should have a consequence.

- Conflict belongs in every scene and in every relationship.

- The magic words "no" and "but" help add conflict to your story.

- The Eleven Steps can help you focus on creating conflict.

- Obstacles test your protagonist and help him grow.

Chapter Fourteen

EVENTS

Can the choice of events in a film story help make it unique? Yes.

Can a writer use events to make clear the passage of time? Yes.

Whether your story takes place over a day or a year, a decade or several decades, you can move your character through it by finding the events that will ground it.

Consider the story bones of **BEAUTY AND THE BEAST,** the classic story by Jeanne-Marie Leprince de Beaumont. In Beaumont's tale, a Prince is put under a spell because of his selfishness and vanity; he is to be a Beast until he can prove he can love and be loved in return. A young woman crosses his path and he captures her, intent on making her fall in love with him. He comes to realize that one cannot demand love, that it has to be earned.

Imagine you are given the task to adapt this story, fill out the characters and the particulars, create supporting characters, and create the world in which the film story will take place.

There are initial decisions to be made: genre, period, location, character traits. And then—events. The events you choose will make your telling different from every other writer's story.

Events Help Make Your Story Unique

In your version of the story, what event will cause the young woman to cross the Beast's path? Is she an inventor? Has her hot air balloon crashed near his castle? Is she a country doctor who is summoned to take care of a strange creature? Is she blinded by blowing debris during a hurricane, stumbles upon him and never sees the Beast's face?

What events need to be constructed to show the distrust between the Beast and the young heroine? What events will *change* that distrust and make it possible for them to be friends? What events need to be fashioned to show a growing friendship? What event will put that friendship to the test and show that the relationship is moving toward love? What event will test that love to show that it is indeed true love?

In Disney's **BEAUTY AND THE BEAST** , what events were chosen? Think of the inciting incident as an *event:* Belle's father gets lost in the forest, goes to the Beast's castle for shelter and is imprisoned. The next main *event* is Belle's arrival to save her father. The next *event* is Belle, seeing her father is sick and afraid, offers to trade places with him; she agrees to be the prisoner of the Beast's castle. Note that there are scenes that connect these events (scenes with the enchanted servants, scenes with Belle realizing her father is lost and in trouble), but those are scenes fashioned to get the character from one important, story-advancing event to another.

In the Disney version, the Beast takes advantage of Belle's offer to switch places with her father. He sends the father home. *Next big event?* Belle's discovery of the rose under the bell jar. How do the writers get there—using conflict and obstacles? First the Beast asks Belle to have dinner with him; she refuses because she resents being a prisoner. The Beast *demands* she have dinner with him, she refuses to leave her room. The Beast goes away, angry. Belle, hungry, accepts the enchanted servant's offer of dinner in the kitchen. Belle has an amazing, magical dinner. (Note that the magical dinner musical number is *not* a story-progressing event. That's why it's called a "show-stopper"; it stops the action of the story and merely entertains.) After dinner, servants offer to show Belle around the castle. She slips away from the enchanted servants and makes her way to the forbidden West Wing. *Next big event:* Belle discovers the rose. She is about to lift off the rose's protective glass when the Beast stops her. His anger and heightened anxiety frighten her, she retaliates with a temper of her own and races out of the castle into a dark, snowy, stormy night. *Next big event?* The Beast saves Belle from the wolves. The scenes that lead up to that event? Belle gets on her horse, ready to leave the castle. Wolves attack her and her horse. Belle tries to save her horse. It looks as if both will perish, but the Beast arrives to save her. There is a battle, the Beast is wounded, but the wolves retreat. *Next event?* Belle nurses the Beast's wounds, the two bond.

By thinking of a script as a series of events, the writer can keep the story moving forward. Every script needs a motor under it, going from event to event can help keep that screen story's motor humming.

Build Events Into Your Story

Arrests. Adopting a dog. Getting a promotion. Trying out for the team. Meeting the girl for the first time. Being stood up. Asking for a date. Getting on a plane for the first time. Buying a new car. Sending the rocket into the air. Losing at the science fair. Saving the planet. A glacier rams into the side of the ship. Wife leaves home, for good. A patient gets a new heart. Aliens steal the Empire State Building.

What *events* are going to be in your story… and how will your character traverse the story that is grounded by a series of events?

Remember to use obstacles and reversals to get from one event to another. Nothing should go smoothly, nothing should be easy.

 E x e r c i s e :

Choose two events from the list below and create a series of obstacles for a character to move from one event to another. Example: A traffic accident and high school graduation. First decide who your character will be—will it be a graduate or a parent or a girlfriend or a best friend or a police officer or a teacher or principal of the high school? Let's say the character in the traffic accident is a high school graduate named Ray. If Ray doesn't make the graduation ceremony, his life will be ruined (of course you have to come up with a reason why). Questions to consider: What is the genre? Comedy? Drama? Horror? Sci- Fi? Has Ray caused the accident or is he the victim? How much time does he have to get from the site of the accident to the high school? Will he need to race off, will he choose to ditch the car, avoid making a police report, will he hitch another ride, will he run, will he steal a bicycle? What obstacles will you build to get Ray from event to event?

1.   A wedding and the honeymoon night.

2.   Getting on a plane and landing in China.

3.   Being sworn in as President of the United States and dancing the first dance at the Presidential Ball.

4.   Being sworn in as President and declaring war.

5.   Winning the Olympic speed skating championship and receiving the medal on the champion's podium.

6.   Getting sworn in as a police officer and the first arrest.

"Munich" Eric Bana, Geoffrey Rush
photo supplied by Globe Photos

Consider the main events of 2005's **MUNICH,** written by Tony Kushner
and Eric Roth, based on a book by George Jonas. This movie chronicles
the aftermath of the Black September slayings of Israeli athletes at the
1972 Olympics.

1.   Avner is asked to lead an undercover group of avengers to retaliate
      against the killings at the Olympics. Avner is flattered, his deceased
      father had been a hero and he wants to be a hero, too.

2.   Avner meets his fellow avengers.

3.   Avner participates in the first murder. Here we see Avner hesitate;
      killing is not natural to him.

4.   Avner goes home for the birth of his child. (We know from the
      beginning of the film that his wife is due to give birth in two
      months, thus we now know two months have gone by. This event is
      a time-telling event as well as one that puts more emotional
      pressure on Avner.)

5.   A series of bombings to show the group is accomplishing their goal.

6.   Avner meets the father of the man from whom Avner buys
      information.

7.   Avner discovers the dead body of one of his fellow avengers.

8.   Avner takes revenge for the murder of his fellow avenger. This event shows a change in Avner's attitude toward killing. It also changes the course of the story because now Avner realizes he is a marked man.

9.   Death by bomb of another of Avner's group. This marks another change for Avner, he no longer has the stomach for the job.

10.   Avner and group's attack on their main target that ends in failure

11.   Avner quits the project and refuses to be de-briefed. He has no sense of being a hero.

12.   Avner goes to the USA to join wife and young daughter. This event gives us a sense of how much time has passed, his daughter is now grown.

13.   Avner's refusal to go home to Israel, acceptance that his country is no longer his home. Not only has he changed his idea about what it means to be a hero, he no longer trusts and believes in those who promised him a hero status.

By finding the main events in the film story, you can see how the plot can be quite simple. Within these events, Avner's character becomes more complex. He makes friends, he experiences pain, loneliness, he questions himself. He struggles to keep his marriage on track. He tries to take care of his mother. He meets strange and interesting characters in the underworld of political plots. But the tent poles, the *bones*, the *events* of the "A" story are very simple. Let the plot be simple and allow the characters to become complex.

Use Events as Runners to Help Show Time Passing

The use of holidays, landmark dates like birthdays or anniversaries, seasonal moments like summer swims or leaves turning to autumn gold… these are visual ways of letting the audience know what chunks of time have gone by.

If it's a growing business, let the new office building go from blueprint to structural skeleton to a building complete with windows and doors to the day the characters move into their offices. If your story lives in the theatre, let the rehearsal process shine a light on time passage. Are actors just being cast? There are costume fittings, dress rehearsals, opening nights.

Every life has events. Choosing to use events can give your story shape, ground the audience and help the audience "tell time" in the story. What events can you use?

Build anticipation for various events. The basketball game coming up next week. Or Christmas. Or New Year's Eve. If your story traverses the time between an engagement and a wedding—you have grounded yourself in two *events.*

Chapter Summary

- Thinking of your screenplay as a series of events can help give a sense of action.

- Choosing specific events can help make your screenplay more unique.

- Explore the obstacles that could be inherent in your chosen events.

- Making a list of your main events can help you more clearly see your plot.

- Use of events can help reveal the passage of time in the film story.

Chapter Fifteen

LOGLINE, SYNOPSIS, OUTLINE, AND TREATMENT

Does the screenwriter need to be able to present
her story in various ways? Yes.

Does the task of summarizing a story help to focus it? Yes.

Logline

A LOGLINE consists of two to three sentences that synopsize your screen story while focusing on character arc and theme. A logline should give a sense of the beginning, middle, and end of a story and, more importantly, a strong, interesting character that embarks on a difficult journey.

A logline is used for many purposes.

1. Building a logline can help you focus the screen story. The more effort you put in focusing what your story is *really* about, what the character's arc *really* is, the better chance you have of writing a successful screenplay.

2. Building a good logline will help you relate the basics of your screen story to others; those in the industry—or just to friends or fellow writers. How many times have you been in a situation where someone is telling you a story and you are hearing so many details or tangential information that you can't follow the thrust or purpose of the story? You wonder *why* you are listening and wonder if this rambling has a point? Building the logline for your screen story will enable you to concisely relay the most important elements: the world, the genre, sense of the plot, the character arc, and the theme.

3. A logline is used when you write a query letter to a producer or agent in hopes of interesting him in your script. In a query letter you need to include a logline so the buyer or representative can determine quickly if your story falls into his area of interest. The buyer, probably, is looking for a certain genre or a vehicle for a particular actor or has

certain budget limitations. From a logline, the buyer or representative can determine if he wants to ask to see the entire script.

Include these things in your logline:

1. Genre
2. Character arc
3. Sense of story
4. Sense of theme

Question: But how can I do my screen story justice in a logline of just a few sentences? My story is complex, there are so many amazing twists and turns and surprises. Won't I be doing myself a disservice?

Answer: No. Of course all the wonderful details of your plot, character twists and your cinematic vision won't be included in your logline, but the buyer or representative doesn't need all the details to know whether or not he is interested in reading the screenplay. Remember, a buyer or representative *wants* to find new properties. If your logline intrigues, you will be asked to send the screenplay.

E x e r c i s e :

Use the template below and fill in the specifics of your screen story. Doing so will give you a sense of what a logline should include. After you have filled in the blanks, loosen the structure, make it your own, but keep in the essential elements. NAME OF YOUR SCREEN STORY is a GENRE about NAME OF PROTAGONIST, AGE, ONE OR TWO VIVID WORD DESCRIBING THE CHARACTER who wants HIS/HER IMMEDIATE GOAL. When THE INCITING INCIDENT happens and ONE MAJOR PLOT POINT, he/she goes on a journey to ACCOMPLISH GOAL and discover/realize/find THEME.

The logline for **MILLION DOLLAR BABY** could have read: **MILLION DOLLAR BABY** is a drama about Frankie, a weathered boxing coach who seeks an understanding of God's purpose. When Maggie, a female boxer who is too old to be a beginner, finally inspires him to coach her, he goes on a journey of renewed human connection. When a tragic boxing incident forces him to choose between God's teachings and new bonds of love and friendship, he follows his conscience, realizing that without risking pain, nothing can be gained.

Once you have your logline worked out, using all the important elements, you can fine tune it, trim it, and infuse it with the tone of your story.

More examples:

LEGALLY BLONDE is a comedy/coming of age story about a spoiled, blonde, Bel Air sorority girl, intent on an MRS degree. When her boyfriend dumps her, Elle pulls out all the stops to get into Harvard Law School to pursue him. At Harvard this wacky but intelligent young woman realizes she has talents of her own that will lead her to a life beyond marriage to the wrong guy.

GODFATHER is a drama about Michael Corleone, the youngest son of a powerful Mafia leader, who plans to break away from the family to live a life outside crime. When his family comes under violent attack from rival mob factions, he discovers his blood ties are too strong to ignore. He joins the family's fight and through his leadership brings about a new era and new hierarchy in the mob.

OUT OF AFRICA is a drama about Karin, an insecure Danish woman who desperately want to control all aspects of her world, including love. She survives a misguided marriage, social prejudice and the destruction of her African farm. When she falls deeply in love with a man who demands trust and personal freedom, she learns that in trying to control all, she loses the very thing that makes her the most happy.

CAPOTE is a true-life drama about writer Truman Capote, focusing on his journey into darkness while researching his novel, In Cold Blood. As he struggles to get into the minds of cold-blooded killers, he is forced to examine his own cold-blooded ambition.

Question: I want to infuse my logline with the personality of the script. Can my logline be funny (or give a sense of horror or irony or…)?

Answer: Absolutely. Make your logline your own, let it show personality. Just keep it short and simple; include your genre, relay a sense of beginning and end for your main character and the theme of your story.

A Logline is Not a Teaser

A logline is meant to *tell the story* in a few sentences. A logline should give the sense of a beginning, middle and end to a character's arc.

A teaser is a marketing tool, to draw audiences into the theatre. Teasers appear on posters, in newspaper ads, in radio and television spots. A teaser leaves an open-ended vagueness to the outcome of the film story. It is not a screenwriting tool—therefore a writer should leave teasers to the marketing group.

Imagine yourself in a studio executive's office. The executive asks you to tell him about your screen story and you (if you had written LEGALLY BLONDE) reply, "A blonde, spoiled sorority girl named Elle follows her ex-boyfriend to Harvard Law School and it's really funny and amazing what happens to her." There would, most likely, be a long pause signaling that the executive is waiting for more. The executive will want to know *what* happens to Elle; does she flunk out and become a waitress? Does she save someone's life on campus and enroll in medical school? Does she meet a biker and become

a Hell's Angel chick? The executive will want to hear the logline and know how Elle changes. He will want to know the basics of the *story*.

Logline reminders

- A good logline can help focus the writer as he is forced to examine the essence of his character's journey.

- A good logline focuses on a character's arc. Character is more interesting than plot. How does your protagonist change over the course of the story? Does she start as an insecure woman who finds strength? Does he start out cocky or irresponsible and finally takes responsibility for his actions? Does your character go from over-confident to seeing she has something to learn?

- Keep the logline short. The best loglines are not over three sentences (and that does not mean massive run-on sentences). Remember, "Oh, tell me *more…*" is a *good* thing to hear. If you relay your logline and pique someone's interest, it means the basics of your story are interesting.

Synopsis

A SYNOPSIS is a simple one page or one and a half page summary of a screenstory. The synopsis should focus on the character arc of the protagonist.

Use the Eleven Step Story Structure as a guide to help you know what to include in your synopsis. Set up the normal life of your protagonist, make it clear what his immediate goal is and why (the why will give a sense of the overall want). Include a logical step or two of how he goes about trying to achieve his goal and how he is denied. This denial closes down logical avenues and your protagonist now has to choose (or not choose) to take advantage of a second opportunity. Include the conflicts and dangers the protagonist assesses about taking this new path. Include how he makes his decision to embark on the new path, follow him as he encounters up and downs on his journey, using broad strokes instead of details.. Include the situation he finds himself in at the crisis moment; emotionally track his feelings about his decision to enter into the climax (or not). Use broad strokes to give a sense of climactic sequences and include the outcome of the climax. Emotionally track the protagonist and include the moment or moments of truth that are revealed at the end of the story. Give a sense of the new normal… and you have a synopsis.

This task is not as easy as it sounds. Writers get attached to the details. Writers don't like to think that their story is simplistic; after all, they have poured sweat into creating a complex, layered story. But trimming the story down to its basic character journey will illuminate the essence of your story.

A synopsis should relay the protagonist's arc, give a sense of plot and action in broad strokes, and emotionally track the protagonist's journey. Remember, one page is optimum for a synopsis.

Basic look of a synopsis:

- Title centered at the top of the page

- Author's name under the title

- One page to one and a half page double-spaced prose

- Use paragraph indentations for an easier to read

Outline

Sometimes the terms, OUTLINE and TREATMENT, are used interchangeably, but there is a difference.

An OUTLINE is a document used by the writer to lay out the basic structure of her film story. It is a tool used to keep a writer on track and on story. This can be shared with a development executive or producer, but in most cases, it is too sketchy to be properly understood by someone who does not intimately know all elements of the story.

An outline should include all elements of the Eleven Step character story. If your protagonist spends a good amount of time in Step #2, Logically Goes For It, your outline should list all the sequences or scenes in that area of the story. Do the same thing for all steps of the story, and you will have an outline.

An outline for Act One of the Hitchcock film **VERTIGO** could have looked something like this:

Question: What do you mean by broad strokes?

Answer: Let me use an example. If your protagonist, Cedric, engages in a series of fabulous and fun battles on his journey through the forest to rescue a damsel held prisoner in a tower, your impulse may be to show how wonderful and clever you are and include all the strange creatures and obstacles he encounters. But you can't go into great detail in a synopsis because you only have one page to tell your *entire* story. So you might *broad stroke* that sequence like this: Cedric, exhausted and near hopeless, enters the forest and faces a wild series of attacks from strange creatures. Against unbelievable odds he finds a magic medallion to that leads him to the damsel's tower. With renewed hope, he steels himself to face his biggest fear…

Question: Why do producers or development executives want a treatment?

Answer: It's a document that can be passed around the office and discussed. It's a document that shows the direction and tone the writer is pursuing. It's a document that allows story problems to be addressed before the writer goes to script (an outline works better for this purpose). It's a document that can be shown to investors to garner financial backing.

p. Scotty and Madeline form a relationship/connection.

q. Drive to the country, visit the Redwoods.

r. Kiss.

s. Midge tries to make a joke of Scotty's obsession and it falls flat. See how far gone Scotty is about Madeline.

t. Scotty has become obsessed; his search for a purpose has become an obsession.

u. Scotty and Madeline go to the Mission for a great love scene. He presses his love, she gets upset and races up the circular stairway to the HIGH tower. Scotty tries to follow but his VERTIGO kicks in, he stops, can't make it to the top of the tower to Madeline.

3. SCOTTY IS DENIED

a. Madeline loses her balance and falls out of the tower. Scotty sees the woman he loves fall to her death.

b. Scotty feels responsible; his flaw (vertigo) caused her death (he thinks).

c. At a "hearing" Scotty's found not guilty but he is not washed of guilt

d. Scotty can't get over Madeline, he visits grave.

e. Scotty has nightmares.

f. Scotty goes into mental hospital, diagnosed with "acute melancholia."

END OF ACT ONE

An outline is the most useful tool a writer can use. Its format is simple; it's easy to go back in for additions or subtractions. Scenes can be easily moved around. It's a clear way to see the events of the film story. It can help determine if each scene or sequence is moving the story forward. An outline forces the writer to concentrate on the main character's journey but allows for space to simply track "B" or "C" stories.

Basic look of an outline:

• Title centered at the top of the page.

- Author's name under the title.

- Divide the story into acts: Act One, Act Two, Act Three.

- Can use bullet points or numbers to indicate new scenes or sequences.

- Writing style can be sketchy, but should include notations that track the character arc throughout the story.

Treatment

A TREATMENT is different in style from an outline and it is also different in purpose. A treatment is a document, 7 to 12 pages in length, that relays the film story in prose style and fully explores the story. It reads, in most cases, like a short story. This is an official document and often used as a sales tool. Sometimes a treatment must be approved by a producer/studio/ executive before the writer gets the green light to go to script. Sometimes it is a contractual step, sometimes it is an "understood" step. Sometimes the writer is paid for a treatment; sometimes a writer is expected to do this difficult task for free. Since the treatment is thought of as a sales tool, it must excite the reader and instill confidence that the story related will serve as a base for a successful film.

Because it is a sales tool, a treatment must be written with style, with carefully chosen words, with an eye to engage the reader emotionally. The thrilling elements of the story must be relayed in an exciting terms; the pathos must tease a tear from the reader. If it's a horror story, the reader must feel the danger. If it's a comedy, the reader must laugh.

Most writers dislike writing treatments because they call on a different skill than screenwriting and the process takes a great deal of effort. There is, in most cases, no dialogue in a treatment. The writer doesn't have the luxury of letting the story unfold with nuance. The special visuals, the pacing, certain structural elements can not be properly expressed. The great action sequences or great emotional outbursts or sense of time and place cannot be properly expressed. In other words, it's not a screenplay and that's what screenwriters want to write. But knowing how to write a treatment is part of the screenwriter's job.

How does one write a good treatment? As in all good stories, concentrate on the main character's journey. If you have written a synopsis of your story, use that as a base and expand it into a treatment. Add details, add descriptions of special scenes. You will still have to use broad strokes to

Question: If I spend so much time writing a treatment and getting it to read like a well-written short story, am I in danger of losing the excitement I feel for my story?

Answer: Yes. That's why, if it is not a contractual agreement, full-blown treatment writing should be avoided. Outlines are helpful, they map a route, they keep your story impulses simple and allow for fresh energy and creativity when it is time to write the scene.

Question: Anything positive about the writing of treatments?

Answer: Anytime you ask yourself to clarify the important story elements that press your protagonist forward on his journey is time well spent.

Question: Where can I find examples of treatments?

Answer: Use your internet search engine to look for SCREENPLAY TREATMENTS or SCREENPLAY OUTLINES. Sites include www.simplyscripts.com and www.filmcampus. info/screenplay_treatments.html

relay complex sequences, but you can include more specifics than you did in your synopsis.

Example: Remember the broad strokes of Cedric's journey in the forest that was relayed in the synopsis? It read like this: Cedric, exhausted and near hopeless, enters the forest and faces a wild series of attacks. Against unbelievable odds he finds a magic medallion that leads him to the damsel's tower. With renewed hope, he steels himself to face his biggest fear....

In a treatment, this section could be expanded to read something like this: Cedric, exhausted and near hopeless, enters the dark enchanted forest. He struggles with his resolve as he encounters strange and violent creatures, hurricane-force winds, quicksand, swamps, toxic gasses and flesh-eating plants. Injured and near collapse, thinking the task is impossible. Cedric stops to drink from a clear, cool stream. The water magically rises around him, he flails to swim free, but he is sucked under. And there, before him, is the magical medallion! He reaches for it- it's his! Bursting from the water, he sees the tower....

Treatments should focus on the protagonist and antagonist, the "A" story. "B" story elements should be introduced and tracked, in most cases, only when they directly affect the "A" story. Keep the relaying of the "B" stories simple.

- The theme of the story should be apparent.

- The writing style should relay the tone of the story.

- The main character's emotional reactions to the story's twists and turns should be tracked.

- There are basic elements of format in the writing of treatments. The most important element is clarity. Infuse the treatment with your personal style.

Basic look of a treatment

- Title on top of the first page-Author's name under the title

  - 7-12 pages of double-spaced prose

  - At the beginning of your treatment, include your logline. (The logline will include genre and give a sense of the protagonist's immediate goals, character arc and theme and prime the reader to the shape and tone of the story.)

- Staple the document.
- Put a header with your name and title of story on each page, just in case the pages get separated.

- Break the story into acts: Act One, Act Two and Act Three.
- Break the prose into short paragraphs. Make it easy to read.

Once you have the treatment complete and approved and you are given the green light to go to script, you can use the treatment to build your script. (An outline usually works better for this purpose but if you are getting paid to write the treatment, that's what you need to deliver).

Tips for Writing the Treatment

Jot down elements of an outline before you start. Know the beginning and middle and end of your story before you start. Don't create your story in treatment format, the expectations of style will, in most cases, frustrate the creative flow. Allow yourself to broad stroke areas of your script. Write it as fast as you can; in one day or allow yourself one day per act and finish it in three days. Polish once. Don't obsess over it.

Chapter Summary

- A logline consists of two or three sentences that synopsize your screen story while focusing on character arc and theme.
- A logline is used in pitches, query letters and outlines.
- A synopsis is a simple one to two page summary of a screen story focused on character arc and theme.
- Use the Eleven Steps to help create a synopsis to ensure you are relaying a complete story.
- An outline is a document used by the writer to lay out the basic film story. It is a tool to help keep the story on track.
- A treatment is 7 to 12 pages and relays the film story in prose form.
- A treatment can be used as a sales tool.
- A treatment is often a contractual step that must be completed before getting the green light to go to script.

What genre of films constantly explore this theme: "Without truth, there can be no peace of mind?" Think of courtroom dramas. Think about love stories that use this theme. Think about films focused on revenge stories. Think about horror films. There is a truism in the theme; most people value the truth and cannot rest until they fully understand a situation.

Many films have themes that explore issues of trust. Many deal with truth. Many deal with respect. Many explore "knowing oneself." Many explore the good and bad sides of love, power, control. There is no reason to try to find an original, never-done-before theme.

When considering your theme, it is the time to be heartfelt, to be sappy, to be political, to be psychological, to show strength of personal conviction. Ask yourself, what am I trying to explore in this screenplay? What does my main character need to find *true* success or happiness or peace of mind? Accept that your *view is valid*. Accept that what you think is important and can push people to think in a fresh way. Accept that there is a life lesson to be learned in every story. In other words, be confident about expressing your theme.

Shakespeare's **OTHELLO,** a story of a man who allows jealousy to consume him, has a strong theme that is hard to miss: "Without trust, love will be destroyed." The story explores trust from various viewpoints; Othello trusts Iago, who is only pretending to be trustworthy. Othello cannot trust his own judgment because it is clouded by jealousy. Othello mistrusts his wife, Desdemona, who is the most trustworthy of all. Shakespeare was clearly exploring the idea of trust. He set out to prove that without trust, one can destroy the very thing he loves.

Themes Are in the Eye of the Beholder

The beauty of stories is they affect people in various ways. One could see **NETWORK** as a film whose theme revolves around the business side of the story: Greed destroys good judgment. One could watch the film and identify with the romance and see the theme: Relationships take under-standing and commitment, and without these elements, true love cannot flourish. Or one could view **NETWORK** as a cautionary tale: Without living real life, the television generation will be cold and unfeeling. The best way to work the theme of your story is through its main character. In **NETWORK**, the protagonist, Max, is going through a mid-life crisis. The world is changing and he feels old and out of touch. The character theme of the film is: Without holding onto your moral and ethical center, one can lose one's soul. This character theme is related to all the above themes, but it is based in character and therefore the writer is able to construct scenes with the character to prove or disprove the theme.

When searching for your theme, try to fill in the blanks: Without ___ there can be no _____.

Examples:

STREETCAR NAMED DESIRE (1951) Without acceptance, there can be no love. Think how this theme relates to Blanche's part in destroying her young lover, how it relates to Stella and Stanley's relationship, to Mitch and Blanche's relationship, to Stella and Blanche's relationship. Each character in this story needs to learn to accept people for who they really are—and when they don't, something important in their life is destroyed.

CHINATOWN (1974) Without facing the truth, there can be no freedom. This theme relates to the protagonist Jake Gittes, to his client and lover Mrs. Mulwray, to her controlling father, to her innocent daughter.

OUT OF AFRICA (1985) Without trust, relationships can be destroyed.

FATAL ATTRACTION (1987) Without taking responsibility, there can be no trust.

BEAUTY AND THE BEAST (1991) Without understanding true love, we are all beasts.

I KNOW WHAT YOU DID LAST SUMMER (1997) Without facing the past, there can be no joy in the future. This theme is explored in the life of every major character.

SHAKESPEARE IN LOVE (1998) Without taking risks, there is no chance at happiness.

GLADIATOR (2000) Without facing your demons, there can be no peace.

SHATTERED GLASS (2003) Without truth, there can be no true success.

SIDEWAYS (2004) Without the ability to move on from the heartaches of the past, there can be no happy future.

Themes Often Emerge During the Writing Process

Writers approach each story differently. Sometimes it *is* the desire to explore a certain theme that draws a writer to construct a story. Consider 2005's **CRASH.** The thematic question is presented in the first scene: Do people need to crash into each other just to feel? The writers explore the idea of lives that intersect in violent ways and bring about a change (or revelation) in personal attitude, prejudice and ultimately, connection.

Exercise:

Explore this theme: Without being true to yourself, one can not earn respect. What characters and situation can you build that will prove that theme? Write a short script, ten pages in length. The script should have a beginning, middle and end. Use no more than four characters.

Sometimes the writer may not know what has drawn him to tell a story. He may not know what his theme is when he begins to write. That's okay. It could be a character or situation that inspires his exploration of the story. The theme, in most cases, will emerge as he writes. If it doesn't, the writer needs to investigate his personal point of view on the situation and characters.

Be willing to embrace theme when you discover it. A writer can challenge. A writer can be sentimental. A writer can believe in something. If you

"Crash" Thandie Newton, Matt Dillon
photo supplied by Globe Photos

Chapter Sixteen: Dramatic Question, Theme, Point of View

believe that love makes one a better person, that's valid. If you believe that love is bogus and it's fear of being alone that draws us to other people, that's valid also. No one has to agree with you. It is your story.

Theme. It may be the impetus that starts the story or it may become apparent as you work on your story. But *it has to be found* at some point. And it can *inform* your storytelling. *It can help shape your scenes.* It can focus your story.

The Author's Point of View

Consider **TREASURE OF SIERRA MADRE.** It's clear the writers believe that a person's moral compass can be lost when greed enters the picture. Consider the X-MEN franchise. It's clear the writers believe that the acceptance of difference can bring peace to the world. Consider **OUT OF AFRICA;** the writer is exploring the nature of control and how the need to control can destroy. Consider **SIDEWAYS;** which character is portrayed as having the most sympathetic point of view? Which character has a different point of view that forces the protagonist to examine his own beliefs? Miles is the protagonist, on a journey that will change his life. His friend, Jack, is pursuing a desire, but this pursuit does not change his life. The authors are telling Miles' story, one that carries hope for change.

The author's point of view, in most cases, is supported in the protagonist's story. With which character does the author wish the audience to identify? Which character is the moral compass? If the main character is evil, does the author hold him or her up as one to be respected, feared or hated?

2004's **JUNE BUG** is a slice-of-life tale of a family that comes together for one week to experience joy, frustration, love, and heartache. Each character is singular and exists within their own sense of right and wrong. The author does not judge any of the relationships or make a decision which character is "more right." What is the author's point of view? That family accepts, that family loves, that life is a learning process and each person must be given room to be an individual.

The author's point of view is often endemic in the storytelling. Subconsciously, or consciously, writers express their beliefs. Is an action fair? Is the world in good shape or in trouble? Is true love possible or not? If you find you are dispassionately *telling* a story, insert your personal point of view on character, on events, on dialogue.

Make your film story one that *only* you can write.

> **Exercise:**
>
> Explore your point of view about friendship. Is it sacrosanct? Would you lie, cheat, steal for a friend even if you did not believe in what you are doing? Or do you believe a true friend wouldn't ask you to go against your principles? What could break a friendship? Write a short paragraph about your point of view of friendship. Then create a ten page short script (with a beginning, middle and end) with no more than four characters that explores the breaking up of a friendship.

Chapter Summary

- The Dramatic Question is the main question posed by the story and should be specific to the protagonist.

- Theme is the unifying moral, philosophical or emotional assumption that the writer wants to explore in his story.

- Themes usually revolve around identifiable human needs and desires.

- A writer should try to explore their theme as well as the anti-theme.

- A story is made more unique and original when the writer instills his own point of view on the material.

Chapter Seventeen

START WRITING: ACT ONE

Does all the preliminary work of outlines and
loglines help in the process? Yes.

Does a writer need to put himself on a schedule to write? Yes.

You've built your story using the Eleven Steps as a guide. You've expanded that document into your outline or sequence sheet. Maybe you've written a full treatment. Now what? Maybe the opening visual or scene you want to write is clear, maybe you've got dialogue and locations and characters set in your mind and you are itching to sit down and write "FADE IN." Go ahead. You've done the character and story work. Write. Don't stop yourself. But if you're not sure of that opening scene or sequence yet, here are a few more things you can do before you take the plunge.

Specific Sequences to Explore in Act One

1. *Fashion a sequence showing the normal life of your protagonist; what are the inherent conflicts and emotions involved in this normal life?* Find a scene or sequence that will inform the audience. What's the most interesting area of your protagonist's life? Work? Play? Hobby? Favorite spot? Friends? Lover? Steer away from a sequence where the protagonist wakes up in bed to a screeching alarm, races to the shower, deals with his messy or neat home in some way, races out of the apartment or house, into his car and drives up to building/school/job; this sequence is overdone. Find a sequence that tells us more about the character and puts the story in motion. Consider starting with a scene in the middle of a situation.

Examples: 1934's **IT HAPPENED ONE NIGHT** begins with an argument between the protagonist, Ellen, and her father over his desire to annul her recent marriage. The sequence ends with Ellen jumping off the yacht and swimming to her freedom. The audience is in the action of the story from the outset. 1988's **RAINMAN** begins with the protagonist, Charlie, dealing with a crisis in his car import/export business. The audience learns money is tight, that Charlie is driven to succeed, that his life is full of conflict .

Question: What if the opening of my film story does not feature my protagonist?

Answer: Start your story where you think best. As long as the opening sequence is a piece of the jig-saw puzzle that fits into the entire story and helps set genre, tone, place and pushes us onto the journey—an opening without the protagonist is fine.

1999's **THE SIXTH SENSE** begins with Malcolm and his wife about to celebrate Malcolm's award from the Mayor for his work in child psychology. This scene is followed by the inciting incident; Malcolm is shot. The audience is shocked into paying close attention. 2005's **CRASH** opens on one of the main characters, Graham, in a car with his lover and fellow police officer. They've been rear-ended in a traffic accident. This scene sets the theme for the film when Graham says, "Sometimes we have to crash into each other just to feel something." 2005's **SYRIANA** begins with Bob Baer, the main character, in an Iranian nightclub that dispels stereotypes. He hopes to get his arms deal into action but has to be patient.

Examples of film stories that do not start with the protagonist: 1998's **SHAKESPEARE IN LOVE** begins with a theatrical producer being tortured to pay his debts. The audience instantly knows the time period, the world, the stakes and one of the important reasons why Shakespeare must write a good play. This scene informs the next scene where the audience is introduced to Shakespeare. Shakespeare is in a "normal life" activity—writing and frustrated with his output. The stakes, should Shakespeare fail, have been made clear in the first scene so there is more tension in Shakespeare's introduction. 1985's **WITNESS** begins with a funeral in the Pennsylvania Amish country. Supporting characters are introduced. Rachel, the new widow, and her son, Samuel, board a train, get off at the Philadelphia station to change trains on their way to Baltimore. Samuel witnesses a murder. This sequence sets the scene for the protagonist, John Book, a tough Philadelphia cop, to enter the story; he's there to solve the crime. By opening in the Amish country, the writers have created a compare-and-contrast of life styles and belief systems between the Amish and the crime world in Philadelphia. This contrast is very important in the telling of this story.

2. *Fashion a sequence that will feature your protagonist's want (Step #1 of the Eleven Steps).* Is he in the middle of a club, watching others dance and clearly wanting a relationship in his life? This sequence could be used to show he wants love. Is she working around the clock as an intern at the hospital to prove to her superiors that she is the best candidate for a residency position? This sequence could be used to show she wants respect. Is he unable to sign up for a track event or chess tournament or stand up to his father or raise his hand in class or, on a police chase, is he unable to scale the fence to apprehend the criminal? Any of these sequences could be used to show he needs to believe in himself. Is she

intent on dominating the conversation or is she attacking burgeoning space colonies or is she at her computer carefully choosing a date from an online service? Any of these sequences could be used to show she wants power and control.

Consider **SHAKESPEARE IN LOVE,** it's very clear in Shakespeare's introductory scene that Shakespeare wants to find a muse; he wants to write the great play. Consider **GLADIATOR,** it's clear in Maximus' first scenes that he wants peace; he wants to go home to his farm, his wife and son. Consider 2005's **40-YEAR-OLD VIRGIN**, it's clear in Andy's initial scenes that he would like to have a sexual relationship (though he has no clue how to go about achieving his goal).

Don't be afraid of letting your character state his immediate goal. If he is self-aware of his overall want, don't be afraid of exploring ways of the character expressing that desire. As you work on your first draft, explore ways to illuminate character and story.

3. *List at least three things your protagonist can do logically to get what he or she wants (Step #2 of the Eleven Steps).* If your protagonist wants a loving relationship, does he ask someone out on a date? Does he agree to a blind date? Does he try to flirt with a co-worker? Does he hit on his best friend? Does he go to a singles vacation spot? Does he ask his mother for help?

Once you have made a list of three or more scenes or sequences where your protagonist goes about pursuing his overall want, construct obstacles to block his path at every logical step. Obstacles can come from character flaws, other characters, bad luck, circumstances, forces of nature—the list goes on. Remember your genre, find the obstacles that will reinforce the genre.

4. *List the scenes or sequences that will mark the biggest denial (Step #3 of the Eleven Steps) that your protagonist will encounter in pursuit of the overall want.* This denial will force the protagonist onto a new path. Remember, it doesn't have to *one* denial—a protagonist whose overall want is respect could be fired, lose her rich boyfriend, break her leg, not be able to pay the rent and lose all sense of self-respect by having to move in with her mother. A protagonist whose overall want is to believe in herself could have her computer. with her nearly completed novel on its hard drive, fall into the ocean, a storm could capsize the boat, she could get konked on the head, lose her memory and have no sense of self in which to believe. Or a protagonist whose overall want is success could test positively for drugs and get kicked off a team, his father kicks him out of the house, his best

Question: What if I am building a character that wants love but he is too shy or otherwise incapable of actively pursuing his desire? How do I make it clear what he wants? How do I avoid writing a passive character?

Answer: Put your character in situations where he *could* actively pursue his goal, but because of his character flaw, he can't be active or successful. (His inability to take action *is* an action.) Let the audience in on his frustration. Construct active scenes to highlight *his avoidance* of the taking a particular action.

Answer: There is no rule. Use as few or as many as you need to create character, character desire and conflict and advancement of story. Remember, each film story will unfold at its own pace. Just remember to keep your main character in pursuit of his want and let him meet conflicts along the way. Once you know your character and he is moving toward his goal—and you have the basics of your plot, it's time to let loose. See where the muse takes you as you strive to tell the story of your character. If you start to feel lost, you will always have your Eleven Step Breakdown to get you back on track.

friend gets arrested and can't help, his college scholarship is gone, his car is stolen and his sympathetic grandmother dies and he now has to pursue the success he desires in new ways. Or a protagonist who wants love loses the beauty pageant, finds out her boyfriend is cheating on her, steps in a pile of dog poop, accidentally dyes her hair green and runs out of gas on her way to a new town to meet a highly anticipated blind date. Of course, this denial step could be just one scene; in **KRAMER VS KRAMER**, Ted Kramer, who has logically set up his perfect life, is *denied* when he arrives home from work and his wife informs him she is leaving the marriage. It's powerful in its simplicity.

Whether it's one scene of a series of scenes, remember, this *denial* needs to propel your protagonist into the very difficult journey of Act Two.

Final Thoughts on Act One

- Have you considered a genre scene to set the tone of your story? This, of course, can include the main characters.

- Are you allowing time for the audience to connect with the main character before propelling him on his journey?

- Are you starting your story as close to the inciting incident as possible?

- Look at different areas of your character's life: Home. Work. Romance. Friendship. Relationships with people in the coffee shop or hair salon or gym or other places he might frequent. Relationship with a pet. Or parents. Or grandparents. Or siblings. Or nature. Or art. Or a book. The list can go on. By showing different parts of your character's life, you make him more real, more relatable; plus you may provide yourself with "B" or "C" stories or a runner or two.

- Have you considered your time line? How many days, weeks, months, years will your story traverse? Are you giving your character enough time to change? To accomplish his goals? By using the language of film, you can take your audience from one important event to another. There is no need to follow your character moment to moment, you can "cut" from day to night, summer to winter, decade to decade…

- Consider giving your story room to breathe. That being said, know that the longer the time span of the story, the more difficult it is to keep the tension taut.

Pace

Not only do you want to make sure each sequence or scene has an action—you want to make sure your story has an *active* feel behind it. That comes from *pacing*. Study some of your favorite films. For the most part, the scenes will be longer in the front of the film, they will shorten as the story progresses (and the audience knows enough about the characters and story to fill in some blanks) and in most sequences in the climax, the length of scenes will shorten even more. Remember: *you lead the audience.* You decide the important elements of the story, you decide which elements to use or toss out. Decide to keep your story moving. An audience knows that if someone makes a date in the morning to meet someone for dinner that night, that life goes on during the day before the assignation. There is no need to show the character at work that day, or dressing for the date unless there's a plot or character advancement to be made. Simply cut to the dinner date and let what the characters are wearing or their attitude or their early or late arrival inform the audience about the rest of their day. Pick the events that will advance the story. Get your character from one event to another.

Make sure each scene counts. If it doesn't have a "point" or advance the story or reveal character, it will end up on the cutting room floor. Scenes that feature brilliant dialogue or stunning visuals but do not advance the story will be candidates for cuts in the editing process.

Enter a Scene Late

Consider starting a scene in the middle of an argument. Or in the middle of an activity. No need for someone to drive up to a house, park the car, walk to the front door, ring the doorbell, wait until someone answers the door—cut right to the door opening if that's where the true action of the scene begins.

No need for the bad guys to get the news that the shipment of gold is arriving, get into their helicopter, travel to the docks, pull on their masks, drop air ladders and steal the loot—the most dramatic, active part of that sequence (the part that pushes the story forward) is the arrival and the stealing of the loot. That is the action that will cause a reaction.

When you think you've entered as scene as late as possible, ask yourself if there's a way to enter even later.

Question: What do you do when one character (let's call him Sam) has been told something, or discovers something on screen—but now must relate that information to another character (let's call her Judy)? How do you get around repeating the information the audience already knows?

Answer: Remember the "enter late, leave early" suggestion? Start your scene *after* Judy has been told or shown the newest information and focus on her reaction. Or cut to a scene where Judy has taken an action that makes it clear that she now does know the information. *The audience can assume she has found out. If it's necessary to find out how she found out, drop it in later. Trust your audience. No need to spoon-feed them.*

Question: But what about all the great character moments and dialogue? If I trim my scenes to the bones, won't it feel like it is all plot?

Answer: Never forget about character. If you are advancing or revealing character, those scenes are the most important element of your script. Just make sure the scene is necessary to track the character's journey and/or plot. Beware of falling in love with dialogue or actions that do not move the story forward.

No need for "Hello, how are you?" "Hi." "Good-bye." "See ya." Cut out the small talk unless it's important to the story. Cut everything that does not cause a reaction that propels the story forward.

Leave a Scene Early

Don't tell us what we are going to see or learn later. Instead of a character saying "Bye, I'm heading off to the diner to see if the bad guys are there…" let the character leave the room and drive up to the diner. Let the audience find out where the character's going once he gets there.

It may feel weird, but once you cut to the most important part of the scene or to just a moment before it, it's liberating. The pace of your story will improve.

You want the readers to be turning the pages of your script with excitement, wondering what will happen next. If you lead them in a way that is too moment-to-moment, the readers may get ahead of the story and the writer wants to avoid that.

E x e r c i s e :

After you write your first draft of Act One, go back and look at the content of your scenes. Are there instances of repeat information? Are you starting too many scenes at a predictable beginning? How long are the scenes? Are they of varying lengths? Can you trim out transition scenes that don't help advance story?

Chapter Summary

• Use the Eleven Steps to help you fashion Act One; it needs to accomplish many things.

• Make sure the overriding genre of your story is clear.

• Set up your protagonist's normal life and his or her overall want.

• Consider starting your script close to the inciting incident.

• Explore various areas of the protagonist's life.

- Use the Eleven Steps to give your story shape.

- Consider giving your story room to breathe, no need to go from moment to moment.

- The writer leads. The audience will follow.

Chapter Eighteen

WORKING ON ACT TWO

Does Act Two need to escalate conflict? Yes.

Does Act Two need to open the scope of the story? Yes.

Does Act Two need to focus on the protagonist's journey? Yes.

Be warned. The process of writing Act Two can test a writer's resolve. Act Two is where many scripts find a nice safe dark spot on a shelf or in a drawer or in a file on your computer and never see the light of day again. This is where writers may doubt their idea, their story, their talent, their career choice, their reason for living. This is where many writers will decide to "take a break" to think or re-energize. This is where many writers get enamored of a new idea and start to work out an entirely new story. And when, after this new Act One is in pretty good shape and they move onto Act Two… the writers hit the same roadblocks, shelve the project for a "re-think" and eventually get enamored of a whole new idea. The cycle is obvious; nothing gets completed.

How does a writer avoid having a screenplay stall in Act Two?

Know Where Your Story is Going

Have your Eleven Step Breakdown at hand. Remind yourself you have done the hard story work; you may not have worked out every detail or sequence, but you know where you are headed. Trust the work. Believe in yourself and your story. Be your own cheerleader.

Set a time for writing every day. This is the time to power through. Don't over-think, don't question. Just follow your outline and crank out pages every day. When you get to the end of Act Two, take a deep breath and *then* assess the script for changes.

Act Two is the Most Important Act For Your Character

I once worked with a studio executive who suddenly got it into his head that a film story did not need a second act. He wanted writers to set up characters and situations in Act One and propel the protagonist immediately into an hour long climax of high-jinx, danger, adventure— whatever the genre of the film dictated. During a meeting, he told me of this new method he wanted his writers to follow. My heart sank. I knew my project was doomed. Luckily, this executive did not keep his job long and I was moved to another executive who understood the value of the second act.

Without the second act, the main character has little chance of going on an emotional or physical journey of change. *The second act is the maturation of the character.* Imagine if, after kindergarten, a person is thrust into a marriage or an operating room to save someone's life or in a position to rule a country. Most people with the skills of a kindergartner would be at a loss. Your protagonist must learn skills in Act Two that will prepare him for the huge demands of the climax. These skills could include understanding himself, understanding others, learning kung fu, becoming a gladiator, going to law school, planning a wedding, learning how the business world really works, learning how to fall in love, learning how to let people in, learning that evil does exist, opening up to the idea that there are ghosts (or not) or….

Without a second act, the protagonist has little chance of learning from mistakes, facing obstacles that will force change, becoming embroiled in complications that will make taking on the climax more exciting. Consider the main second act complication of **THE BOURNE IDENTITY;** the growing relationship with the love interest. Without this "B" story, the film would not be as compelling. Bourne's actions now affect another person for whom he cares. Consider the main second act complications of **THE GLADIATOR;** Maximus' new life as a slave forces him into new friendships and understanding of the lives of the common Romans. Act Two allows time to pass so that Maximus' rise to the spot of top gladiator is believable. The Senate's plot against Commodus has the time to take hold and Maximus is able to put himself in a position to be part of it. Maximus' relationship with Lucilla is explored. Commodus' cruel reign is made clear. All these elements are parts of good storytelling and without them—the film's climax cannot truly grip the audience.

You want *serious complications in Act Two.* Your main character needs to get into territory that is totally unfamiliar—emotionally or physically. He needs to find himself in a new situation where he will gain new experiences. He will have to find new ways to deal with problems. Never make it easy! The talents of your protagonist are not good enough; he must grow. An uncomfortable, questioning character who doesn't have all the answers is more interesting than one who makes all the right decisions and feels at home everywhere.

Divide Act Two Into Two Parts

Why? There are practical and artistic reasons. First, you won't be facing the task of filling 50-60 pages, but 25-30 pages. You will make this part of your script feel more manageable. Second, by knowing where your midpoint is, you can build to a moment of change for your protagonist.

Part One: Start with the Second Opportunity (Step #4) and work your way to the MIDPOINT of your film story.

Midpoint

The midpoint is halfway through your script. If your script is 100 pages long, this is page 50. Your protagonist is on his path, trying to attain his overall want. At the beginning of Act Two a second opportunity presents itself—a path that is a bit foreign to his nature or skills. He pursues this path, facing obstacles and reversals. Now, at the midpoint, it is time to add another curve, maybe a drop off, maybe a cross in the road where now there are two paths—and he needs to choose which way to go. The writer must raise the stakes. A writer must add a complication. New information can present itself. Something new could be revealed. New feelings could surface. This midpoint shift will heighten the stakes of the story, add new conflicts and propel the protagonist toward the all important crisis at the end of Act Two.

Recap of Act One

Think of the first three steps of the Eleven Step Story Structure as Act One. Remember that your Act One can be long or short, it doesn't have to hit a specific page count. But it *does* need to include certain story elements:

1. Set up the protagonist's *overall want* and *why* he wants it.

2. Follow the protagonist as he *logically goes about achieving his overall want;* he does this by going after his immediate goal or goals. These logical attempts will backfire or fail or not bring about the desired goal—creating obstacles and reversals and conflict for your protagonist.

Question: Act Two seems like such a huge chunk. How can I keep from getting lost?

Answer: First of all: Don't forget your Eleven Step Breakdown and your sequence sheet or outline. Use them. This will help you go from event to event, keep the pace of the story going. You want to keep the story moving forward. Second: Divide Act Two into two parts.

Answer: There is no rule here. Your story will dictate how long your spend in each step of the Eleven Steps. Just keep in mind that whether you are in an area of your script where things are going well for the protagonist or in an area where things are falling apart, if you are at the halfway mark, consider a plot twist that will heighten the stakes even more, broaden (or tighten) the world even more and force your protagonist to switch gears.

Question: Do many films place the midpoint at the end of All Goes Well (Step #8) and the beginning of the All Falls Apar (Step #9)?

Answer: Yes. But remember, it's not necessary.

3. Finally the protagonist, while pursuing his goal, will hit an emotional or physical wall that cannot be scaled. *This is a denial that will force the protagonist to consider a new path, a new option, an alternate course as he pursues his overall want.*

Take a look at the chapter that includes Film Breakdowns. You will see how each film story handles these same basic story points differently. Every story will have its own pace and spend different amounts of time in each step.

Let's move into specifics of ACT TWO.

The First Half of Act Two

The exciting blush of Act One—setting up the world and the great characters and interesting situations—is over. Now the hard work begins.

The Second Opportunity

Step #4. In Act One, your protagonist has failed to achieve her goal. Most, or all, logical paths have been explored and have not led to success. Your protagonist needs to find a new way to continue the pursuit of her goal. Does a Fairy Godmother appear? Does the protagonist get a new job? Experience a divorce? A death? Is she the victim of a crime? Does she make a decision to become a criminal? Does he move out of his parents' house? Remember, the Second Opportunity does *not*, necessarily, have to look like a positive option. Does Maximus, in **THE GLADIATOR,** *want* to become a slave and gladiator? No. But this terrible circumstance is the opportunity that eventually allows him to achieve his goal.

The protagonist doesn't know the outcome of his journey. He doesn't know what is really needed to get him to the desired end. Maybe he does meet a genie and get three wishes. Or maybe he does meet the girl of his dreams. Or maybe the second opportunity for your main character initially is looked on as a disaster or even a tragedy.

The Second Opportunity Can Bring the Protagonist Into a New World

It's time to raise the stakes and go into new and risky territory. Consider **THE BOURNE IDENTITY;** Jason Bourne, suffering from amnesia, has taken the logical steps to find the truth of his identity. All attempts fail and the police are chasing him. He reaches out to a stranger and asks for a ride to Paris. The stranger ascertains that he is a wanted by the authorities. Will she give him a ride? Will she trust him? Is she someone he can trust? Should he put someone who is not involved in his problem at risk? This decision propels him into complications that force his character to grow and change. Consider **TOY STORY;** Woody wants to be the top toy in Andy's toy collection. When Bud Lightyear arrives and usurps that position, Woody logically tries to prove that Bud is not worthy of the other toys' respect. When his attempts fail and Bud Lightyear falls out the window, Woody is forced into venturing out of his safe world to rescue Bud. This is Woody's only chance to regain the respect of his fellow toys— but this new world includes great risks including trucks, pizzerias and the sadistic boy next door.

What is the "new world" your protagonist will enter? Consider Ariel in Disney's **LITTLE MERMAID;** she has given up her fishtail for legs and now lives on land in the Prince's castle. Elle, in **LEGALLY BLONDE,** is now at Harvard Law School. Michael Dorsey in **TOOTSIE** enters into a world where he is accepted only if he continues to pretend he is a woman. The family in **THE SQUID AND THE WHALE** enter a new world in Act Two when the parents decide to divorce. Whether the new world is completely different or slightly different, Act Two should introduce a change in the status quo of your protagonist's life; one that forces him into a world that is not familiar.

Broaden the Scope of Your Story in Act Two

Can your protagonist's journey now affect a wider group of people? Consider **SILKWOOD:** In Act One, the protagonist, Karen, is concerned with a friend's health after the friend has been exposed to radiation. In Act Two, Karen is contaminated, making the personal stakes even higher. Finally, she is fighting for new laws for safer working conditions and her actions affect her boyfriend, best friend and all her co-workers at the chemical plant. In Disney's **BEAUTY AND THE BEAST,** Belle begins by wanting a new life for herself. She enters into a new world and soon her desires affect Gaston, the man who wants to marry her, the Beast and the enchanted servants and her father. Her story widens until the whole community is involved. Elle, in **LEGALLY BLONDE,** broadens her world; she's tries to fit in at Harvard Law School, she makes friends with a manicurist and she enters the professional world of law. This broadening of her world serves to aid her in finding her true sense of self. **MILLION DOLLAR BABY;** Frankie finally agrees to coach a woman boxer; something he has never considered before. **A BEAUTIFUL MIND:** John Nash is now out of University and is a respected mathematician and he moves deeper into his world of fantasy.

Conflicts About Taking Advantage of the Second Opportunity

Step #5. Remember: Drama equals conflict and conflict equals drama. If your protagonist has no conflicts about taking advantage of the Second Opportunity, you are making it more difficult for yourself to write an engaging Act Two. Find the emotional, moral, mental and physical conflicts your protagonist faces. Is she putting herself at more risk? Is he naturally passive and now he has to be active and he has no clue how to do that? Do parents (or someone close) disapprove? Do the actions have to be secret and the protagonist is bad at keeping secrets? Is she breaking a promise? Does she have a broken leg? Is he fearful of commitment? Is he going behind someone's back? Munny, the protagonist in **UNFORGIVEN** has many conflicts about going back to life as a hired killer: He promised his wife he would reform and if he goes back on his word, the chances of seeing her in heaven are gone. He has to leave his children alone with no adult to care for them. He has lost some of his skills, can no longer shoot or even ride his horse well. He worries that once away from his remote hog farm, he may succumb to old habits such as heavy drinking. His best friend refuses to join in the venture, highlighting Munny's own reversal on his promises and increasing his guilt.

Conflicts for Michael Dorsey in **TOOTSIE** when he decides to take advantage of the second opportunity to prove he can be a working actor: He has to pretend to be a woman. He has to get up extra early and shave closely. He needs a new wardrobe. He has to lie to his best female friend. His roommate thinks Michael is losing his mind. It's difficult to pursue his love interest. The director doesn't like him. The producer wonders about him. The father of the woman he loves is attracted to him as a woman.

Setting up these conflicts give the writer a great number of scenes that *need* to be written in the film. What is the outcome of all these conflicts? Will the protagonist deal with them well? How will each rise to the surface to make the journey more difficult?

Look at the film breakdowns included in this book. Note how important this step is in the character's journey.

 Exercise:

Make a list of 3–5 conflicts for your protagonist as he faces the decision of taking advantage of his Second Opportunity. Make sure you consider emotional, physical, mental, moral conflicts. Once you have these listed, write a sentence or two about a scene or scenes that you could include in Act Two that explores each conflict. Example: In **UNFORGIVEN,** Munny has promised his wife he'll give up alcohol. Once in the town, he needs to enter a saloon. There he is faced with a decision; to drink or not. The first time he is able to say no to the offer of whiskey. Later in the story, when circumstances are more dire and tense, he succumbs… and faces the consequences.

Goes For It

Step #6. The main character decides that, despite all the conflicts and/or advice against taking advantage of this second opportunity, she must pursue her *overall want*. Remember, if your protagonist is wishy-washy about achieving her goal, the audience will not connect. Whether it's winning a soccer game or saving the world, the goal has to be all-consuming. This is the most important thing in the protagonist's life at this moment. The rest of her career or love life or existence rests on the outcome of this story. Never allow your protagonist *not to care*. She may profess that she doesn't care, but the audience *has to know* that down deep, her need is paramount to her happiness or satisfaction. Find a scene that will show the decision the character makes: Will she give up or go forward?

All Goes Well

Step #7. Give your protagonist a taste of success. Let her glimpse it. Or experience it. This will make the moment when it falls from reach even more tense and powerful. If your story spends a good amount of time in this step, as does **SHAKESPEARE IN LOVE**—you must make sure there is conflict at all times. Possibility of failure needs to be present at all times. Nothing can be easy.

All Falls Apart

Step #8. Consider the emotional, physical, mental, moral areas of your film story. Consider everything that touches your protagonist's life. It's not just work that has become untenable, it's also familial life, friendships, dreams, opportunities, beliefs.

This is the part of your story where your character needs to tested. Physically and emotionally. And nothing goes right. In action films, each sequence makes the hero's plight more difficult. In romantic comedies, feelings are shattered, events are misunderstood, decisions are made for all the wrong reasons. In a drama, the protagonist might be on a downward spiral or facing death or divorce or destruction with no relief in sight.

E x e r c i s e :

Make a list of 10–12 events or things that can go wrong for your protagonist. Look at each item on the list and ask yourself how you can make this bad thing even worse. Once you have your list, write a sentence or two about the scene or sequence that will illuminate each All Falls Apart moment.

Take a look at the Film Breakdown chapter to see that a high percentage of films spend a good deal of time in the All Falls Apart area of the story.

Crisis

Think of the Crisis (Step #9) as the end of your Act Two. In classically metered screenplays, this happens around page 75 to 80. But remember, depending on the structure of your screenplay, hitting story points on a certain page is not necessary. The aim is to make the screenplay yours and yours alone and if you have a short Act One, a mid-size Act Two and a longer Act Three, your story will still work. You need to include all the classic character-story points, but not necessarily on an exact page. Audiences have been watching films for a long time; they subconsciously know the structure of film stories. Films that vary from the norm, and yet fulfill all the desired story points, are a welcome change.

There are three things that make a good crisis.

1.   Your main character should be at his *lowest point*, emotionally or

physically or both and have a moment to assess his situation. Maybe all friends are gone. Maybe family is gone. Maybe the rescue team is late, or not on its way or maybe it's been re-routed and there is no possibility of rescue. Maybe a lover has left, looks like for good. Maybe the coveted job is now out of reach. Maybe New York City is flooded, the hero has two broken legs, is bleeding profusely and nearly passed out from lack of oxygen and his girlfriend has been seduced by the antagonist. Things look dismal, the protagonist realizes his predicament and *giving up is an option.*

2. It looks as if there is *no-way-out for the protagonist.* The audience should wonder *how* this dilemma will ever be made right. Write yourself into a hole. Keep in mind character traits; it could be an *emotional* no-way-out, or it could be *physical.* If you can find a way to do both, your script will be all the better. (And then—of course- the writer must surprise the audience by creating an exit from this no-way-out situation—while still remaining true to character, story and genre.)

2. *Decision.* This is the most important part of the Crisis. The protagonist *must* make the decision to dig deeper into his soul, into his reserves of strength, into his desire to survive than he has ever dug before. The protagonist must *decide* to enter the climax. If he does not, you risk constructing a passive character who is merely swept along toward the completion of the story and his new life. Giving your protagonist a decision to make at this juncture is important. Characters, for the most part, are more interesting and compelling when they are actively engaged in the outcome of the story. If the protagonist achieves his goal through luck or through someone else's hard work, the story is not as satisfying. Let the hard work be done by the protagonist.

Note: The Crisis point works best where there is a strong possibility that the protagonist will choose another route. Therefore, the odds have to be stacked against him. Will he give up? Will he choose to go forward and face the greatest odds? Put himself and others in danger? Make that ultimate bet? Enter that darkest room? At the altar, will she choose to marry the rich, handsome man who can help make her career or will she disappoint family, friends and expectations to run off with the poor, not so handsome man who is a lonely fisherman on a deserted island because he sparks something special inside her?

Rick's crisis point in **CASABLANCA:** Ilsa has come to Rick's room in the dark of night. It's clear she loves him, he loves her. If they decide to be together, it affects their lives, it could affect the war effort against the Nazis. Ilsa is torn and asks Rick to "do the thinking for both of them." Rick now has a dilemma and the audience does *not* know what he will do. Will he choose love? He loves her, he has a strong ego and will feel validated to show others that Ilsa chooses him over a great war hero. Or, will Rick choose honor? Will he choose to take a side in a war in which he has steadfastly worked to stay neutral? Rick's crisis: Will he choose personal happiness or the chance to contribute to the greater good of the world?

Dorothy's crisis point in **WIZARD OF OZ:** Dorothy, Tin Man, Scarecrow and Lion finally (after a wild Act Two where they have dealt with the Wicked Witch and know she's powerful and evil) get to see the Wizard. Dorothy thinks her journey is over, that she will now get to go home. But the Wizard tells them that they have to fetch the broom from the Wicked Witch in order to gain his help to get Dorothy home. Will Dorothy decide to face the evil witch again? Put her friends in danger? They could die in the process. She could stay in Oz forever, it's pleasant, she's adored. She could give up her dream and live here with her friends. Wouldn't that be easier? But does she decide to take the easy route?

Max's crisis point in **COLLATERAL:** Max, the taxi-driver, has to decide whether to wreck his own cab and possibly kill himself (and Vincent the hit man) in order to stop Vincent from continuing his killing agenda. Does Max save his own skin and say to hell with others? Or does he put himself on the line?

Ellie's crisis point in **IT HAPPENED ONE NIGHT**: Ellie thinks Peter has left her and she goes home to her father to marry the fortune hunter. (Note: In romantic comedies, *giving up* at the crisis point is a well-used option. Of course, in the climax, the two lovers usually reverse and take an active role in making their relationship work). The climax is all about two questions: Will Peter be able to get through to Ellie before the wedding takes place? Will Ellie reverse her "wrong" decision?

John Book's crisis point in **WITNESS:** Book sees Rachel bathing. He loves her. She's beautiful. She is making herself available. He has to decide

"Witness" Harrison Ford, Kelly McGillis
photo supplied by Globe Photos

whether to pursue making love to her or not… knowing the life-changing consequences of his decision.

Act Two Advice

1. Keep your subplots working. Your "B" and "C" stories should be heading more and more in the direction of your protagonist's "A" story. In Act Three you will want all your stories to intersect or affect each other, so don't let them veer off into a land (no matter how interesting) that has nothing to do with your main story.

2. Runners! If there's a "running gag" or "running visual", find the most powerful spots to place them. A runner should be used at least 3 times (or it's not a runner).

3. Keep your theme going. Write a few scenes or sequences that support the theme. Make the scenes or sequences organic, but don't shy away from having your point of view shine.

4. Character development. All main characters have to change. *Show* the audience how it is happening over the Second Act. Show the audience the factors that are affecting the character. Don't let the change happen all at once at the end of your screenplay.

5. Make sure all your subplots and secondary characters are introduced. You don't want to introduce characters in Act Three just when you

need them to tie up the plot. If you do this, Act Three will seem too "easy" and "convenient" and your audience will feel cheated.

6. Reversals. So you're writing along and things seem to be going in the right direction for your main character. Don't let things go too smoothly for too long. Pull the rug out from under him. If things are going badly, maybe add a glimmer of hope. Keep the audience guessing.

7. Pace. Don't let things slide. You can take a breather to do a character or theme moment....but keep the action going. There should be a sense of the action quickening in its pace (even in a drama) as you head into the latter part of your screenplay. Consider making the scenes shorter to give a sense of pace.

8. Let new information come out. This is important. This will keep the story growing. Let the story broaden in scope.

9. At the end of Act Two, your main character needs to be at his CRISIS point. Will he be strong enough to go forward into the climax for the final battle or will he give up? Let your main character be in charge of his actions, his choices. Create a decision point for the protagonist.

Chapter Summary

- Act Two can be divided into two parts for better manageability.

- Use the Eleven Steps as a guide to make sure there are highs and lows in Act Two.

- Act Two focuses on Steps #4 through #9 of the Eleven Step Structure.

- Act Two needs to open the scope of the story and the character's world.

- The Midpoint should feature a shift in stakes or the story.

- Act Two should explore character growth, physical and emotional.

- Act Two must prepare the protagonist and the audience for the climax of the film story.

Chapter Nineteen

WORKING ON ACT THREE

Can a weak Act Three make the entire film experience disappointing? Yes.

Can a writer construct an Act Three that satisfies and surprises? Yes.

Your protagonist has to earn the end of his story. Imagine if you had saved up for years to get tickets to the Super Bowl. You love the game of football; the competition, the fight, the hoopla, the excitement. You're in your seat, it's the middle of the fourth quarter and the game is tied. Suddenly the ref calls the game and everyone goes home. You have been robbed of the cathartic joy or sorrow you would have experienced at the end of the game—depending if your favorite team won or lost. You feel as if your hard-earned money was ill-spent. You feel cheated.

The audience goes to a film with the same expectations of going to a sporting event. They desire a cathartic experience. They have picked their genre, they have arrived with certain expectations. Give them an exciting experience; it could be thought-provoking, it could be akin to a roller coaster ride, it could be an emotional experience. Make them cry. Laugh. Scream. Think. They have paid their money—they deserve a story with an ending that will make them feel their money was well-spent.

Some producers want to know what the end of the film is before talking about the rest of the story. In their opinion, if there isn't an exciting, meaningful, stunning end to the story—there won't be a good film. There's something to that.

The climax of your film story must top all the other moments of the story. In action or emotion or in revelation.

The final truths about the character and the situation revealed after the climax is over need to be satisfying and challenging. A writer should include a sense of future for the protagonist. Not all questions about the protagonist's new outlook or situation have to be answered, but the audience needs to know that one chapter of the main character's life has come to some sort of closure, and that he is moving onto another.

Audiences have committed to your story, they have become involved in Acts One and Two. Now you must deliver on their hopes and expectations. Surprise them, as you wrap up the story. Don't disappoint your audience.

Climax

The climax (Step #10) is the culmination of all the story elements set up in Acts One and Two. The crisis pushes the main character into a final commitment to her goal—and straight into the climax. Once in the climax, the protagonist can't turn back. All is at risk. Dangers abound. The best climaxes are emotional and physical, and often bring about a catharsis or epiphany for the protagonist.

The climax of your film story needs to test your protagonist in a way in which she has never been tested before. She is either up for the task or not. She will win or she will lose. There is nothing in between.

The writer of an action film must design a climax full of difficult challenges and tasks. If the tasks are too easy the audience will not feel that surge of emotion when the protagonist defeats all and is triumphant. Remember: Nothing can be easy.

If, in a comedy, the complications of the climax do not rise to a high level of absurdity or craziness or level of emotion so that the protagonist has to face the most outrageous challenges of the film, the audience will be disappointed. Laughing feels good. Film-goers will choose to pay money to see a comedy because they want to laugh. Don't disappoint your audience.

If, in a romance, the climactic moments before the lovers unite (or not) are not highly charged, if the characters do not face impossible odds (emotional or physical or both) to express their love, the audience will not feel that intense worry and vicarious heartache that romance junkies long to feel.

Protagonist Faces the Antagonist

Make no easy choices. Let your protagonist be resourceful, smarter than he's ever been (smarter is better than lucky). This will help ensure that your protagonist has to call on unknown talents, rise above his personal best to triumph. Don't forget that the antagonist has to be as smart/strong/resourceful as protagonist. The protagonist and antagonist are in the final battle for dominance. Both of their flaws come into play. Who will be strong enough to rise above their weaknesses and triumph?

Gather All Key Characters Together For the Climax

The climax should bring the "A" and "B" and "C" stories together.

Consider **WITNESS.** The key characters include John Book, the Philadelphia police detective, Rachel, the Amish widow and her son Samuel, Rachel's father, the dirty cops from Philadelphia and the Amish community. These characters have affected one another throughout the film but have never been in the same place at the same time before the climax. The climax is the time to bring all story elements and characters together. Disney's **BEAUTY AND THE BEAST:** The climax brings the Beast, Belle, Gaston, the enchanted servants and the villagers together for a final battle. **KRAMER VS KRAMER** brings the major characters together for a courtroom battle. **FINDING NEVERLAND** brings all the major characters together for an emotional climax: J.M. Barrie, the ailing Sylvia and her sons, Sylvia's mother and the play, "Peter Pan". The play speaks to all of their hopes, dreams and relationships. **THE GRADUATE** brings all the major characters together at Elaine's wedding for a climactic stand off. The climax of **THE STING** brings all the major characters together for the ultimate con.

The battle of the climax—emotional or physical or both—will be richer and more resonant if the "A'," "B", and "C" stories merge.

Climaxes are stronger if they affect all the major characters.

"The Graduate" Anne Bancroft, Dustin Hoffman
photo supplied by SMP/Globe Photos

Location of the Climax

Does it matter? Yes, it does. If the writer is constructing a shoot-out for the climax of an action film, he must consider a location with an emotional significance. Think of the climactic moments in **THE GODFATHER,** all unfolds while the baptism of Michael's godchild takes place in a church. Consider **ON THE WATERFRONT:** The climax takes place on the docks of New Jersey—an emotional location for all the characters. The climax of **VERTIGO** is staged at the location of the protagonist's biggest heartache —the Mission's tower. The climax of **THE GLADIATOR** takes place in the largest stadium on Rome—an emotional place for the protagonist and the antagonist—and all major characters witness this final battle.

Consider whether the climax takes place during the day or during the night. What makes it feel more dangerous? What will make it more emotional?

The Climax is a Race to the Finish

In most cases, the pace of the film story quickens in the climax. Scenes tend to be shorter. Many films take advantage of "the ticking clock"; a certain task has to be completed before a deadline. Before a wedding. Before a bomb goes off. Before the ship sails, before the plane takes off. Before graduation. Before the aliens gain ultimate power. Before summer ends. Before the big game or sporting event. In **THE STING** all must be accomplished in split second timing, before the con is revealed, before the authorities track down the con artists. In **LEGALLY BLONDE** Elle must present her defense in court on a certain day at a certain time or her client will be sentenced to prison. In **FINDING NEVERLAND,** all must be accomplished before Sylvia dies. In **GOOD NIGHT AND GOOD LUCK,** Edward R. Murrow's broadcast needs to be completed (researched, written, presented) by a deadline imposed by the television network. In **HUSTLE AND FLOW,** the demo tape needs to be completed in time to give it to the star musician who has come to visit his old neighborhood. Consider the ticking clocks in **LORD OF THE RINGS, DAY AFTER TOMORROW, INDEPENDENCE DAY.**

Exercise:

Make a list that includes all the elements of your "A," "B" and "C" stories. Consider how they can all come together in the climax. Make a list of the major characters. Consider how they will be part of the climax. Make a list of possible locations for your climax. Consider which will have the most resonance.

Stay Consistent with Your Genre

Be true to your genre. The climax must deliver the expected in an unexpected way. You don't want to add a Broadway musical number to the climax of a thriller in the vein of **SILENCE OF THE LAMBS.** You don't want to add a terrorist attack to the climax of a comedy in the vein of **KICKING AND SCREAMING.** Suddenly switching genres in the climax is disconcerting and ultimately disappointing to an audience. They have learned to trust your story, they have paid for the ride they want to go on. Give them surprises, give them the unexpected—but stay true to the genre.

The Truth Comes Out

(Step #11) The final moments of your screenplay. Answer the questions that need to be answered. The ones that don't need to be answered to bring about a satisfying conclusion to the story do *not* need to be answered.

Cinderella *did* lie and go against her stepmother's wishes. She *does* love the prince and wants to marry him. In **KRAMER VS KRAMER,** Ted's wife *does* love her son, *does* see how Ted has changed and *does* see that Ted should have primary custody of their child. In Disney's **BEAUTY AND THE BEAST,** Belle *does* love the Beast and the Beast *is indeed* a prince. In **HUSTLE AND FLOW,** the protagonist *does* go to prison, he *does* get his music out into the world and it *is* appreciated. He *will* be more generous than the rap artist who disappointed him. In **LEGALLY BLONDE,** Elle *is* at the top of her law school class, she *has* dumped her loser boyfriend, and she *will* be proposed to that night by a worthy suitor.

Question: How does the writer make a climax feel new and original and still stay true to his overriding genre?

Answer: It comes back to character. Trust your character and the singularity you have created for him. Each character will react to the stressful demands of a climax is his own way. Staying true to your characters will keep your climax fresh and new. Choose a location with resonance. Be specific about supporting stories and how they affect the "A" story. Work in surprising obstacles and reversals. Test ways of letting the protagonist *fail.* Write yourself into a corner and then *find a way out.* Ultimately, don't strive for "new and different," strive for making the climax as difficult as it can be for your very singular main character.

The New Normal

What is your protagonist's new life? What is her future likely to hold? How has this journey affected his life and choices? Is he now alone? Is she now moving on to freedom?

Give your audience a sense of the future for your protagonist. Consider **CASABLANCA;** Rick, after giving up the love of his life, clearly commits to being part of the war effort—he walks into the fog with Captain Renault, "Louis, I think this could be the beginning of a beautiful friendship…." **KRAMER VS KRAMER;** Ted is surprised when his wife gives up primary custody of their child. There is a satisfying conclusion to the story *and* an intriguing question set up about the future of this separated family. **FINDING NEVERLAND;** J.M. Barrie is given partial custody of the deceased Sylvia's children. He will share custody with Sylvia's mother, a woman with whom he has not gotten along. A definite future and conflict are ahead, it's intriguing to the audience. Consider GLADIATOR; Maximus, after being killed, is floating over the peaceful wheat fields, leaving earthly life to join his wife and child in the afterlife. The audience is left to imagine the reunion…

The Discussion After

A writer wants to ignite discussion. Because a writer is exploring a point of view, exploring a character and exploring a theme, there will be room for audiences (or readers of scripts) to agree with the writer's vision or not. *Disagreement is good.* Controversy is good. Friendly arguments are good. A writer hopes the audience will ruminate on his film story. Creating a sense of future—the new normal—will help build an afterlife for your film. Let audiences wonder about the new normal; will she make it as President of the United States? Will the criminal become a worthy member of society? Will the runaway father really become a good dad? Do just the words, "I'm sorry" really repair damage to a relationship? Will the romance last? Consider **JERRY McGUIRE;** the outcome to the romantic relationship is not a sure thing.

There is no need to tie up all the ends. There is no need for a neat, perfect wrap up.

The Protagonist Must Earn the End of His Story

She surmounts the greatest odds. He makes it through the difficult test that proves his true love. She digs deeper than she has ever dug, found hidden strength or talents to achieve her goal. He finds emotional strength or a moral compass he never knew he possessed—and he can own it. The odds are specific to the character and the story. In Acts One and Two, the writer sets up a strong antagonist, the protagonist's fears and flaws and the obstacles that stand in the way of her completing her journey and reaching her ultimate character change. In Act Three these obstacles need to get more dangerous, more insidious, more far-reaching. And then the protagonist succeeds (or not).

Rarely does one hear from an audience member, "Oh the beginning of the film was great, therefore it was a fabulous experience." If *only* the beginning of the film catches their imagination, the experience will not be remembered as a good one. Rarely does one hear, "That middle section of the film makes me want to see that story over and over again." Obviously it is the good storytelling of an *entire* film that will solidify the audience's affection, but remember—the last moments are the most powerful because they leave the final impressions.

Act Three Advice

- Keep your main character's overall want consistent. Remember, immediate goals may change, but the protagonist's overall want (respect, love, power, control, sense of belonging etc.) needs to remain the same.

- Biggest battle. Biggest problem. Act Three has to top the other acts. Accelerate pace, deepen problems, raise the stakes.

- All stories should come together. The "A'," "B", " "C" stories should merge or cross paths and contribute to the conflicts and problems for your main character.

- Nothing should be easy. Or convenient. Don't let your character, who is in need of money, win the lottery. Don't let your character, who secretly loves someone, find a letter in which the object of his affection admits her love for him. That's too easy. The protagonist must earn the end of the story.

Question: What about the film stories where there is a goal (sporting event, election, battle over the love of the same man, etc.) and the protagonist does not achieve her goal but is, nonetheless, happy with her "new normal"?

Answer: Remember, it's not the *immediate goal* that has to be achieved in order to have a satisfying ending for the protagonist. Immediate goals are invented in the screenplay to move the protagonist toward his *overall want*. What is the emotional want or need that the protagonist is pursuing? If he loses the football game but gets his best buddy off steroids and brings the team together as a unit—he has gained the respect he desired? If a protagonist does not win the prom queen election but gets her family back together—has she gained the sense of belonging she desired?

- The stakes *must be* high. Life or death. Happiness or regret for the rest of the protagonist's life. A hopeful future or one that denies hope. If the stakes are not high (personal, familial, the fate of the company or world or universe or...), the audience will not be able to totally engage in the story and enjoy a cathartic experience. If the main character regards the stakes as high, the audience will too.

- Let the antagonist and protagonist really duke it out now. Face to face. No more messengers or go-betweens. They must be worthy adversaries Never take the easy way out.

- Jeopardy, tension, surprises. Emotional and or physical. In the climax, the writer wants the audience to still be wondering *what* is going to happen and *how* it is going to happen. The main character should be in danger of losing it all.

- Stay consistent in the tone of story. Stay away from sudden switching of genres.

- Let the audience get a sense of what the future holds for the characters. What path will the character be on? Does the path look promising? Does it look dangerous? We've grown attached—we've gone with them on a journey. Let us know what lies ahead. Give a sense that life *does* go on.

Chapter Summary

- Act Three must top all the other acts—it leaves the most lasting impression on the audience.

- Producers will often want to know what the Act Three includes before committing to a film story.

- The climax should be true to the overriding genre.

- Careful choosing of the location of the climax can add resonance.

- A protagonist must earn the end of his story.

Chapter Twenty

CHECKLISTS

Act One Checklist (Steps 1–3 of the Eleven Steps)

1. Introduce the world. When does the story take place? Does it take place in present day? Past? If it's a historical piece, what era are you setting your story? Future? How many years into the future? What are the rules of the societies? Make the world and its rules clear.

2. Set place. New York City? Smalltown, Montana? Los Angeles? Kansas City? Different areas of the country have different customs, different ways of speaking, different politics. Does the story take place in Africa? Europe? Asia? Is it a rural or cosmopolitan story?

3. Set tone. Is the story full of dark humor? Is the story silly and "dumber than dumb"? Does the story have intellectual overtones? Is it a rough-edged drama filled with irony? Is it ingenuous and sweet? Let the audience into the tone of the piece.

4. Set genre/genres. Horror? Comedy? Romantic comedy or romantic drama? Coming of age? Western? Mystery? Thriller drama? Remember that most films are a combination of genres—and it's a good idea to know the *overriding genre.*

5. Introduce the main character (protagonist) in such a way that will make the audience interested in spending time with him. Is it a visual introduction? Verbal? Put your protagonist in a *place* that tells the audience something about his character. Put your protagonist in the middle of an *action* that will help reveal character. Explore the character's *normal* life before the inciting incident.

6. Is your story based around one main character? Are nearly all the scenes centered around that person? There's a practical reason: Films are "star"-driven and a prominent actor will be attracted to a film in which he is the center of attention. Of course there are ensemble films and "buddy" films, but most of those, too, have a dominant character.

7.   Consider *where* you start your main character's story. Are you too close to the end of her journey? Are you too far away from the end of her journey? There is no reason for scenes that do not advance the story. Start your story as close to the *inciting incident* as possible.

8.   Have you chosen the most intense events that will contribute to the character's journey?

9.   Make the protagonist's overall want clear. (The *why* can come now or later, depending on how you want to tell your story.) If your main character is self-aware, he can voice his overall want or need. If your main character is clueless (or in denial) of her overall want or need, let another character make an observation that gives a clue to the audience. It's possible for the protagonist's want to be obvious, therefore there is no need for dialogue. How you handle clarifying the overall want of the protagonist depends on how you want to tell your story; but it has to be clear.

10.   Make sure to distinguish the difference between the immediate goal and overall *want* (need) of the protagonist. The immediate goals can be accomplished without the character achieving the overall want. The immediate goals can change, heighten, or morph as the plot plays out. Example: **LEGALLY BLONDE:** Elle's first immediate goal is to get engaged to her boyfriend. When that fails, her immediate goal is to get into Harvard. Once accomplished, her immediate goal is to join her ex-boyfriend's study group and find friends. When that fails, her immediate goal is to earn the valued internship at her professor's law firm. Elle's *overall want* (desire for respect) never changes.

11.   Make sure your main character has a flaw. Something that could hinder him from accomplishing his immediate goals and overall want at this moment in time. Make it clear what your main character lacks at this point; a reason why she can't realize this want or need at the beginning of the film. Do the same thing for the antagonist.

12.   Make sure you have considered your protagonist's biggest fear. Is it the opposite of his greatest want? Is he afraid of never being loved? Is he afraid of being powerless? Is she afraid of being poor?

13. Make the protagonist's immediate goals and overall want difficult to achieve. Nothing should come easily. Set in obstacles and reversals. Have you had your main character attempt to reach his goal; has he taken the most logical steps?

14. Introduce your antagonist. In almost all cases, you will want the antagonist to be present and active in Act One.

15. Make clear what your antagonist wants and how it relates to the protagonist's overall want. If their desires do not clash, you may have chosen the wrong antagonist for the story. Make it clear why your antagonist wants to stop the protagonist from achieving his goal.

16. Consider opportunities for telling the story visually. Consider cutting dialogue when the visual can tell the story.

17. Consider opportunities to construct active scenes. Let your characters *do* something. Allow actions to help reveal character. Sports? Projects? Hobbies? Household chores? What the characters *do* will help reveal character. (Just sitting and talking is *usually* not the most interesting choice.)

18. Introduce other characters that will affect the main character's journey. Use friends, family, love interests, bosses, co-workers, neighbors to aid in the storytelling. Set up anyone of importance in Act One, you don't want people popping up late into Act Two, it will seem as if you are just adding them because you need to bend and shape your story. Make sure each character serves a purpose. Make sure you don't have two characters doing the same thing when one character can serve the purpose. Example: In **THE GODFATHER**, the three brothers (Sonny, Fredo and Michael) are all different and serve different purposes in the story.

19. Look at different sides of your character: home life, love life, work life, friendships, the relationship with the person in the coffee shop, or at the hairdresser or the… Is there a relationship with a pet? What about parents, grandparents, siblings? Perhaps you want to explore a relationship that seems outside the main plot, one that will be used to help add dimension to the protagonist and see how that can eventually be woven into the "A" story. Example: In **LEGALLY BLONDE,** Elle finds friendship with the manicurist in the beauty salon.

20. Consider how many days (or weeks or months) you need to convey the events in Act One. Are you moving too slowly, too "moment to moment"? Would adding time (night to morning, morning to night to next afternoon, week day to week end) give you more opportunity to go from one story-progressing event to the next important event? Remember, you are in charge, the audience will follow your lead.

21. Consider introducing a runner that can be repeated as needed in Act Two and Act Three.

22. Let your main character hit a major roadblock, the *denial*. He now has to change course in order to achieve his overall want. All the small obstacles and reversals you have built into Act One will force your protagonist to consider a different option—one that will thrust him into uncomfortable territory. This denial should shut down the logical steps available to the protagonist and force him to consider a more out-of-the-box alternative.

Act Two Checklist (Steps 4–9 of the Eleven Steps)

1. Have you set a writing schedule for yourself? Are you committed to powering through this longest act?

2. Are you broadening your story's conflict? Consider letting the problem facing your protagonist be more far-reaching than he or the audience originally expected. Does the story now affect more people? Does your protagonist's actions/desires/consequences affect a wider world?

3. Are you challenging your protagonist? Are her known talents/ connections/ resources failing her? Does she have to learn new ways to accomplish her goal?

4. Check to see if the overall want of your main character is consistent. Example: Jane wants love; she thinks she's in love with Joe so she pursues Joe. But then her estranged father becomes ill and she has to leave Joe's side to nurse her father and hopefully rekindle a lost paternal love. Meanwhile, Joe has cheated on her and she falls out of love. Then her best friend Sam is revealed as her soul mate and despite swearing off romantic love due to her broken heart, she falls for Sam because love is what makes her life feel meaningful. Her original overall want is the same (desire to find love).

5. Intensify the need to achieve the immediate goals and overall want.

6. Are you using the flaws of your protagonist and antagonist to add complexity to the story?

7. Have you introduced all the subplots and secondary characters? If you add plots and characters too late, they will seem like devices inserted to help facilitate the end of the story.

8. Continue to develop your story's subplots ("B" and "C" stories) simultaneously with the main story line. These subplots should relate to the main story line. Let them have their own arc.

9. Continue using obstacles and reversals (red lights/green lights). Remember, nothing can be easy.

10. Construct consequences for every action, physical and emotional. If the protagonist confronts a new prejudice, is he now less naïve? If the protagonist finds out her lover is cheating on her, is she now more hardened and distrustful?

11. Follow the emotional path of your character. Plot is necessary, but character growth is most important.

12. Have you fashioned a midpoint of your film that raises the stakes for the character and/or twists the plot?

13. Are you revealing new information about character and/or plot?

14. Have you found an opportunity to give your protagonist a taste of success? Let things go well for a short while, tease the protagonist with a sense of victory. Then reverse the circumstances.

15. Have you thought of everything that can go wrong for your protagonist? Build on this area, it's usually the most compelling.

16. Are your "B" and "C" stories contributing to the downward spiral of your protagonist's story? Consider letting *all* areas of his or her life fall apart.

17. Are you keeping the tension high?

18. Check to see if you are starting scenes as late as possible and leaving them before the tension dissipates.

19. Keep the motor running under your story. Keep the audience wondering *what* will happen next; stay ahead of them.

20. Make sure you are not repeating information.

21. Are you thinking big? Remember, this is a story. Heighten reality. Go for the bigger choices.

22. At the end of Act Two, at the crisis moment, are you putting your protagonist in a position to make a decision? Will he go forward or give up? What path will she choose?

Act Three Checklist (Steps 10–11 of the Eleven Steps)

There is a saying among screenwriters: If Acts One and Two are constructed properly, Act Three will write itself. This, in most cases, is *almost* true. Of course the act won't write itself, it will require the same blood and tears it took to write the first 75–80 pages. But, if Acts One and Two *have* set up the protagonist and antagonist and problem of the story and crisis moment in such a way that the climax is inevitable (not predictable), the writer should know *what* he needs to write. That takes the pressure off—so hopefully the writer can complete Act Three at a quicker pace.

1. Make sure the main character's overall want remains the same. If your protagonist wanted respect at the beginning of the story, is she still in pursuit of it? Either from others or from herself? The immediate goal may be different, but the overall want needs to be consistent. Example: The protagonist may have thought she wanted respect from her father but she realizes, in the climax or resolution, as long as she has *self* respect, she can be happy.

2. Make sure all stories are coming together. Are the "B" and "C" stories affecting the "A" story and vice versa? Do all the stories' main conflicts and subplots cross paths and create even bigger and greater problems for the main character?

3. Make sure all the major characters are affected by the outcome of the story. How has the world changed (in a large or small way).

4. Are you testing your protagonist's moral and physical and emotional strength like no other place in your story?

5. Are the stakes as high as you can make them? Is your character going into her biggest battle? Facing his biggest problem? Her biggest fear? Will all defenses crack?

6. Are you accelerating the action? Are the scenes getting shorter?

7.   Have you allowed the antagonist and protagonist to really confront each other? Face to face. No more messengers or go-betweens. Never take the easy way out.

8.   Have you created surprising and exciting climactic scenes for your story?

9.   Is your main character in danger of *losing it all?*

10. Have you avoided tying up everything in a bow?

11. Have you created a surprising but satisfying ending? When the truth comes out and the new normal is revealed, is there a sense of the future?

Just a Few More Reminders

1.   Know your audience. Ask yourself, who will be interested in the story I am telling. If the answer to that question is "everyone" or "all teens" or "horror film lovers" or another large segment of the movie-going population, then full-steam ahead. If not, then know that you may be writing a smaller movie that will be harder to get produced. But if you are passionate about it, full-steam ahead.

2.   Does your screenplay have a point of view? A theme? Is it trying to say something about the human condition or the world?

3.   Have you done the research you need to lend real detail to your story?

4.   Are your main characters complex? Are they "this but also that…" Examples: Strong but insecure. Loveable but neurotic. Intelligent but a bad judge of character… Heroes with faults are more believable and more interesting than perfect heroes. Villains with some moral code are more believable and interesting than villains who are evil, love evil, pursue evil in every shape and form.

5.   Have you built characters who are different from one another? Do they disagree? Do they argue? Do they have different beliefs? Do they have different speech patterns? Different educations? Different backgrounds?

6.   Is there a dramatic question driving your screenplay? Will she find true love? Will he find the treasure and save the world? Did he pull

the trigger? Will the audience be hooked into the question and enjoy the ride?

7. Have you created obstacles that seem insurmountable—both emotionally and physically? Is your screenplay full of reversals and surprises? Not just in the plot but in individual scenes? Every scene should accomplish something.

8. Have you been true to your genre? If it's a comedy, is it funny? If it's a horror film, is it scary? If it's a drama, will tears be in the eyes of the audience? If it's historical, is it true to the period?

9. Have you told your story visually? Have you used sound, weather, time of day, location to help set mood and lend story elements?

10. Emotion. Emotion. Emotion. Build characters who feel deeply. Don't be afraid to cull your own emotional depths as you write. If you don't feel it, the audience may not either.

11. Are you committed to finishing your screenplay? Set a schedule. Have readings of finished acts to spur the creative process. Write even when you don't feel like it. Get it done!

How Your Script Looks is Important

Competition in the screenwriting world is fierce. Readers, executives, directors, producers have a wide array of screenplay choices. They will only recommend a few for serious consideration. You want your screenplay to get produced; that is your end goal. Give yourself *every* opportunity—and that starts with making sure your screenplay is in proper format. *Never* turn in a script that is not up to industry standards.

- There are good books on proper formatting. These include: Cole and Haag's *The Complete Guide to Standard Script Formats* and Christopher Riley's *The Hollywood Standard: The Complete and Authoritative Guide to Script Style and Format.*

- Screenwriting programs such as Final Draft have proper formats built into the program.

- Screenplays found on-line or in bookstores are wonderful resources but be careful about using them as format guides. Some will be production drafts, where each scene is numbered; the draft of your screenplay that goes into the studio or into the speculation market should *not* include production scene numbers. Other caveats about using on-line scripts or published scripts as template: Downloading inconsistencies (either to your computer or from the original manuscript to the website) can occur. Published screenplays are formatted to fit book size and publishing needs. Rarely are they published in industry standard format.

- Your screenplay should be a good, fast read. Don't over explain things that don't need explaining.

- Stay away from including camera direction; you are writing a story, not directing the camera.

- Let the set designer design the set, let the set decorator decorate. All you need to do is let the reader know the location and a few adjectives about the sense of the place. Messy? Neat? Modern? Maybe one specific element if it speaks to character. No need to tell the reader who designed the chairs or painted the pictures (unless is *affects* the story).

- Let the director block the actors' moves. Blocking should not be included unless "standing up" or "sitting down" is pivotal to the storytelling moment. Chewing, taking a breath (beat) are details best left out. Crossing to the door, turning the knob, opening the door and stepping out and closing the door is extraneous detail (you can write simply: the character strides out or limps away ... or simply "exits").

- Create the mood. No need to be specific about the lighting unless it is pivotal to a story or character arc.

- Respect the reader. No need to repeat information in action lines and/or in dialogue.

- For the most part, keep the dialogue short, crisp, character-true and as natural as possible. No need to build complete sentences, people rarely talk in complete sentences.

- Shoot for a page count close to 100. An overly long screenplay is not a professional calling card.

- Keep the plot simple, let the characters become complex.

- Know *clearly* what your film story is about—if you don't know, chances are the reader will not be able to glean it from your screenplay.

Chapter Twenty One

THE BUSINESS OF BEING A SCREENWRITER

Can a screenwriter ignore the practical business side of the film business?
No.

Can a screenwriter find a way into the business? Yes.

A writer writes. He doesn't just talk, for years and years, about that one screenplay that's **almost** finished.

Once you dip your big toe into the world of screenwriting, you will meet a hundred, maybe a thousand people who are "in the process" or who "have an idea they want to get totally worked out before they put pen to paper" or "who have been stuck in Act Two and are waiting for the cataclysmic breakthrough with their screenplay before they get it to the right producer"…

Most of these people will never finish their scripts. You don't want to be one of these people. They are talkers, not do-ers.

You want to be a do-er.

You can be quiet, you can be the life of the party, you can shout your brilliance to anyone who will listen or just, unobtrusively, finish your scripts and send them through the right channels to the right producers, directors or agents, contests… any personality is fine in the screenwriting world.

The only thing that is absolutely necessary? That you *finish* your work. That you complete what you set out to do. Half finished screenplays are of no value. Ideas—and even treatments or outlines, by themselves are not enough. The finished, polished, well-executed screenplay is the business card you need.

How do you make sure you are a do-er and not a talker?

Put Yourself on a Schedule

Know when you work best.

I am an early morning person. I get up, maybe 4:30 or 5:00 am and head to my local 24 hour coffee shop (so I am not tempted to go back to bed, clean the house, decide what to get out of the freezer for dinner or browse the internet—yes, I avoid internet cafes—too distracting.) I find if I start my day focusing on my story or script for two or three or four hours, then I can take a break (do an errand or attend a meeting) and be able to reconnect with the piece any time during the rest of the day. The creative problems I am struggling with have gotten into my psyche first thing and live with me all day. An average day of writing? Seven to eight hours.

I asked other writers to share their methods:

Emmy winning screenwriter and film director Jane Anderson (**PRIZEWINNER OF DEFIANCE OHIO, NORMAL** and other feature films) has her routine: "I go along like any good writing stiff; I hit the computer from nine to five, five days a week, an hour for lunch, a few breaks in between to stretch out the kinks in my neck. But if I hit the wall about two or three, I stop. I used to make myself plow through the exhaustion point but nothing decent ever gets written when your muse cries 'uncle.'"

Screenwriter Tom Benedek (Golden Globe nominated **COCOON, ZEUS AND ROXANNE** and other feature films) has a routine: "I go to my desk every morning and stay there for three hours. Eventually I start to write. And I never know if it is good or not. I will believe I am having the best day of my life at the computer just because it is flowing easily. And another day I will struggle and struggle and think what I am doing stinks. My assumptions are sometimes correct, sometimes not. In the afternoons, I take my notebook and my outline and the pages I have written and review. I never know as I write. It is only in the rewriting that I really understand what I have."

Screenwriter Diane Lake (Academy Award nominated **FRIDA**) has her own way of working. "I'm not driven by schedule, I'm driven by characters and scenes. Depending on where I am in the writing, I may wake up and run to the computer with the solution to a problem I've been pondering. Or, I may wake up and spend the day judiciously avoiding writing because there's a problem I have yet to figure out with the scene I am on. But I do have one consistent writing pattern; when I am near the end of a script I cannot stop—literally. If I've done my job and everything's set up as it should be, those last 20 pages just pour out of me. It's a tremendous feeling… like when you were 10 and riding a sled down the biggest hill in town!"

Award winning screenwriting partners Raymond Singer and Eugenia Bostwick (**MULAN, JOSEPH KING OF DREAMS, HBO'S IRON-JAWED ANGELS**) have separate routines. Raymond: "My day always begins with not writing. I take my daughter to school, have a cup of coffee with friends at the local hang-out and then, about 9, find myself at my desk. I usually know how I'll begin because I've stopped the day before where, even though the characters may have stopped talking to me, the Big Picture is clear and I've made notes the previous day to jumpstart me in the morning. I work till I get to the scary place of 'not knowing what's next' and then write some more. The 'some more' is usually what I rewrite the next day to get into the flow of it all again. I'm never without a small notebook and bits of paper and yellow pads pile up on my desk like snow in winter. Or litter on the beach. Take your pick." As partners, Raymond and Eugenia initially work separately on different areas of the script (from an outline they have agreed on) and then exchange pages and polish each other's work. At the end of the process, they finally work in the same room and discuss (argue) over each sentence, word or image and do the final polish on the script together.

Every writer will have his or her routine. Some like to work in coffee shops or libraries. Some need it quiet, some need noise or music in the background. Some write in huge streaks after weeks of "thinking" and taking notes. Whatever the routine, the most important thing is that the work gets completed, polished and out into the world.

The Spec Script

This is a script written on speculation (no one is paying you to write it). Most writers start here and most writers continue to write spec scripts throughout their career. Spec scripts are very important. Put it in your mind that you need to write at least one spec script a year. Even if you are being paid to write, try to squeeze in time to do your original work. Not only will it keep you in touch with your singular point of view, your own voice, your own interests (*you* are choosing the topic, the characters, the story, the voice—not the producer or production company) but you will also, at the end of the process, own your work.

Question: What if you are holding down another job while you are trying to find a paying gig as a screenwriter?

Answer: Obviously, your day to day writing schedule will reflect your other commitments. But know that *other* screenwriters, who are also holding down other jobs, are using their weekends, their early mornings, their late nights to finish their screenplays. If you want to compete—you have to put in the time to *finish and polish* your work *as well as* find a path for it to get into the hands of people who will make a difference in your career.

Question: What if I
get a specific note from
a producer and he has a
specific way he wants
the note addressed. Can
I tell him I found a
better way to approach
the problem?

Answer: First, try to
address the note the
way the producer
suggested. You want
him to be invested in
the script emotionally
and this is a way to get
achieve that. And his
suggestion might work
great. If, after you've
given it a solid try, you
feel the note is better
addressed in another
fashion, *show* him the
work you did doing it
his way—and then
gently suggest that it
might be approached in
another way—and
which way does he like
best? If this is a spec
script and you are not
getting paid to write or
rewrite it, it's ultimately
your decision. If the
producer is paying for
the script, it's a good
idea to make his idea
work.

Always writing on assignment may fill your bank account, but at the end of the process, you don't *own* your work. Whoever has paid you to write the script—he or she owns it. If the film does not get produced (and a very high percentage do not) you are not in the position to try to sell it to another studio or production company because it is not your property. A writer should have pieces all her own, that are her brain children, that she can try sell or produce or direct herself.

Taking Notes

There are few people who can give notes without bias. Each person has different values and life experiences, different senses of humor, different points of view. It is the writer's job to be strong (not inflexible) and to believe in his or her own vision. Yes, a friend or an agent or peer who reads many scripts might have valid and helpful suggestions and may give fabulous notes that will enhance your script. But there are also friends, peers and industry professionals who give notes that can take the life out of a story. No one but the writer truly understands how changing one detail of character or story can completely unravel an entire script. Protect your work. Know why you wrote it, know your theme, know what makes it important to you. Let notes give *your* vision more clarity. Don't rewrite just to please someone else.

Sometimes an agent, producer, director, friend or whoever is giving you notes that will point to a problem in the screen story. You may agree or disagree that the story element *is* a problem. If you get the same note from multiple sources, it's usually time to consider the note's validity. There probably is a problem. All of those readers may have had different suggestions for *how* to fix the problem area. Don't get confused. It doesn't matter how you fix it, just that it gets fixed. *You* will come up with the fix *your* way. Follow your own path.

Be grateful for all notes. Someone has taken the time to read your work and put some thought into it. Even if you don't take the notes, thank the reader for his time and assure him that all notes will be considered. There is no need to get defensive, just write down all the comments, go home… and sit with your script and consider if the notes are something you want to implement—or not.

Note: *Remember, a writer who writes for the existing marketplace could miss the mark. Films take time to write, produce and distribute. If a writer sets out* *to write a script in the vein of the film she just saw in at the local multi-plex, by the time the script is finished, the vogue may have changed. There's no predicting what will catch an audience's imagination. A writer's original work should always reflect the characters and stories that the writer is passionate about—a writer needs to follow his own muse.*

On Assignment

When you are hired to write a script for a production company, director, producer or friend or other entity—and there is payment involved—this is called writing "on assignment." By accepting payment for writing, the screenwriter is put in a position of trying to please the boss. There needs to be a sense of collaboration. Some producers will want the writer to take the lead, others will want to help shape the story and script. If you work on assignment, be open to collaboration.

The Pitch

The pitch is a verbal presentation of your film story. Development executives and producers hear pitches nearly every day, looking for that story that might make a box-office hit. If the pitch catches the imagination of the producer, a deal would be made and you would be hired to write the screenplay of the story that you "pitched". A good pitch should be no more than ten minutes, should concentrate on the main character's growth and journey, set up the world and major conflicts of the story, sketch in the opposing and aiding forces and be as exciting as you can make it. Be creative, bring in simple visual aids if available, but keep it short. Using the Eleven Step Story Structure as a guide will ensure that the pitch has a solid beginning, middle and end and includes a series of conflicts and character changes.

Agents

An agent is the writer's representative in the film business. The writer agrees to pay his or her agent ten percent of each writing assignment or sale.

There are two kinds of agents: Agents who love the written word and have opinions about material and get passionate about your work and are interested in the sale of your material … and agents who rarely read a script, rely on coverage of readers and assistants to form their opinions and are *only* interested in the *sale*. Both are acceptable, both have pros and cons.

Question: Do the studios buy a lot of pitches every year?

Answer: Selling a story on a pitch is not easy, especially for a writer with no credits. If you are passionate about the project and are lucky enough to get into a room to pitch your story, go for it because it's a chance to make contacts in the professional arena. Don't be disappointed if the pitch is not bought. Don't stop believing in your story. Just be working on the screenplay as you pitch it around town. Ultimately, a script is more easy to sell than a pitch.

Question: How can you tell if an agent is legitimate?

Answer: Reputable agents will be signatories of the Writers Guild, the union that represents writers in film and television. This means they have agreed to abide by the rules, regulations and industry standards set by the Guild.

Question: What if an agent or writer's representative asks me for money before they will read my script?

Answer: This is not allowed under the WGA contract. Most likely this person is not a reputable writer's representative.

The agent who actually reads your screenplay and has opinions and wants to give you notes can be helpful or harmful. Are the notes of value? Do the notes enhance your vision? Would the notes change your screenplay significantly and in a way that would take a detour from your original impetus? Is the agent trying to fashion your screenplay to fit the current marketplace? Or to fit his version of your story? Is the agent reluctant to put your work into the marketplace for some reason? Does he believe in it or not?

The agent who is not a reader and relies on assistants to form opinions for him can also serve a purpose. If this agent is an incredible salesperson and can sell your screenplay—that can totally be sufficient. The agent has done his job. Some writers depend on mentors or peers or family for feedback on their work and do not need the extra eye of an agent.

Find an agent who approaches your work in a way that makes you feel comfortable.

The most important thing a writer must remember when working with an agent: *An agent is a businessperson.* An agent needs to pay the rent, keep his or her job, impress the boss. Most want to make a mark on the industry, just as the writer does. Agents can make their mark only through their clients. They want you to be good, they want you to be prolific, they want you to make their job easier.

Agents expect writers to network, make contacts, keep contacts, and be able to work with the various personalities of producers and directors. Once you have an agent, don't sit back and wait for the phone ring.

Agents will focus on clients who are bringing in the most return. That's reality. The writer's job, when not on assignment, is to keep writing on spec so the agent has product to move into the marketplace.

Managers

Managers seek out work possibilities and contacts for their clients. Managers usually work in tandem with agents or attorneys to identify and set up meetings with buyers/producers/directors/executives. They will help identify available jobs and are expected to know the marketplace. Managers usually deal with a smaller client pool and are more readily accessible to the writer than an agent who works in a large company and has a long client list. Managers take another percentage of the writer's paycheck; usually this percentage is negotiated on an individual basis.

Attorneys

Writers would be wise to employ an entertainment attorney to look at any contract or deal memo they are interested in signing. Since it is the studio and production company attorneys' job to write contracts designed to keep as much money and control in their employers' pockets, writers need attorneys who have *their* best interests in mind.

A studio or production company's attorney keeps his or her job by finding ways of keeping rights, residuals, bonuses, monies, sequel privileges, participation in toys or books or television shows based on the writer's material safely in the studio or production company's control. A writer's attorney's job is to find a way for his or her client to participate in anything that emerges from the writer's material.

An entertainment attorney who is on the writer's side and has a wide knowledge of the industry players, the studio system, and all areas of the film business is a necessary adjunct to the working screenwriter's life.

How Does a Writer Get an Agent or Manager or Attorney?

The most simple answer is this: by getting a writing job and proving you are a person who will make money as a screenwriter. Remember, agents and managers and attorneys are businesspersons and to them, the making of films is more a business than an art.

This true story exemplifies a road to getting an agent: After I had moved to Los Angeles and landed a few feature writing jobs as well as worked on staff on a television show, I recommended a talented friend to my agent. She had a spec half hour comedy script that was hilarious and I knew she could be successful in the television area. I asked my agent to read the script. A year went by and he never found the time (yes, this is a 30 page script, double-spaced). My friend did not wait for this agent to tell her she was good. She did not wait for him to agree to help her find work. She continued to make contacts herself. She participated in a writing seminar at the WGA in New York. There she met the head writer of one of the most successful situation comedies on network television. This head writer responded to her seminar contributions, read her spec script, thought she would be a good addition to his staff and hired her. When I called my agent to tell him the good news, he suddenly had "Just read her script last night and had planned to call her today about representing her". He asked me to please call her and tell her that he would be happy to negotiate her new contract for her.

Question: What if my friend or brother or uncle or niece is a lawyer in Oklahoma who specializes in tax law? Can I ask him or her to look at my contract?

Answer: Yes, of course you can. But you are putting yourself at a disadvantage. First of all, this lawyer will not have the expertise or the knowledge of the film business. He or she may not be able to point out certain areas in the contract that need to be questioned or adjusted. Advice: Find an attorney who has specialized in the entertainment business.

Question: How long does it take to find an agent or manager?

Answer: The competition is strong and there are many pulls on an agent and manager's time. Don't put your eggs in one basket, send your query letters and/or sample scripts out to more than one person at a time (as many as you want). Ask friends, fellow writers, family members if they know anyone in the business, try to make as many contacts as you can. Follow up your query letters or submissions with polite phone calls. Demands, over-calling, bribes etc. are considered unprofessional. Avoid letting your frustration be felt. There is no set time for expected responses. Small agencies may be better for the writer with no credits. Younger agents looking to find a new hot client may be more likely to read fresh material. Target those first.

How to get an agent's attention? Get a job. How to get a manager's attention? Get a job. How to get an attorney's attention? Get a job.

Finding Your First Job

How does one get a job without an agent or manager or attorney? Write your spec scripts. Send them into contests. With a contest win or honorable mention, you can make yourself look more bankable. Make contacts. Enroll in classes or workshops. You might learn something, but beyond that, you will begin to network with people with similar goals and interests. Once you make a connection, stay in touch. Chances are someone will land a job or an agent or manager and pave the way for friends to take advantage of that contact.

Go to screenings and be open to meeting people. Find an online chat room for screenwriters. Of course, always use your best judgment, find writers as serious as you are and don't get bogged down in critiquing others work if it takes time from your own writing. Be your own judge, find fellow writers whose work you admire and stay in touch.

The WGA (Writers Guild of America) holds seminars and events; some are open to non-WGA members. The Academy of Television Arts and Sciences in Los Angeles holds regular events where industry professionals answer questions or give presentations; some are open to non-members.

Send out query letters asking agents, managers, producers, development executives to read your work. What does a query letter look like?

Query Letter

A query letter is written in hopes of interesting a buyer or writer's representative in reading your film script. First, let them know who you are—in one sentence. Are you new to Los Angeles? Are you a lawyer or doctor or minister or cowboy who has turned to screenwriting? If you have been referred to them by someone, let them know that. In one sentence.

Fill in the blanks in this letter—and then extrapolate and make it your own.

Your Name

Your Email Address
Your Telephone Number
Your Street Address
Your City and State and Zip

Name of Agent/Manager/Producer/Actor
Name of Their Company or Affiliation
Their Street Address
Their City, State, Zip

Date

Dear Ms. Or Mr. _____,

My name is _____, (add one personal thing about you as a writer). I have recently completed an original screenplay entitled _____ .

TITLE OF YOUR FILM SCRIPT is a (FILL IN GENRE) about a (FILL IN WITH YOUR LOGLINE) . Add one or two short sentences (not run-on sentences) about plot or character that you think is relevant and will pique their interest.

What strikes most people as unique about this script, is that my main character is (FILL IN DETAILS WITH JUST A FEW SENTENCES). In my opinion, this script could attract actors like _____ or _____.

I am hoping you will consider reading my script because I admire your work on (MENTION THE FILM HE OR SHE WAS INVOLVED IN—OR THAT THE AGENCY HAS A GREAT REPUTATION OR....)

I'll give your office a call next week to see if it is possible to send in my script for your perusal—or feel free to contact me. Of course, I am willing to sign a release agreement.

I am hoping you will find my script of interest.

Thank you,
Your Name
(Repeat your Email address)

Keep it short, add a bit of personality if you feel the urge. Remember, this is a *business* and proper business approaches are expected. Check out the websites http://www.breakingin.net or http://www.wga.org for more Query Letter advice.

Contests

Enter writing contests. One of my agents told me he is more inclined to read a script that has won (or received honorable mention) in a screenplay contest.

Screenwriting Groups

There are screenwriter support groups that meet on a regular basis. Some meet in coffee shops, some meet at members' homes. Groups are usually organized like this: Screenwriters meet once a week or once a month to read their work aloud. The screenwriter may read the script, or it may be read aloud by others in the group, each taking a different character. All or parts of the script may be read in one session. The writer is then given feedback on his work thus getting support and suggestions from fellow writers.

When I moved to Los Angeles, I joined a group called the Writers' Bloc; to this day those writers remain some of my closest friends and the ones I ask to read early drafts of my screenplays. I value their opinions. Many went on to be successful, produced screenwriters and we still get together once a month to share our work and information on the business.

Be open to starting your own Screenwriting Group. Invite writers whose work and work ethic you admire.

Write. Write. Write.

Write. Write. Write. When you are finished with one screenplay, write another screenplay. When you are finished with that screenplay, write another. Get your screenplays out into the world. Ask people to read them, ask them to pass them along to anyone who might be helpful in getting the scripts into a position to be bought or produced.

Take a Meeting

Be willing to meet people in the business, people on all levels. Everyone has to start someplace and working friendships can blossom from unexpected sources.

Note: *Be protective of your time. Your main job is to write. Filling every day with meetings may not be the most productive use of your time. Put the writing first.*

Writers Guild of America

The Writers Guild of America (WGA) is a labor union composed of writers of feature films, television shows, news programs, documentaries, animation, CD-ROM and content for new media technologies. The most important duty of the WGA is to represent the member writers in negotiations with film and television producers. The WGA has constructed a collective bargaining contract that sets pay scales, health coverage contributions, credits and residuals.

The WGA contract sets minimum salaries for writing services. If a producer hires a writer, negotiations will start at the set minimum salary. In the feature arena, there is a scale of minimums that correspond to the expected budget of the film. In the television arena, there are different minimums for network and cable productions.

Employers who are signatories of the WGA (those producers who have agreed to abide by the most recent WGA collective bargaining contract) pay a small percentage, on top of the writer's salary, into the healthcare program set up by the WGA.

The WGA is responsible for determining writing credits for films and television programs. This is an important issue and the WGA takes it very seriously. A writer who receives onscreen credit will not only receive artistic recognition but he will participate in the financial rewards that an onscreen credit assures in the WGA writer's contract. The WGA has a system of arbitration; when more than one writer works on a produced project, each writer will prepare a written statement of credit expectations. The WGA has a core of arbitrators, made up of member writers who volunteer to sift through all drafts of the scripts. These arbitrators determine the percentage of work done by each writer involved in the project and thus determine onscreen credits.

The WGA monitors and collects residuals for its members. Residuals are payments for the reuse of films and television programs; if a film written by a WGA member plays on network or cable, the writer will receive a payment for its usage. If a television program is in re-runs, the writer will receive a payment for each re-run. This is a job that the WGA takes on, as one can imagine, keeping track of what films or television programs are featured in subsequent markets is a massive task.

The WGA Registry is the world's largest screenplay registration service. The main reason for registering your original work is to establish the completion date. If, at some point in your career, you feel your work has been plagiarized, you will have a registered script at the WGA that is available for any legal action you may take.

There is the WGA West, with its main office in Los Angeles and the WGA East, with an office in New York City. WGA's website is www.wga.org. Great Britain and Canada have similar unions and all work well with each other.

Favorite Websites

There are new and useful websites cropping up regularly on the internet. Here are a few of the good ones to check out:

http://www.imdb.com – Internet Movie Database. Include film credits, industry news, filmmaker dialogues and more.

http://www.moviebytes.com – Moviebytes is a good source for contests, industry news, what's selling and what's in production.

http://www.boxofficemojo.com – Online movie production and box office reporting site. Also includes reviews, industry bios and more.

http://www.wordplayer.com – Wonderful site aimed at screenwriters, with articles written by screenwriters.

http://www.script-o-rama.com – Drew's Script-o-rama is a great place to start to look for the produced screenplays you want to read or download.

http://www.screenplayguide.com – This site deals with format questions.

http://www.scriptsales.com – This site features Done Deal, a listing of recent sales of books, scripts and pitches. It also includes lists of agents, managers, law firms, production companies, and more.

Use your search engine to seek out other sites that might be of interest to you. Technology has made it easy to get answers to most of your questions. Take advantage. I have had students find writing and production jobs through Craig's List!

Chapter Summary

- A knowledge of the business if being a screenwriter is necessary for success.

- The most important thing is to continually produce (write) product for the marketplace.

- Agents, managers and attorneys can help the career of a screenwriter.

- Create a network of writers and business associates in the industry.

- Write. Write. Write.

ELEVEN STEPS FILM BREAKDOWNS

Breaking down successful films can illuminate good structure. All of the films included in these Eleven Steps breakdowns are award-winning and well-respected films. Note how the breakdowns focus on character and the character's journey. They all begin with the protagonist's want and show how all the elements of the screenplay focus on that facet. Watch these great films again; once you understand the screenwriting process, you will never look at a film the same way again.

ALL ABOUT EVE

(1950)

written by Joseph Mankiewicz

In the theatre world, an actress is only as great as her last role. An actress is only as young her audience will believe. An actress is only a star until the public doesn't want to hear about her anymore. Beauty as well as the affection of a fickle public changes over time. How does an aging actress find peace with herself as she sees her star begin to wane? What does she discover to be most important in life? Adoration of her fans or true friendship and love?

Margo is the main character. She has been a star actress for years now, but she lives in constant fear that as she ages, she will lose all she has worked hard to gain. We see this in three areas of her life: her career, her love life and her friends. The story becomes universal because it deals with her love life and her friendships; remember to round out your characters, deal with many aspects of their lives.

Eleven Step Breakdown and Notes

1. MARGO WANTS to be appreciated and loved and feel secure. WHY? Fear of aging and losing her appeal. She is insecure and covers it with bite and anger. Margo's character flaw is her insecurity and her sharp tongue. This flaw threatens to undo her.

2. MARGO LOGICALLY goes about getting what she wants by

   a. Playing parts that still portray her as "young"

   b. Constantly demanding attention

   c. Testing Bill, the man who loves her by accusing him of not caring about her because he has plans to go to Hollywood to pursue opportunities in his directing career

3. MARGO IS DENIED a sense of security

   a. When Bill heads off to California for work

   b. Critics comment on her age

    c. A deep-seated fear that she can't shake takes hold; she is convinced that aging will cost her all she holds to be important

4. SECOND OPPORTUNITY FOR MARGO TO GET WHAT SHE WANTS: Eve comes into Margo's life. Eve flatters and fawns and makes Margo feel important and respected. This give Margo a sense of security.

5. CONFLICTS ABOUT TAKING ADVANTAGE OF THIS OPPORTUNITY

    a. Margo's dresser is not too happy or trusting of Eve.

6. MARGO DECIDES TO GO FOR IT

    a. Eve is set up in Margo's home as personal secretary/assistant

7. ALL GOES WELL FOR MARGO

    a. Eve thinks of everything, flatters Margo and waits on her hand and foot. Margo can't remember how she got along without Eve.

8. ALL FALLS APART FOR MARGO

    a. Margo begins to sense that Eve is overstepping her bounds; that she is stealing affections of friends

    b. Eve remembers Bill's birthday and arranges a call from Margo (who hasn't remembered); Margo wonders if this was staged to put Margo in a bad light

    c. Margo sees Eve "pretend" to play Margo's part on stage. Suspicions and insecurities grow.

    d. Margo's lover, Bill, doesn't come directly to her when he returns from California, he talks to Eve first

    e. Margo's friends defend Eve

    f. "BUMPY RIDE" disastrous party where Margo offends everyone

    g. Margo finds out that Eve has been given the job as Margo's understudy without Margo's permission; this signals Margo's falling power

    h. Margo and Bill argue and break up

    i.   Friends try to get Margo and Bill back together. They arrange circumstances for Eve to go on one night as understudy; give Margo and her lover time together to patch up quarre

    j.   Margo is waylaid in the country

9.   CRISIS

    a.   Margo has to decide whether to accept the inevitable; will she pull out all the stops to get back to the theatre in time to make the curtain or will she let her ambition rest for moment to reflect on what's most important to her—the love of Bill or holding onto her career.

10.   CLIMAX

    a.   Eve is huge success as understudy

    b.   Critic writes anti-Margo—pro- Eve

    c.   Margo has to decide to "out" Eve and reclaim her friendships and position

    d.   Margo knows that Eve makes a play for Bill.

    e.   Margo knows Eve politics for part in new play by Margo's friend playwright—a part that was meant for Margo. Margo knows she is too old for the part but will she be able to face the truth and move on?

    f.   Margo reclaims her friends and place in the theatre

11.   TRUTH COMES OUT TO MAKE THINGS RIGHT

    a.   Margo's lover makes it clear he wants her. Margo finally accepts that his affections do not rely on her staying one age or staying as the reigning diva of the theatre

    b.   All are aware of Eve's manipulations and underhanded-ness. Margo's friends stand by her. She has found appreciation and security in the community of her friends and lover. She has found peace.

Eve's Character Arc

As the antagonist, Eve also has an arc that is as interesting as Margo's (the protagonist). Eve is a bit of cipher. Film-goers have varying views of her duplicity; was it all a plan from the very beginning, or did her plan of taking over Margo's life hatch over time? Is she the supreme manipulator or did she "become" a manipulator as she struggled to succeed in the world as a professional actress? My opinion? Eve is clever and had a plan from the very beginning. As the antagonist, she needs to be working against the protagonist from the very outset. Remember, every protagonist needs a worthy antagonist.

Eleven Step Breakdown and Notes

1. EVE WANTS to be appreciated, loved and feel secure. (Note it's the same as Margo's, but while Margo is already a star, Eve is at a different point in her career.) WHY does Eve need to be appreciated and adored? There's something lacking in her history, never clear just what—but we know she's made up stories about herself to make herself feel important/special.

2. EVE LOGICALLY goes about trying to get appreciation, love and security by

    a. Making sure people (especially Margo's best friend Karen) see her every night at the theatre. She finally speaks to Karen and wangles an introduction to Margo. Once inside the dressing room, she wangles herself into a job working for Margo.

    b. Getting all of Margo's friends (save her dresser) to think Eve is wonderful. Becoming friendly with them.

3. Eve's DENIED when Margo starts to catch on to Eve's ways and begins to distrust her intentions. Eve rightly feels her days may be numbered…

4. SECOND OPPORTUNITY FOR EVE TO GET WHAT SHE WANTS. Eve manipulates Karen into getting Eve an audition to be Margo's understudy.

5. CONFLICTS ABOUT TAKING ADVANTAGE OF THIS OPPORTUNITY

a. Eve's game is getting more complicated. She has to juggle a lot of balls/personalities. Eve has to keep the fact that she is going to audition from Margo for as long as possible.

b. Addison, the theatre critic, is watching and getting wise to her. They are common souls, he understands Eve and sees her for what she is; an ambitious manipulator.

c. Eve knows her "assistant to Margo" days will be over and there is a clock running; it's now or possibly never.

6. EVE DECIDES TO GO FOR IT—she auditions for the part.

7. ALL GOES WELL

a. Eve gets understudy role.

b. Eve manipulates Karen again (or takes advantage of Karen's desire to get Margo and Bill back together). She convinces Karen to set up a circumstance where Margo will miss a train back the city, thus missing a performance. Eve goes on in the star role when Margo is waylaid in country.

c. Eve's a hit. She gets reviewed. She is now the hottest thing in town.

d. Eve starts a campaign to convince Karen's husband, the playwright, to give her the plum role in his new play. She is also after his affections and he is interested.

e. Eve and Addison become close allies, he helps her by writing about her in the paper.

f. Eve gets the part in the new play and she feels she has won Karen's husband also.

8. ALL FALLS APART

a. Seeds of doubt about Eve's intentions begin to grow throughout the community of her allies.

b. Eve's arrogance is starting to show; she thinks she indestructible now and begins to show her true colors.

c. Karen sees her for what she is and retracts her friendship.

d. Addison is now her only friend.

e.   Eve is snubbed by Margo loyalists at a fancy restaurant.

9.   CRISIS—Eve, realizing that Karen is now totally on to her, makes the decision to blackmail Karen to keep her manipulations secret. Karen will not succumb and Eve no longer has a hold over Karen.

10. CLIMAX

a.   Addison is tightening his hold on Eve. He refuses to let her pursue her desire for Karen's husband.

b.   Addison tells Eve she now belongs to him—Eve cannot outwit Addison, he's as clever and devious as she is.

NOTE: Addison is Eve's antagonist....

11. TRUTH COMES OUT TO MAKE THINGS RIGHT

a.   The final Theatre Awards Ceremony. Eve is a success (she gets what she wants) but at a price... no friends, no one she can trust.

b.   All are aware of Eve's manipulations and underhanded-ness and Margo's friends stand by Margo.

c.   Then, of course, the chilling truth: there is a young, ambitious actress waiting for Eve in her apartment. This young actress begins to play Eve's game... we know she is an Eve in the making and history will repeat itself.

NETWORK
(1976)

written by Paddy Chayefsky

Paddy Chayefsky started his television work on **PLAYHOUSE 90,** back in the 50's. Incredible writer; wrote short stories, radio plays, theatre plays, early TV dramas, his feature credits include **MARTY** (Academy Award Winner that was expanded from his TV script), **THE HOSPITAL, THE AMERICANIZATION OF EMILY;** he had his named removed from **ALTERED STATES** because he didn't like the way the movie turned out…

When I think of writers who put their whole being into their work, he always comes to mind. His POINT OF VIEW of the world is always evident; basically right in your face. His characters have opinions, he shows both sides of an argument/idea. His characters are real, have deep emotions and human frailties.

Eleven Step Breakdown and Notes

- Set up of place and time; USE OF VOICEOVER—omniscient, we don't know who's voice it is. Gives us a quick background; Howard Beal, super news anchor, is experiencing falling ratings… he's been given his two weeks notice.

- Set up that television news is changing—it's becoming all about ratings.

- SET UP OUR MAIN CHARACTER: Max (William Holden) and his friendship with Howard Beal. We learn of both of their passions for television news; going beyond the pale to get the story—the excitement of producing news, the immediacy of producing news.

1. MAX WANTS to feel that rush of excitement again in his life. WHY? He has felt it in the past through work and he has blown his past excitements up to be iconic moments in his life. He also wants to be ethically sound and successful as a network news producer as well as being a good friend.

2. MAX LOGICALLY TRIES TO KEEP EXCITEMENT ALIVE AS WELL AS BE ETHICALLY SOUND IN HIS WORK

a. He continues in his job as head of news.

b. He laments that news is becoming all about ratings.

c. He laments the firing of his friend, Howard.

d. He tries to arrange a way for Howard to leave the network with dignity.

3. MAX IS DENIED

a. Max can't do anything about Howard being fired.

b. Hackett wants to muscle into Max's News Division, Max fights against it.

c. Max presses his desire to focus on REAL news, but he is being pushed to go sensational for the ratings.

d. Diana shows her chops and her ambition, threatens Max's position.

e. Max is shut out of a big stockbroker meeting and no one will give him information. He feels shut out and is angry. Max figures he'll be fired too. Max allows Howard to go back on the air and say "Bullshit" as revenge.

f. Max gets fired.

g. Max packs up his office and feels old (where is that rush of excitement he used to feel?) He tells stories about the past glories again to his staff.

4. SECOND OPPORTUNITY FOR MAX TO FEEL EXCITEMENT AND HOPE OF DOING HIS JOB WELL.

a. Howard is a bit hit with the viewers and he is put back on air to do his "truth" routines.

b. Max, due to his friendship with Howard, is re-hired.

5. MAX'S CONFLICTS ABOUT TAKING ADVANTAGE OF SECOND OPPORTUNITY.

a. Max knows the network is in upheaval.

b. Max knows Diana will be fighting him for his position.

    c.   Max thinks Howard is becoming unbalanced. He feels leaving Howard on the air is wrong; Max is going against his best moral judgment.

6.   MAX GOES FOR IT

    a.   Max takes the job back.

7.   ALL GOES WELL

    a.   Howard continues to be a bit hit with the television audiences. Thus Max's job is intact for now.

    b.   Diana flirts with Max as she tries to sell him on whacko news ideas; she also sparks a competitive thing too—telling him she wants to run his division. He asks her for dinner (she excites him…)

        i.   We get exposition here about Diana seeing Max talk to her University when she was a student… (reminding him of his age, and flaming his feelings of mid-life crisis).

        ii.   Diana coolly cancels a date to be with Max; we see she's heartless in all areas of her life.

        iii.   Over dinner, a lot of exposition comes out. This is a good place for it, we are interested in these people by now and we want to know more about them.

    c.   Diana and Max sleep together; affair begins.

    d.   Howard begins to hear voices in the middle of the night and becomes even more interesting as a TV personality.

8.   ALL FALLS APART

    a.   Max's friendship is more important to him than ratings. He doesn't want to take advantage of Howard's instability, he wants to get him to a doctor. He goes against the grain of the network and the men in charge do not appreciate it.

    b.   Max finds out that Diana has been given Max's position as head of news; this signals end of affair.

    c.   Max, fired again. He's at home with family to watch Howard's rain-soaked crazy diatribe, "I'm mad as hell and I won't take it anymore…"

d. Diana hires terrorist group to have a "news" show—all the things that Max abhors and sensationalizing the news has come to be—news is now Sybil the Soothsayer etc.

e. Ed Ruddy dies (Max's friend).

   NOTE: This is a place where Paddy goes wild with giving a point of view (through Beal)—a diatribe against TV. He can do it because it AFFECTS the story.

f. Hackett announces big profits.

g. Funeral services for Ruddy—Max and Diana hook up again. Remember Max's overall want of excitement and feeling like he makes a difference. The deaths of his peers and friends is making him feel that he is marking time in his life… he can't stand that.

9. CRISIS

a. Max tells his wife about his affair with Diana.

   NOTE: another place where Paddy goes into verbal warfare— Max's wife (Beatrice Straight, who won a Best Supporting Actress Oscar basically for this scene), gets to point out the unfair world; that she does not get her husband's winter passion.

b. Max knows Diana's flaws, but still can't help the DECISION he makes. He moves out and moves in with Diana.

10. CLIMAX

a. Jenson (head of the corporation who owns the network) calls Howard in and takes advantage of the unstable Howard. Howard becomes Jensen's mouthpiece—that money/business is what runs the world. Max witnesses his friend's mental health decline even further.

b. Howard as Jensen's mouthpiece is not a ratings hit. Diana hates this and it affects her relationship with Max.

c. Max breaks up with Diana.

   Note: Max gets HIS SAY—about human decency and love and how he misses being LOVED and that Diana, finally, he realizes is incapable of really loving. She agrees and HATES that he wants that. She chooses to answer the phone and deal with business rather than deal with EMOTIONS.

    d.   Max moves out. He is afraid that Diana will crack, he really cares about her.

11.   TRUTH COMES OUT

    a.   Max wants to go back to his wife "if she'll have him."

    b.   Hackett and Diana and heads of network decide to kill Howard on the air so that they can get a show with better ratings.

    c.   Howard killed on the air, proving that there is no moral code in TV.

This is a powerful film with a message; it leaves the audience a bit shocked. But the whole idea is supported in the film's characters; they stay true to their codes.

KRAMER VS KRAMER

(1979)

screenplay by Robert Benton
based on novel by Avery Corman

This is Ted Kramer's story, even though Joanna Kramer goes through a major change also. The audience stays with Ted (portrayed by Dustin Hoffman) as he embarks on this journey; as he learns to be less self-centered, to put someone else before his own immediate desires, as he learns to be a friend, an empathetic person and most importantly, a parent.

Check out how Robert Benton shows the audience time passage. He uses two Christmas holidays. It's a way for us to know that Ted's journey was a long one, that he has put in the time and energy, that he did not change overnight.

Use of repetition of certain scenes works well also. The first breakfast scene is a disaster; dad and son are not connected at all. The last breakfast scene is perfection; dad and son have become a team, they have earned a routine. Those scenes are also emotion-packed; they are character growth scenes.

Another scene that is repeated three times: Ted dropping Billy off at school. Each time we see it we see the progression of Ted's knowledge of his son (first time he doesn't even know what grade he is in, the second shows a concerned dad who has the lunchbox routine and schedule down, the third reveals Joanna (portrayed by Meryl Streep) watching Ted and Billy and commitment to being a parent. You can also think of these repeat scenes as "runners." They help show the progression of the relationship and time passage.

This is an "issue" movie; it's an exploration of mores and conceptions about family and roles of husband and wife, parent and child. What keeps it from being preachy? What keeps it from being a "lesson"? It's the emotion; the humor, the anger, the growth of character. The audience is shown, not told. The final courtroom scene stays emotional; it does not become a lecture. The audience is left to make their own decision; no one is painted as perfectly right, no one is painted as perfectly wrong.

Eleven Step Breakdown and Notes

1. Self-centered TED KRAMER WANTS his vision of a perfect life. To him that is career success and providing a good life for himself and his family. WHY? It's what he assumes is his role, it makes him feel like "the man."

2. TED LOGICALLY GOES FOR IT

    a. He has put together the pieces of a young, successful career man.

    b. He has a beautiful wife and beautiful son.

    c. He puts in extra time with his boss /he is getting promoted.

    d. He has provided a nice apartment for his family.

3. TED IS DENIED

    a. When his wife, Joanna, leaves the family unit because she feels stifled and stuck—and leaves him to raise his son alone.

4. TED'S SECOND OPPORTUNITY TO PROVIDE A GOOD LIFE FOR HIMSELF AND HIS FAMILY: Learning how to be a single dad.

    NOTE: This does not look like a welcome opportunity for him at the time. Remember, the second opportunity doesn't have to look like a Fairy Godmother who has dropped in to solve all your problems. In retrospect the character may see it as a mixed blessing; a certainly hard way to learn what he is to learn on this story's journey.

5. TED'S CONFLICT about taking advantage of this opportunity.

    a. Worried his work will suffer.

    b. Doesn't know the basics of child-rearing/taking care of a household.

    c. Doesn't know his son.

6. TED GOES FOR IT.

    a. Ted rejects his boss' suggestion that he send Billy away to relatives so that his work won't suffer. Ted (whose want is to provide a good life for himself and his family) decides he can do it all.

7. ALL GOES WELL

    a. Ted and Billy get to know each other.

b. Ted does a pretty good job explaining to his son the reasons Joanna left the family.

c. Ted and neighbor Margaret gradually become friends and Ted learns more about a woman's point of view regarding mothering and need for personal satisfaction outside the home as well.

d. Ted continues to work hard, but he is stretched thin.

e. Billy tests Ted but Ted doesn't give up on trying to be a good dad.

f. Ted, who has tried to expunge Joanna's existence from the apartment, lets Billy have a picture of Joanna by his bed because he comes to understand that emotionally, this is what is good for Billy.

g. Ted starts to understand why Joanna left him.

h. Ted teaches Billy how to ride a bike.

i. Ted shows up at the school play.

j. Ted carries Billy to the ER when he gets hurt in the playground, is with him while he gets stitches.

8. ALL FALLS APART

a. Joanna comes back to NYC and wants custody of Billy.

b. Ted's lawyer tells him it won't be easy for Ted to retain custody of his son.

c. Ted gets fired from his job.

d. Ted's lawyer tells him that without a job, he has no chance of getting custody of Billy.

9. TED'S CRISIS

a. Knowing he can't fight Joanna in court without a job, Ted goes all out to get a job in 24 hours. He makes a DECISION to put himself on the line and demand an answer to his job application during a company Christmas party.

10. CLIMAX—THE COURTROOM

a. Joanna's emotional testimony.

b. Ted's emotional testimony.

11. TRUTH COMES OUT AND THINGS ARE MADE RIGHT

    a. Lawyer informs Ted that Joanna was awarded custody

    b. Ted tells Billy how the custody thing is going to work. He has become a loving good parent who is trying to do what will make his son understand fully the situation

    c. Joanna Kramer comes to get her son, and realizes she can't do it. She tells Ted that Billy is home—with Ted.

    d. Ted is clearly a changed man. He is able to see Joanna clearly, as a person, not as *his wife*—all her pain and turmoil—and understand her.

It's a very simple movie, and a very emotional one. No big car chases. No special effects. It's about family, understanding, love. Most importantly, this movie has a very strong point of view. It does not shy away from the hard questions. It does not shy away from making characters unsympathetic. No one is perfect. It feels real. That's why it works.

RAINMAN

(1988)

screenplay by Barry Morrow and Ron Bass

This film story features two characters as opposite from one another as can be imagined. Cocky, street-smart, ambitious, insecure and callous Charlie (portrayed by Tom Cruise) is in financial troubles. The other is sweet-tempered idiot savant Raymond (portrayed by Dustin Hoffman). Raymond is unable to exist in the world alone, he has no ambition, he is very content with his life Add the element that they are brothers, that one holds the control over the inheritance from their father. Add the fact that Charlie, at the outset of the story, didn't even know his abnormal brother exists. Add that Charlie has a problem with his father that he cannot fix now that the father has passed away. Add that Charlie lives on the West coast, Raymond on the East. Add that Charlie plans to bust his abnormal brother out of a protective facility for mentally challenged people and transport him across country. Add that Raymond's fear of flying is so intense, the option becomes an impossibility. Add that travel has to be by car, the brothers are forced to get to know one another.

It's clear that opposites were set up and pushed as these characters were designed. Doing this helps create conflict—and conflict is good.

This is not a story of "who gets the inheritance". The story elements that deal with this question are just *plot*. The overriding story explores the *emotional* journey of the cocky brother who learns he was loved—and now learns to love. He realizes that having a strong familial love is what he lacks in his life. When Charlie makes the right choice concerning his brother's future, he has completed a full journey of change.

Eleven Step Breakdown and Notes

1. CHARLIE WANTS to feel loved and feel validated. WHY? He had a difficult parting with a father—a father from whom Charlie never felt love.

    Note: Throughout the movie that there are references to how Charlie's interests are very much like his father. Even though they are estranged, Charlie's life reflects his father's interests: most specifically cars. Nice touch, works on a layered level throughout the film. Remember Charlie looking at dad's car collection in the garage? They travel by car. These elements *add* resonance to help make Charlie's unconscious desire more apparent.

2. CHARLIE LOGICALLY TRIES TO GAIN A SENSE OF VALIDATION/LOVE

    a. Charlie works hard at his car business, thinking being rich will be the answer.

    b. Charlie has a girlfriend, thinking that love will be enough.

    c. Charlie goes to pick up inheritance when he finds out dad has died, thinking this will be the answer to his money problems.

3. CHARLIE IS DENIED SENSE OF VALIDATION /LOVE FROM FATHER

    a. Charlie only gets rose bushes and a Buick.

    b. Charlie does not receive good or loving words from his father, even in the will.

4. CHARLIE'S SECOND OPPORTUNITY TO GAIN SENSE OF VALIDATION/LOVE

    a. Charlie finds out the money was left in the hands of Dr. Bruner.

    b. Charlie finds out he has a brother; the three million has been left in trust for his care. Charlie thinks he can somehow get his hands on some of it. NOTE: Not so easy, his brother is an idiot savant.

    c. Charlie meets his brother; thinks if he "takes" his brother and becomes his guardian, then he can get hands on the money.

5. CHARLIE'S CONFLICTS ABOUT TAKING ADVANTAGE OF SECOND OPPORTUNITY

    a. Charlie's brother is an idiot savant; smart in some ways but incapable of functioning in the real world.

    b. Charlie's brother can't make a decision about his finances.

    c. Girlfriend is not supportive of Charlie's plan.

6. CHARLIE GOES FOR IT

   a. Charlie decides to "kidnap" Raymond, calling Dr. Bruner and threatening to keep Raymond if he doesn't get half of the money.

7. ALL GOES WELL—CHARLIE IS STARTING TO BECOME CONNECTED TO RAYMOND—BEGINNING OF FAMILIAL LOVE

   a. Charlie and Raymond get to know one another and Charlie learns to understand some of Raymond's quirks.

      Note the addition of a ticking clock; Charlie needs to get back to Los Angeles for business.

   b. Charlie's girlfriend leaves them. Note: This relationship supports Charlie's need for change. Although she loves Charlie, he cannot really commit or really connect with her because he's not "whole" emotionally. She is used well in the script here because she can be the "audience's voice of "you're being a jerk, Charlie."

      c. Raymond is not able to get on a plane so Charlie agrees to go by car.

      d. Charlie and Raymond begin to bond.

         Note: Throughout the bonding—there is ALWAYS CONFLICT. NOTHING COMES EASILY. EACH STEP IS HARD, FRUSTRATING.

   e. Charlie finds out the SECRET, he learns why Raymond was put in the facility. Raymond's actions had put young Charlie in jeopardy, so to protect Charlie, Raymond was institutionalized. Charlie understands more about his father, feels that his father must have cared.

   f. In Las Vegas Charlie sees that Raymond's talents can be put to use. They make money. Charlie, by this time, has become attached to Raymond emotionally – and now it looks like it will be a financial gain as well.

   g. Charlie decides that he wants Raymond to stay with him, they will become a FAMILY in Los Angeles.

8. ALL FALLS APART FOR CHARLIE

    a. Las Vegas security asks them to leave the casino

    b. Charlie and Raymond arrive in Los Angeles. It's clear Raymond can't stay by himself while Charlie works. **Note:** By now the slick, always in control, uncommitted Charlie is no more. We see him as a more real and emotionally connected person.

    c. Dr. Bruner offers Charlie money—if he will send Raymond back to the institution. **Note:** Money used to be the driving factor in Charlie's life. We are now on Charlie's side; we have seen how much he will sacrifice to have this "family" in his life.

    d. Raymond almost sets Charlie's apartment on fire. Raymond is emotionally distraught and Charlie, for the first time, is forced to be realistic about this new life he has set up for Raymond.

9. CRISIS

    a. Charlie doesn't know if he can "keep" Raymond, care for him the way he needs to be cared for. Charlie visits the psychiatrist and knows he needs to make a decision.

10. CLIMAX

    a. Court decides Raymond should go back to hospital.

11. TRUTH COMES OUT

    a. By letting go of Raymond and doing what is best for him, Charlie shows more love than he would've if he had tried to "keep" Raymond. Validation of doing the right thing,.

    b. Plans to visit.

    c. Sense of family, finally.

WITNESS

(1985)

screenplay by William Kelly,
Earl Wallace and Pam Wallace

Perfect juxtaposition of characters; a man, John Book (portrayed by Harrison Ford) who lives by his wits and who has accepted a level of violence in his life as he struggles to keep justice in the world and a woman, Rachel (portrayed by Kelly McGillis) who has grown up in a protected society that eschews violence and contact with those who, for right or wrong, perpetrate it.

The Dramatic Question of the film: Can these two very different people find happiness in each other's worlds?

Eleven Step Breakdown and Notes

1. JOHN BOOK WANTS justice. WHY? It makes his world make sense. He is a police detective. He likes to control his world, he wants things to be right. His sister even says it to Rachel "John always thinks he's right."

    Note: An important element of his character is that he is willing to use violence to attain justice. This violence is in direct opposition to the beliefs of the Amish, the world he will have to enter in order to solve the crime.

2. BOOK LOGICALLY TRIES TO GET JUSTICE

    a. Book goes through interview process with young Samuel, the only witness to the murder, in an attempt to find the murderer of another police detective. He refuses Rachel's request to keep her son out of the investigation.

    b. Book goes to a seedy neighborhood bar to grab a suspect. His use of violence in apprehending the suspect is evident.

    c. Book tries to get Samuel to ID suspect.

d. Book, in order to retain Rachel and Samuel in the big city so he can use Samuel to help solve crime, arranges for them to stay with his sister overnight.

e. Book has Samuel go through mug shots at precinct.

f. Once Samuel has identified Officer McPhee as the murderer; Book goes to his Captain to report.

3. BOOK IS DENIED JUSTICE

a. Book realizes that the Captain is in on the crime.

b. Book is shot and badly wounded.

c. Book has to leave town and job and partner to save Samuel, Rachel and himself; knowing he has to stay alive and his witness has to stay alive in order to get the justice he desires.

4. SECOND OPPORTUNITY TO FIND JUSTICE/MORALITY IN HIS WORLD

a. Book goes to live with the Amish.

5. BOOK'S CONFLICT IN TAKING ADVANTAGE OF THIS SECOND OPPORTUNITY

a. Book is injured, has to recover from gunshot.

b. This world is foreign to him, he doesn't know how to act.

c. The Amish do not want him in their lives, he is an outsider who could bring great danger to them.

d. He's attracted to Rachel.

6. BOOK GOES FOR IT

a. Book has no choice, he has to recuperate and regroup. He is not strong enough to go back into the fray.

7. ALL GOES WELL

a. Book gets well physically.

b. Book learns about the Amish ways.

c. Book begins to make a good relationship with Rachel and family.

    d.   Book helps raise a neighbor's barn, others begin to accept him.

    e.   Book's feelings for Rachel grow; a sense of how justice and "right" can be found in an alternate place.

8.   ALL FALLS APART

    a.   Book's partner, via phone, is keeping him informed about the latest events in the crime and that the search for Book is increasing in its pace.

    b.   Tensions in the Amish community about Rachel's actions/ feelings.

9.   CRISIS BLENDS WITH THE "ALL FALLS APART" IN THIS FILM

    a.   Book and Rachel can't deny their physical attraction. He has to make a DECISION; will he sleep with her? Will he complicate her life, ruin her reputation in the Amish world? Is he willing to turn his back on his world and accept hers? Will love win out? His decision to sleep or not to sleep with Rachel at this point is massive. There are so many ramifications to consider…

    b.   Book finds out his partner has been killed. He makes a decision to call his Captain, swears revenge.

    c.   Book rides back to farm with Eli, chooses to fight with the tourist/local who makes fun of the Amish.

    d.   Book (off screen) tells Eli he's going home.

10.   CLIMAX

    a.   Rachel finds out Book is leaving, they run to each others' arms and we assume consummate their love.

    b.   McPhee, Captain come after him.

    c.   Book has to protect his Amish friends in the only way he knows how. All the relationships he has made in the community now play out. Will they stand by him? Will he be able to protect them?

    d.   Shoot-out.

11.   TRUTH COMES OUT

    a.   Book confronts Captain; asking the question that shows that Book is now a changed man. Enough! He has a newfound understanding of using violence to further one's desires. He questions if violence is the answer? Will violence bring about justice? And more importantly he sees that violence begets violence and wonders if there will ever be an end to it.

b. Book knows he has to leave Rachel. Their love is not enough to bridge their two worlds.

c. Book leaves the Amish, knowing he does not belong. But he is a changed man.

SHAKESPEARE IN LOVE
(1998)

written by Marc Norman and Tom Stoppard

The main character is Shakespeare (portrayed by Joseph Fiennes). Shakespeare is the person who makes the story happen. It is his need to create that puts all events into action. Viola (portrayed by Gwyneth Paltrow) has an important and emotional arc also. Most good romantic comedies will feature strong arcs for both romantic leads.

Eleven Step Breakdown and Notes

1. SHAKESPEARE WANTS a muse. WHY? Ego. Writer's need to create. Also he needs to pay off his debts. He wants to have a theatre to do his work.

2. SHAKESPEARE LOGICALLY goes about trying to get what he wants.

   a. He tries to write.

   b. He goes to an alchemist (16th century type therapist) who gives him a bracelet to give to a woman so she will dream; this dream of hers is predicted to unleash his writer's block.

   c. He chooses Rosalind who he thinks will be his muse. He gives her the bracelet.

   d. He goes to theatre to talk to Burbridge about his stake in theatre.

   e. He goes home to write, thinking the muse will soon be his.

3. SHAKESPEARE'S DENIED

   a. He finds his muse having sex with the Queen's theatre "cop."

   b. Burbridge decides to produce Marlowe's play

   c. He throws away what he has written

   d. He talks to Marlowe and feels inadequate.

4. SHAKESPEARE'S SECOND OPPORTUNITY TO GET WHAT HE WANTS

a. Marlowe gives him some story ideas.

b. Thomas Kent (Gwyneth Paltrow disguised as a boy) auditions and inspires.

c. Shakespeare goes to a dance/ sees Viola, he's inspired by her beauty.

5. SHAKESPEARE'S CONFLICTS ABOUT TAKING ADVANTAGE OF THIS SECOND OPPORTUNITY

a. Thomas Kent runs off, Shakespeare has to pursue to meet this actor who spoke his words so well.

b. Shakespeare tells Nurse to give Kent the news that he is cast.

c. Shakespeare finds out that Kent is indeed Viola.

Note: The runner of Shakespeare pretending to be Marlowe is started here. This runner has an arc of its own.

6. SHAKESPEARE GOES FOR IT

a. Shakespeare goes to Viola's window that night and declares love. (She has become his muse.)

7. ALL GOES WELL

a. Inspired, Shakespeare writes through the night.

b. Kent shows up for rehearsal and inspires other actors.

Note: The "All Goes Well" section of this movie is longer than most. The reason it holds up so well is that *as* things are going well for Shakespeare, tension grows. Will the lovers be found out? Will Viola's acting in the guise of a boy be found out? Will the theatre be able to afford to put on the play? Will the Queen shut down the theatre? Will Shakespeare's lie about Marlowe being Viola's lover be found out? Will Viola's fiancé catch the lovers? Will Viola find out Shakespeare is married? The more Shakespeare's love for Viola grows, the more emotionally the two are committed.

8. ALL FALLS APART

a. Viola has to see the Queen and have her marriage to Wessex officially sanctioned. Shakespeare realizes he is going to lose Viola. The wedding is in one week.

Note: Putting the time clock on the piece here helps with the pace and the tension.

b. Shakespeare names Marlowe as Viola's lover.

c. Burbridge finds out that Shakespeare and his mistress had an affair.

d. Burbridge starts a sword fight with Shakespeare.

e. Viola and Shakespeare's pain at knowing they will soon part grows more intense.

f. Viola finds out Shakespeare is married.

g. Shakespeare finds out Marlowe is killed, blames himself.

h. Shakespeare goes to church to pray for forgiveness.

i. Viola is told of death of playwright/poet, thinks the victim must be Shakespeare. Even through she finds out Shakespeare's alive, she realizes that Shakespeare's life is in danger if she doesn't marry Wessex.

j. Webster sees Viola (dressed as Kent) and Shakespeare make love.

k. Viola is outed.

l. The theatre is shut down.

m. Viola marries Wessex.

9. CRISIS

a. Shakespeare makes the decision to accept Burbridge's offer to present his play despite loss of Kent in the lead and despite his heartache.

b. Viola, after wedding to Wessex, decides she must go to the play.

10. CLIMAX

a. The man playing Juliet has a vocal problem; he can no longer play in falsetto.

b. Viola takes a chance and plays Juliet in the play. This is against all laws at the time.

Note: This playing out of the high points of the play creates a strong climax—at any point we know Viola could be kicked off stage/ discovered and Shakespeare's play and his love could be destroyed.

11.   TRUTH COMES OUT TO MAKE THINGS RIGHT

    a.   The Queen's theatre "cop" tries to force Viola off the stage but the Queen intercedes because it is a good play.

    b.   Queen gives Viola and Shakespeare time together, but decrees that Viola will be off with Wessex to America.

    c.   Viola and Shakespeare talk of how their love will never age, never change.

    d.   The muse continues. Viola spins a story with Shakespeare (that becomes one of his most beloved plays; Twelfth Night).

Viola's Arc

1.   VIOLA WANTS (and note that she says it baldly in one of her first scenes) "poetry in life and adventure and great love"… WHY? She's a woman ahead of her time. She is more independent and wants more from life than she is being offered.

2.   VIOLA LOGICALLY GOES FOR IT:

    a.   She dresses as a boy and auditions for Shakespeare's play.

    b.   She falls in love with Shakespeare

    c.   She convinces her nurse to help with the subterfuge and begins a love affair.

3.   VIOLA'S DENIED—

    a.   She finds out she is promised to Lord Wessex in marriage.

4.   VIOLA'S SECOND OPPORTUNITY TO GET WHAT SHE WANTS:

    a.   She takes Shakespeare to bed and wants to get as much love and adventure she can before she is forced to marry…

    b.   She continues on in the play rehearsals

5. CONFLICT ABOUT TAKING ADVANTAGE OF HER SECOND OPPORTUNITES

    a. Her affair needs to be secret.

    b. Her acting in the play needs to be secret.

    c. Wessex is suspicious.

6. VIOLA GOES FOR IT

    a. Love cannot be denied.

7. ALL GOES WELL

    a. Shakespeare is a great lover and creative soul mate.

    b. They maintain the secrets.

8. ALL FALLS APART

    Note: This is when Shakespeare and Viola's stories get on the same track....

UNFORGIVEN
(1992)

Screenplay by David Webb Peoples
Nominated for Academy Award for Best Screenplay

This is a classic ANTI-HERO story. An anti-hero uses dishonorable actions to achieve an honorable goal. In other words, DOING THE WRONG THING FOR THE RIGHT REASON.

Notice how the situation of Munny's life is set up: a visual of a man digging a grave. Even though it's necessary to set up the inciting incident in the town at the saloon in order to start the story—this initial visual lets us know that there's an important character who will join the story.

WHAT NEEDS TO BE SET UP IN THE WORLD OF THE STORY: The idea of women who are treated as property. That this is the Wild West, violence in the way of life. The antagonist is introduced—the Sheriff Little Bill who has a violent streak and no empathy for the women's plight. Alice (portrayed by Frances Farmer) is introduced, she leads the prostitutes in their need for justice. She comes up with the idea to offer as a reward for any man who will kill the attackers of one of her fellow saloon girls.

Eleven Step Breakdown and Notes

1.   MUNNY WANTS to live a good, clean, lawful life and take care of his family. WHY? He made a promise to his wife and even though she is now dead, he wants to be true to his promise.

2.   MUNNY LOGICALLY TRIES TO GET WHAT HE WANTS

   a.   Gives up old life of being a hired killer.

   b.   Becomes a hog farmer even though he's not good at it.

   c.   Takes responsibility for his kids.

   d.   Stops drinking.

   e.   Says 'no' to an offer to kill for the reward, even though he could really use the money for his family and farm. **Note:** This is where we get a lot of the exposition about Munny's life before – how he was a cold-blooded killer.

3. MUNNY IS DENIED

   a. Hogs get the fever and Munny has no way to keep his family going.

4. MUNNY'S SECOND OPPORTUNITY TO LIVE UP TO HIS PROMISE TO HIS WIFE—

   Note: Anti-hero actions: DOING THE WRONG THING FOR THE RIGHT REASON.

   a. Munny decides to go for the reward so that he can take care of his family.

5. MUNNY'S CONFLICT IN TAKING ADVANTAGE OF THIS SECOND OPPORTUNITY:

   a. Munny's moral conflict; he knows he's doing something his wife would not approve of.

   b. Munny can no longer shoot as well as he had in the past.

   c. Munny has to leave kids alone.

   d. Munny's even out of shape as a horse rider.

   e. Munny's friend, Ned, doesn't want to join him.

   f. Munny can't stop questioning himself.

6. MUNNY GOES FOR IT—

   a. Munny decides that even without Ned, he has to seek the reward. He sees no other choice; he has to earn money to support his kids.

7. ALL GOES WELL

   a. Ned decides to join him.

   b. Ned and Munny hook up with Kid, Kid accepts Ned. **Note:** This is where the writer gets in some of his own point of view-through the Kid's questions: Kid thinks killing will make him feel strong and powerful, Ned and Munny have their own thoughts about killing: There's a dead feeling that the shooter gets for every person he kills.

     c. Munny finds some "moral" right in what he's doing; that no woman deserves to be cut up.

     d. Munny is able to say no to offer of liquor.

8.   ALL FALLS APART for Munny

     a. Munny arrives in Big Whiskey—feels ill (has fever). The Sheriff beats him up while Kid is upstairs talking to Alice about reward.

     b. Munny thinks the fever is sent by the angel of death, fear of dying, fear of hell. Note: The author takes advantage of this moment to explore how a person deals with the sins he knows he has committed.

     c. Munny can't move on in his life; when Delilah offers him kindness, comfort, he can't accept. He is stuck—trying to please a dead wife and deal with his demons.

     d. Ned can't shoot the guilty cowboy—can't kill anymore.

     e. Munny shoots one of the cowboys who were responsible for the cutting of Delilah. The kill depresses him more.

     f. Ned quits and is ready to go home.

     g. Sheriff is getting posse together to go after Munny, Ned and Kid.

     h. Sheriff captures Ned, tortures him.

     i. Kid realizes after his first kill that the kill was not invigorating, but demoralizing.

     j. Ned killed by Sheriff, put on display.

     k. Munny starts drinking.

     l. Kid tells Munny he doesn't want to be a killer, he never wants to be a man like Munny.

9.   MUNNY'S CRISIS

     a. Munny gives the money to the Kid and decides to go after the Sheriff to avenge Ned's death.

10.   CLIMAX

     a. Munny takes on the Sheriff and deputies. Munny shows his strength and violent nature.

b. Munny wins. He is the best killer of all.

11. TRUTH COMES OUT

   a. Beauchamp wants to write Munny's story.

   b. Munny heads home—we find out that he took his family to San Francisco to start a new life in Dry Goods.

Eleven Step Breakdown and Notes for the Character Arc for Antagonist Little Bill (Sheriff):

1. SHERIFF WANTS to keep his power base and keep the hired killers out of his town. WHY? Power. Ego. His sense of right and wrong.

2. SHERIFF LOGICALLY GOES FOR IT

   a. Sheriff passes his judgment on the crime against the whore—decrees that the exchange of a horse will make things right.

   b. Sheriff uses violence to get English Bob out of town.

   c. Sheriff beats up Munny.

   d. Sheriff kicks Ned, Kid and Munny out of town.

3. SHERIFF IS DENIED

   a. Saloon ladies put Munny, Ned and Kid up in a barn and take care of them.

4. SHERIFF'S SECOND OPPORTUNITY TO RETAIN POWER

   a. Continues to try get Munny, Ned, Kid out of town.

   b. Sheriff captures Ned, beats him for information.

5. SHERIFF'S CONFLICT ABOUT TAKING ADVANTAGE OF SECOND OPPORTUNITY

   a. Antagonist doesn't need to have conflict over his actions—he thinks he's in the right.

6. SHERIFF GOES FOR IT

   a. Sheriff tortures Ned for information.

7. ALL GOES WELL FOR SHERIFF:

   a. Ned names Munny.

8. ALL FALLS APART FOR SHERIFF:

    a. Munny comes after Sheriff.

9. CRISIS

    a. Sheriff realizes Munny is not going to back down and decides to challenge him.

10. CLIMAX

    a. Shoot-out.

11. TRUTH COMES OUT

    a. Sheriff, as bad guy, gets "what's coming to him".

B Stories and Runners:

B STORY AND ARC: English Bob and Sheriff's battle of wits and will. (Arrogance is shot down and the Sheriff's ego is raised.)

B STORY AND ARC: The saloon girls getting their revenge. (Start with vengeance in their hearts, learn how violence breeds more violence.)

B STORY AND ARC: Kid's realization that killing is not romantic. (The arc: Kid thinks it will be great but at the end of the movie he has completely changed.)

RUNNER: SHERIFF BUILDING HIS HOUSE.

RUNNER: BEAUCHAMP WANTING TO WRITE A NOVEL ABOUT THE BEST GUNSLINGER IN THE WEST.

TOY STORY
(1995)

screenplay by John Lasseter, Peter Docter, Joss Whedon, Andrew Stanton, Joe Ranft, Joel Cohen, Alec Sokolow

Eleven Step Breakdown and Notes

1. Woody WANTS things to stay the same; he wants to keep respect. WHY? He's in charge, he's loved best; it makes him feel IMPORTANT.

2. He LOGICALLY plays with Andy, organizes other toys, keeps things in ship-shape form in Andy's bedroom. He sends out troops to scope out the new birthday toys. He IS in charge.

3. He's DENIED (notice how there's a sequence here).

    a. BUZZ LIGHTYEAR arrives.

    b. Woody, insecure, tries to show up Buzz, telling him he can't really fly; but this ploy backfires because by a fluke, Buzz looks like he's flying.

    c. When Buzz is accidentally bumped out of window, other toys blame Woody; it reflects badly on him and he's lost their respect.

4. SECOND OPPORTUNITY—Buzz shows up in car heading to Pizza Planet. Woody thinks he can "save" him and get him back to Andy's home and everyone will be happy.

5. CONFLICTS ON TAKING ADVANTAGE OF THIS OPPORTUNITY

    a. Buzz hates Woody at this point and doesn't want to be with him.

    b. Has to lie to Buzz and let Buzz think Woody thinks he's a real astronaut to get him to go into Pizza Planet.

6. GOES FOR IT—Lies, doesn't think he has a choice.

7. ALL GOES WELL

   a. Gets Buzz into Pizza Planet.

8. ALL FALLS APART

   a. Sid shows up.

   b. Sid takes Buzz and Woody home.

   c. Weird toys.

   d. Sid puts Buzz on a rocket.

9. WOODY'S CRISIS

   a. Woody asks his friend toys for help, they don't trust him. He will have to do it himself.

10. CLIMAX

   a. Dog.

   b. Buzz sees commercials and realizes he's a toy and gets depressed.

   c. Woody has to get him out of his depression!

   d. MOVING VAN is coming (setting in time clock).

   e. Can't get into moving van, toys still not trusting.

   f. Gets idea for go-cart help.

   g. Uses the match! Fly into ANDY'S CAR!

11. TRUTH COMES OUT TO MAKE THINGS RIGHT

   a. Bo Beep says Woody was telling the truth.

   b. All are friends again.

SHREK

(2001)

screenplay by Ted Elliot, Terry Rossio, Joe Stillman, R. Schulman
based on a book by William Steig

Eleven Step Breakdown and Notes

This is a comedy, obviously. And it's a satire/spoof. So FLIP everything - what's white is black, what's up is down, what's sexy is not the norm…

1. SHREK WANTS to be accepted/ loved for who he is. WHY? He's lonely. He's tired of having his feelings hurt. He's tired of people throwing things at him. But because this is a story that is poking fun at the "typical" fairytale, this hero is acting in his own worst interests. What he *thinks* he wants is to be left alone. He sets out to DENY himself what he really wants because he's too vulnerable and is really a softie, emotion-wise (which again, is the opposite of what you think an OGRE would be).

2. Shrek LOGICALLY goes about getting what he THINKS he wants by putting out NO TRESPASSING signs and scaring off the local fairytale characters.

3. Shrek is DENIED when DONKEY decides he wants to move in with Shrek to keep out of sight of Lord F's goons. Ogre can't seem to get rid of him. And the Fairytale creatures won't leave him alone, they want his help.

4. SECOND OPPORTUNITY—Shrek agrees to help the Fairytale creatures. If he succeeds, he will give him back his privacy.

5. CONFLICTS ON TAKING ADVANTAGE OF THIS OPPORTUNITY

    a. Donkey wants to come with him.

    b. Lord F is a terrible, sadistic guy.

    c. Shrek has to leave his beloved home.

6.   GOES FOR IT—Shrek and Donkey head out

7.   ALL GOES WELL

    a.   Get to Lord F's castle.

    b.   Learn of contest to get Princess Fiona for Lord F.

    c.   Get the better of the guards who try to capture/kill them.

    d.   Lord F hires Shrek and Donkey to go get Fiona; if they are successful he promises Shrek can have his swamp.

    e.   Shrek and Donkey set out to do their task.

    f.   Shrek shows he's clever and smart getting Donkey across bridge.

    g.   Successfully fight dragon.

    h.   Princess thinks Shrek (in helmet) must be the prince who was sent to save her.

    i.   Shrek saves Donkey from dragon.

    j.   Takes Fiona and off they go—heading back to Lord F.

    k.   Fiona thanks Shrek.

    l.   Fiona sees Shrek's face and is disappointed.

    m. Fiona is difficult/ wants to be in a place—alone—before sunset.

    n.   Donkey and Shrek by fire.

    o.   Fiona cooks them a rat for breakfast.

    p.   Burping contest.

    q.   Fiona helps them vanquish Robin Hood and gang.

    r.   All having a great time together.

    s.   Shrek and Fiona really connecting.

    t.   See the castle in the distance but decide to spend another night together, they're having too much fun.

    u.   Shrek and Fiona almost kiss, interrupted by Donkey.

    v.   Donkey encourages Shrek to tell Fiona he loves her.

8.   ALL FALLS APART

   a.   Donkey finds Fiona in her ogre-look.

   b.   Shrek overhears Fiona tell donkey it's a curse. He thinks he's being rejected.

   c.   Fiona decides to tell Shrek she's an ogre too—but Shrek is gone.

   d.   Fiona and Shrek mis-communicate, argue.

   e.   Lord F arrives, Fiona realizes Shrek went to get him and it looks like he selfishly turned her over so that he could have his "swamp."

   f.   Fiona agrees to marry Lord F.

   g.   Shrek and Donkey head off, they fight, Donkey leaves Shrek.

   h.   Shrek is all alone. Sad.

   i.   Fiona is getting ready to marry Lord F. Sad.

   j.   Donkey and Dragon. Sad.

   k.   Donkey shows up at Shrek's, claims his part of the swamp. They fight.

9.   SHREK'S CRISIS

   a.   Donkey lets Shrek know that Fiona was in love with him (not letting on that she is an ogre—of course—that would take the final reveal away and if you let that out here to Shrek—the story's tension would dissipate). Shrek DECIDES to go save Fiona from ugly, short, mean Lord F.

10.   CLIMAX

   a.   Shrek and Donkey go to rescue Fiona.

   b.   Fiona and Lord F are married!

   c.   Fiona is revealed at wedding to be an ogre! Lord F's true nature revealed, as long as he's KING, he doesn't really care.

   d.   Shrek has to fight off army.

   e.   Lord F eaten by dragon (AHHH! Fiona is a widow so soon!)

11.   TRUTH COMES OUT TO MAKE THINGS RIGHT

    a.   Shrek tells Fiona (as ogre) he loves her.

    b.   Shrek and Fiona kiss.

    c.   True love's kiss turns Fiona—into her real self—she stays on ogre!

    d.   Both feel good about who they are: true love means more than anything.

    e.   Fairytale creatures celebrate!

This is a ground-breaking film in the fact that it takes the "typical" fairytale and turns it on its head. But the message is similar to a lot of the classics: Without self-acceptance and commitment to being yourself there can be no real happiness. Of course there's also the lesson: "Don't judge a book by its cover."

ADAPTATION
(2002)

written by Charlie Kaufman and Donald Kaufman
inspired by the novel THE ORCHID THIEF
by Susan Orleans
Nominated for Academy Award for
Best Adapted Screenplay

Genre: Dark Comedy Drama

The protagonist, Charlie, portrayed by Nick Cage, is a brilliant screenwriter and an insecure man. He wants to please, but needs to stay true to his vision of the world. He wants answers, he wants to find the passion in his life and wants to find the strength to pursue it.

This film story is interesting on many levels—take note how it unravels in two different time periods. Charlie's story is "present day". Susan's story starts three years earlier. By the end of the second act, Charlie's story has caught up to Susan's—and then both continue in "present day". The audience is treated to Charlie's story in a more moment to moment way, whereas Susan's story is told through the larger events that lead up to the climax of her relationship with LaRoche. It is Charlie's discovery of the passionate secrets in the Susan/LaRoche relationship that cause him to come to grips with his questions.

Both Charlie and Susan are seeking out passion and the ability to act on their passions. The common theme—*Without finding and following the passion in one's life, one cannot truly feel alive…* enables the film story to be about *one thing*.

Charlie Kaufman is the screenwriter. Donald Kaufman is not a real person. The addition of Donald's name to the film credits is a nod to the film story itself; that one must stay true to oneself when creating a work of art, but one must stay open to react and take in outside forces and relationships that will add to the creative process.

Eleven Step Breakdown and Notes

1. CHARLIE WANTS/NEEDS answers to what makes a good script, what makes a good life. WHY? He wants to be able to follow passion, he needs to let go and stop trying to do things right, he needs to get out of his head. He is unhappy, tortured. He can't allow passion to take over in his relationship with Amelie. He can't unlock the answers to the screenplay, he doesn't have a ghost orchid in his life. **Note:** The NEED is added here because in some stories, the main character is not aware of what he NEEDS to accomplish a buried WANT. It's clear to the audience what Charlie wants, Charlie is somewhat self-aware but still cannot act on his desires.

2. CHARLIE LOGICALLY TRIES TO find the answers to his script and his life

    a. Charlie takes the job adapting a book about passion/orchids/specialness.

    b. Charlie tries to write the script.

    c. Charlie tries to impart to his brother, Donald, the real truth, according to Charlie, of what makes a good script.

3. CHARLIE IS DENIED finding the answers

    Note: More than half of the film story takes place in this area.

    a. Charlie's advice to Donald is not taken as the truth, Donald decides to take Robert McKee's class.

    b. Charlie's script writing is not going well, he can't find the story.

    c. Charlie isn't able to make the commitment to passion with his girlfriend, Amelie.

    d. Charlie doubts anyone has the answer to the secrets of life.

    e. Donald's social skills make Charlie feel inadequate.

    f. Charlie's dreams are always interrupted.

    g. Charlie has to listen to Donald's pitch, hates it.

    h. Charlie is on the set for his latest film, the actors/crew do not acknowledge him, don't even know who he is. Donald, however, is making friends readily—including a girlfriend.

i. Charlie asks the waitress for a date, she says no.

j. Charlie goes to the orchid show alone, tries to unlock answers to what make women "tick", finds no answers.

k. Donald is figuring out his script, he's having fun.

l. Charlie is not figuring out his script, he is tortured. He rambles into tape recorder… but nothing seems to work.

m. Charlie's agent calls to tell him the script is overdue.

n. Charlie dreams of having sex with Susan, the book author. Interrupted by sounds of Donald having real sex with his girlfriend.

o. Charlie meets with agent, his agent is not helpful.

p. Donald gives Charlie Robert McKee's 10 Commandments of screenwriting. Charlie rejects the idea that the answer is formulaic.

q. Charlie runs into film executive in restaurant, he is invited to meet Susan in person, he cannot face it and leaves.

r. Donald finishes his script. Charlie hasn't really started.

s. Charlie goes to NYC to talk to Susan, the author. He can't make himself do it and doesn't talk to her.

t. Charlie's agent loves Donald's script and is going to sell it for a lot of money. Agent suggests Charlie ask Donald for help on the orchid script. Donald is a success… Charlie feels as if he is a big fat failure.

4. CHARLIE'S SECOND OPPORTUNITY to feel good, to get answers

a. Charlie signs up for McKee's class and asks a question; what if nothing happens in life. What if characters don't change? McKee puts him down, tells him that things happen every day in life, that people make huge decisions, go through great highs and lows. This shakes Charlie's thinking process up—he wants to be one of those people that things happen to… who feels and does passionate things. How can he make his characters (and himself) come alive?

5. CHARLIE'S CONFLICTS ABOUT TAKING ADVANTAGE OF THE SECOND OPPORTUNITY

    a. Charlie has denigrated McKee.

    b. Charlie doesn't want to believe that one has to go outside oneself (sometimes) to find the answers.

    c. Charlie doesn't want to be in a room with other screenwriters looking for answers, he wants to feel special.

6. CHARLIE DECIDES TO GO FOR IT

    a. Charlie waits outside the class and finds the strength to stop McKee and ask for his help.

7. ALL GOES WELL—Charlie is finding answers and feeling good about taking action

    Note: At this point Susan's story (which has been taking place in the past), and Charlie's story (which has been taking place in the present) connect. From here on out, both stories are in the present… and affect one another moment to moment.

    a. Charlie and McKee have a drink and Charlie tells McKee the script story.

    b. McKee gives advice that helps Charlie.

    c. Charlie decides to ask Donald to come to NYC and help him with his script.

    d. Donald comes to NYC, he helps Charlie with script.

    e. Donald impersonates twin brother Charlie—interviews Susan. He feels she is lying and Donald and Charlie research more into Susan's life and find she is one of the females on LaRoche's porn site.

    f. Charlie and Donald follow Susan to Florida and spy on her and LaRoche. The story is now "out of Charlie's head" and physical.

8. ALL FALLS APART

    a. Charlie is caught spying, Susan and LaRoche decide he must be killed—he has uncovered Susan's passionate affair with drugs and with LaRoche.

b. Charlie and Donald are at the swamp, Susan and LaRoche there too—trying to kill them.

   c. Charlie and Donald escape and are chased through the swamp.

   d. Charlie and Donald hide.

9. CRISIS

   a. Donald tells Charlie that "You are what you love…". Donald tells Charlie he is a wonderful person who must believe in himself and believe that he can follow his passions… and in doing so—will become a more complete and happy person.

10. CLIMAX

   a. Charlie and Donald make a break for it—get into the car. They speed off—

   b. A truck crashes into the car.

   c. **Note:** This crash mirrors the crash LaRoche experienced—the one that killed his mother and caused his wife to divorce him.

   d. Donald dies. Charlie has to tell his mother.

11. TRUTH COMES OUT

   a. Charlie, back in Los Angeles, is lonely without Donald. The house feels empty. Charlie truly misses Donald.

   b. Charlie finishes script and turns it in.

   c. Charlie meets up with Amelie and admits his love for her. He kisses her.

   d. **Note:** Charlie's new normal? The audience gets the feeling he is stronger—he will be able to follow his passions… act on his desires… Amelie now has another boyfriend but there is a possibility she and Charlie could get together. (Charlie and Donald's personas have merged here.)

Breakdown and Notes for Susan Orleans Story

The film story is really in two parts… Susan's story takes three years before Charlie's story begins. Charlie is clearly the main character, Susan's story complements his journey.

1. SUSAN WANTS answers. She wants to feel passion, she wants to want something badly. WHY? Her life is safe, her marriage comfortable, her friends are homogenous, she feels as if she is in a rut.

   Note: Susan's desire is the same as Charlie's. They are searching for the same thing—this allows the screenplay to hold a common theme.

2. SUSAN LOGICALLY tries to find answers

   a. Susan decides to write an article about a man who lives his life by his passions (LaRoche).

   b. Susan becomes fascinated with an orchid—one so rare that legend has it that a person, gazing on its rare beauty, will understand life in a new way.

   c. She questions LaRoche? Can passions change? Can love just disappear? Do people adapt and change?

3. SUSAN IS DENIED

   a. Susan feels great dissatisfaction with her husband and friends at a NYC dinner party. This life holds no answers for her.

4. SUSAN'S SECOND OPPORTUNITY to find answers

   a. Susan's article in the New Yorker is a great success. She is asked to expand it into a novel. Hollywood studio executive wants to buy the piece (and soon-to-be book) to adapt into a film.

   b. Susan agrees—this sends her back to Florida to spend more time with LaRoche.

5. SUSAN'S CONFLICTS about taking advantage of this second opportunity

   a. Susan is feeling as if LaRoche and she are bonding, he comments that people are attracted to him because they are lonely. This hits Susan hard; is her search so transparent?

6. SUSAN GOES FOR IT

   a. Susan keeps up the relationship with LaRoche, wanting to know more about him. She is hoping that by understanding LaRoche, she will find the answers she needs to unlock new passions in her life.

7. ALL GOES WELL

    a. LaRoche tells her more about his life.

    b. Susan pursues the sexual attraction she feels for LaRoche, asks him to take her into the swamp so she can see a real ghost orchid.

8. ALL FALLS APART

    a. LaRoche cannot find the ghost orchid, they get lost.

    b. LaRoche is shown to be fallible.

    c. They finally find the ghost orchid, but in gazing on it, Susan does not find "answers".

    d. LaRoche finds out the Seminoles are extracting the drug from the orchid, that they are not appreciating the orchid for its beauty and singularity.

    e. LaRoche suggests Susan take the drug, that the drug will surely help her understand her feelings and needs better.

9. CRISIS

    a. Susan hesitates, but decides to experiment with the drug.

10. CLIMAX

    a. Susan gets high. The drugs unlock her inhibitions with LaRoche, they start an affair.

    b. Susan meets Donald (pretending to be Charlie) and lies about her affair and relationship with LaRoche.

    c. Susan goes to Florida for more sex and drugs with LaRoche.

    d. Susan discovers Charlie spying on them, decides Charlie must be killed to protect her career and marriage and "old life".

    e. Chase through the swamps.

    f. Susan sees LaRoche eaten by an alligator.

    g. Susan struggles to get LaRoche out of the swamp.

11. TRUTH COMES OUT

   a. Susan holds LaRoche in her arms as he dies.

   b. Susan blames Charlie for shining a light on her passionate secret, for ruining her life.

   Note: The main character's story takes over here (Charlie's)... Susan, as a supporting character—causes Charlie to find answers...

SIDEWAYS

(2004)

written by Alexander Payne and Jim Taylor
based on a novel by Rex Pickett

Genre: Dark Comedy

The protagonist, Miles, portrayed by Paul Giamatti, is a depressed man. He is still in love with his ex-wife and can't move onto a new relationship. He is a novelist who cannot find a publisher for his work, his self-confidence is low. He lies—to himself and others—and can't seem to get his life "going". He has planned a week in the wine country with his best friend who is about to get married. Miles oversleeps, procrastinates, picks up his friend late, he steals from his mother, he won't face facts. He's let himself get out of shape, he is annoyingly self-deprecating. Why does the audience get behind him?

Because he is not the most unlikable person on the screen.

Miles' ally—and antagonist—is Jack, portrayed by Thomas Haden Church, a friend from college days. Jack makes things miserable for Miles, pushes him, embarrasses him, and, in the end, doesn't act like most best friends are supposed to act. Jack is selfish, his ego always comes first, he is about to get married and sets out to bed women before he ties the knot. Miles expects a weekend of male bonding, Jack is only interested in finding sex. Jack lies, he's impatient, he's incorrigible and insensitive.

In comparison, Miles looks like a great guy.

Jack's dual role as ally and antagonist is interesting. By pushing Miles to face facts and move on with his life, he is helping his friend. But when Jack's selfishness threatens to end Miles' venture into a relationship with Maya, portrayed by Virginia Madsen. Miles has to finally confront him and "battle" for his own sense of self.

Other reasons why Miles is likeable? He has a passion for wine, so much so it becomes humorous. He feels inadequate—therefore he is an underdog and audiences like to root for underdogs.

Eleven Step Breakdown and Notes

1. MILES WANTS/NEEDS to feel good about himself and move on with his life. WHY? He is depressed, nothing in his life has worked out the way he would like. **Note:** The NEED is added here because in some stories, the main character is not aware of what he NEEDS to accomplish a buried WANT. It's clear to the audience what Miles wants, but Miles is not self-aware at the top of the story.

2. MILES LOGICALLY TRIES TO feel good

   a. Miles plans a week away with his best friend to a favorite place; the wine country.

   b. Miles buys special wines for the trip.

   c. It comes out that Miles sees a therapist and takes anti-depressants.

   d. Miles allows Jack to give him advice (not ready to take it but…).

   e. Miles eyes Maya, asks her to join them for a glass of wine.

3. MILES IS DENIED feeling good

   a. Maya asks if they have plans for the evening and Miles tell her they are going back to the motel—tired after the drive. He shuts the door on the possibility of getting to know her better.

   b. Jack tells Miles he plans to get laid on the vacation. This makes Miles feel unappreciated.

   c. Miles and Jack meet Stephanie, Jack arranges a double date for Miles and himself.

   d. Miles resents Jack's desire to spend time with women instead of just him.

   e. Jack tells Miles his ex-wife, Victoria, has gotten remarried.

   f. Miles realizes Jack and Victoria have been discussing Miles' problems behind his back. (Miles runs into a vineyard, angry and upset, this is the culmination of all the denials).

4. MILES' SECOND OPPORTUNITY to feel good

   a. Miles and Jack get ready to meet Maya and Stephanie for dinner.

5. MILES' CONFLICTS ABOUT TAKING ADVANTAGE OF THE SECOND OPPORTUNITY

   a. Jack tells Miles he cannot bring the night down with his depressive thoughts. Also he cannot be upset if anyone wants to drink Merlot.

   b. Miles is nervous about a date with Maya (Jack has lied to Maya about Miles' book being published and Miles did not correct him).

6. MILES DECIDES TO GO FOR IT

   a. Miles goes with Jack to meet the women for dinner. He agrees to be on his best behavior.

7. ALL GOES WELL

   a. Miles and Maya have a wonderful time at dinner.

      Note: Things are going well, but Miles puts a call into Victoria, still upset about her remarriage. She tells him not to call her while he is drunk.

   b. Miles and Maya have a nice chat about wine at Stephanie's house . They have a lot in common, they both love wine and the making of wine.

   c. Miles tells Maya about his "special wine" that he is saving for an extra special occasion—and about his book.

   d. Miles and Maya kiss.

      Note: There is great tension in this area because Miles is having a hard time following his impulses, taking chances.

8. ALL FALLS APART

   a. Maya does not respond to Miles' kiss—awkward.

   b. Miles has to cover for Jack when Jack's fiancé calls.

   c. Jack leaves Miles for the day—he's off with Stephanie.

   d. Miles spends a lonely day.

   e. Miles has to listen to Jack's doubts about upcoming wedding.

   f. Miles has to hang out with Jack, Stephanie and Stephanie's family.

    g. Miles spends the night alone with his wine and porn magazine.

    h. Miles goes to see Maya—she's not working, doesn't see her. Gets drunk on his own.

    i. Miles plays golf with Jack, Jack is pushing him to go forward with his life. Golfers give them grief, Miles and Jack act crazy.

    j. Miles tells Jack he's tired of being a failure.

    Note: In this section, there are ups and downs… Maya and Miles do spend time together and have a good time (always let things go up and down/ obstacles and reversals…

    k. Picnic: Miles and Maya have a great time and spend the night together.

    l. Nearly immediate reversal: Miles accidentally spills the information that Jack is getting married in a few days.

9.   CRISIS

    a. Miles tells Maya the truth about Jack and his wedding (this is done off-screen).

10. CLIMAX

    a. Maya gets mad at Miles, he should not have been part of the lie.

    b. Miles gets news that his book was rejected, goes berserk in the winery.

    c. Stephanie beats up on Jack, Jack knows that Miles told Maya.

    d. Miles is left again by Jack when he goes after the waitress.

    e. Miles has to sneak into the waitress' house to retrieve Jack's wallet.

    f. Jack drives Miles' car into a tree.

    g. Miles and Jack arrive back at Jack's fiancé's house. Miles will not go in—doesn't want to deal with Jack's lies.

    h. Wedding. Miles sees ex-wife, finds out she's pregnant.

11. TRUTH COMES OUT

   a. Miles drinks his special bottle of wine—no longer saving it for
       a special occasion.

   b. Miles drives up to see Maya—hopeful ending—he has put the
       past behind.

SHORT GLOSSARY
OF SCREENWRITING TERMS

You want to know the language of the screenwriting world. You want to know what your fellow screenwriters and those executives are discussing. You want to be able to go through your work and ask yourself, have I used all the tools available to tell my story? You need to know these terms; most will become second nature as you work on your screenplay.

"A" STORY: The foremost plot of the film story that focuses on the main character's journey to achieve his or her goal.

ANTAGONIST: The character who gets in the way of the hero (see Protagonist); this character can be actively trying to stop the protagonist because of conflicting goals or it can be a character who, by nature, acts as a stopping block. Sometimes the antagonist is called a nemesis, sometimes a "bad guy", sometimes the "evil force," sometimes the "villain."

ANTI-HERO: The protagonist who does the wrong things for the right reason. A character who acts in a dishonorable way to achieve honorable goals. (Example: Michael in **GODFATHER,** Munney in **UNFORGIVEN,** Donnie in **DONNIE BRASCO.**)

ARC: A story that has a complete arc will have a beginning, middle and end. To create a satisfactory arc, characters, the state of the world and other elements should go through a change. (See Character Arc and Character Development.)

"B" STORY: A supporting subplot of the screen story that will directly affect the outcome of the "A" story. The "B" story will have its own arc; beginning, middle and end. In a story of a man climbing the corporate ladder, the "B" story could be the love story that pushes him to stand up for himself. In a crime drama, it could be the detective's home life, or his struggle with his own vices.

There can be more than one "B" story in a screen story. There can also be "C" or "D" stories that take up less time, but still have an arc of their own.

BACKSTORY: The events that make up the life of the character up until the moment the film story begins. These events bring the character to his or her readiness to take on the action of the story. Backstory helps answer the question of why the character is acting on and reacting to the forces of the story.

BEATS: Those silent moments within scenes that are charged with emotion; humorous or dramatic. Actors take beats within their scenes, directors and editors create beats in scenes to make sure an emotion or meaning is successfully conveyed.

BUTTON: Usually the last line in a scene that signals its completion. Often used in comedy scripts, as in a final word or line that "buttons" the joke.

CHARACTER ARC: The change in a character from the beginning of the screen story to its conclusion. Examples: A character goes from shy and retiring to being able to stand up for himself. A character goes from egotistical and completely self-serving to realizing that helping others also has its rewards.

CHARACTER DEVELOPMENT: Your main character will go on a journey in your story; starting at point A and ending at point Z. Or B. Or H. (It all depends on how much your character changes.) A character *must* change or you run the risk of your story being static. A character can grow from irresponsible to responsible, from naive to wise, or from fearful of love to willingness to take the risk of emotional commitment. Emotional growth is most important. Physical growth (as in a sports story) should always go hand in hand with emotional growth. The story you tell *must* force the character to take a hard look at himself and, in doing so, create the environment for the change to occur.

CLIMAX: The most exciting and important part of your story. This is usually in Act Three when your main character is fighting against all odds to achieve her goal. There can be no turning back. All is at risk. The Antagonist and opposing forces are at their most dangerous. The best climaxes are emotional and physical. The climax can bring about a catharsis. All story elements help lead up to the climax that will forever change the main character's life.

CATHARSIS: The moment when your character experiences some sort of revelation about himself or others, usually in a moment of great stress. This revelation usually brings about acceptance of self or situation and allows the main character to realize that she is forever changed.

CONFLICT: *"Drama is conflict and conflict is drama,"* is the crux of screenwriting. The hero rises to a great challenge and succeeds or fails, and along the way faces great conflict, both emotionally and physically.

CONFRONTATION: Characters facing their fears, their enemies, or obstacles. Screenplays are built on confrontation; nothing can come easily.

COVERAGE: Production companies and studios hire readers to write synopses of scripts that are sent to them. The reader will summarize the story, assess the writing skills, give an opinion on the commercial possibilities of the film story. This coverage is sent to the upper level executives with a recommendation: Read or don't read. An executive will choose to read the entire script if the coverage interests them.

CRISIS: A moment of decision usually found near the end of Act Two when the main character finds himself in the deepest darkest hell imaginable. She has to *decide* to give up or go forward or to take a path that looks dangerous either emotionally or physically or both. By making this moment one of decision, the writer ensures that the protagonist is retaining an active role in the story.

DEUS EX MACHINA: A Latin phrase referring to the use of an improbable character or unconvincing event used to resolve the plot. Example: The hero, in the climax of the film, is up against all odds and his success is in question. Suddenly an angel or powerful person or god or some character who is not indigenous to the story appears to "make things right." In most cases, the writer wants the hero to be responsible for the determination of his future. By using a deus ex machina, the writer is taking the outcome of the film story out of his protagonist's hands.

DEVELOPMENT EXECUTIVE: The person at the film studio or independent film company who will read your script/ hear your pitch/ help (or not help) you on the way to getting your film made.

DIALOGUE: The words the characters speak in the story.

DOUBLE-BIND: The main character faces an emotional or physical "either-or." A major choice that will affect the outcome of the story. Examples: The need to choose between family and career. The need to choose between lying to make things seem better, or telling the truth and stirring up possible havoc.

DRAMA: The portrayal of the human struggle to maintain value and give meaning to the actions taken in life. The more exciting and difficult this struggle is; the more drama. The more drama, the more conflict. Film stories are best when filled with conflict.

DRAMATIC QUESTION: The question that pertains to the central dilemma of the main character in the story. Example: Will he have the patience to win the girl's love? Will she have the strength to destroy the alien? Will he find the confidence to expose the crime?

ELEVEN STEP STORY STRUCTURE: A breakdown of a film story's structure, focused on the main character's physical and emotional journey.

EPIPHANY: A character's intuitive leap of understanding, when he "gets it" in a sudden burst of recognition. This can happen when a strong action occurs, or when he hears a certain word or sees a certain visual. A moment of understanding on a deep level.

FLAW: The character element that makes your characters *human and relatable.* A flaw can be physical or emotional; sometimes both. Examples of flaws:: insecurity, low self-esteem, dangerous pride... agoraphobia, short term memory loss, envy, greed, etc. Every good protagonist and every antagonist should have a flaw that affects their journey in the film story.

FORESHADOWING: Visual, action, dialogue or event that hints at situations or story points to come.

FORMAT: The proper arrangement of headings, slug lines, action lines, dialogue and character names on the page that make up a professional screenplay.

GENRE: The kind of story you are telling; is it a drama, comedy, thriller, or horror film? Is it a western, bio-pic, or sci-fi story? Most audiences choose which films by genre. Each genre calls for specific story elements.

HANDLES: Dialogue additions to make the characters' words seem more natural or specific. Examples: "Well,..." "Oh,..." "Just in case, ..." "Don't'cha know, " etc. Be careful of using handles too much, they can really slow down the pace of a story. Be vigilant, not every character in your film should use handles—or the same handle.

HIGH CONCEPT: A story idea that can be pitched and understood in one sentence or less. Examples: **TWISTER** (A tornado wreaks havoc, tornado chasers to the rescue.), JAWS (A shark attacks Martha's Vineyard, a new sheriff who is afraid of water must lead an unlikely crew of shark-chasers and save the town.) Other high concept films include **GLADIATOR, TITANTIC, BIG, FINDING NEVERLAND, MUNICH, WALK THE LINE, BROKEBACK MOUNTAIN...**

HOOK: An idea, sequence, character revelation or incident near the top of the film story that piques the audience's interest and brings the audience into the story.

IMDB: Internet source for film credits and other information on the business of film. (imdb.com)

INCITING INCIDENT: The event or moment that changes the normal life of your protagonist and sends her on the journey of the film.

LOG LINE: Two to three sentences that relate the basics of the film story, focusing on character arc and theme. Example: **GODFATHER** is a drama about Michael, the resourceful and determined son of a powerful Mafia leader who has decided to break away from the family to live a straight-laced "American Dream." When his family comes under attack by rival mob factions, he goes on a journey to discover that honor, duty and familial ties are the most important thing in his life.

LOW CONCEPT: A story idea that is not high concept. Low concept stories need more detailed explanation to understand the thrust of the film story, They usually turn more on character than on plot. Examples: **ADAPTATION, CHINATOWN, THE ENGLISH PATIENT, SIDEWAYS, NETWORK, THE SQUID AND THE WHALE…**

MISDIRECTION: The writer uses misdirection to guide the audience in a direction that will (hopefully) illuminate the story, but not necessarily answer the most immediate question posed by the character or plot. Example: **CHINATOWN;** Jake Gittes finds eyeglasses in the saltwater pond at Mrs. Mulwray's house. The audience (as well as Jake) is led to believe that this points to Mrs. Mulwray as a murderess. Only in following the misdirection does Jake find out the truth.

MOTIF: A recurring element in your story that can become an emotional benchmark. Think music, or a catch phrase, or a necklace, or park bench, or car or whatever element that becomes a symbol for the audience and helps reveal the character's emotional state.

OBSTACLE: Large and small problems or roadblocks (emotional or physical) that are put in the path of the protagonist that hinders his progress in attaining his goals.

OPTION: Payment for the privilege of using a literary piece (newspaper, book, poem, short story etc.) or biographical story or event for a certain length of time. Every option agreement will be different, in price and length of time.

OUTLINE: A document used by the writer to lay out the basic structure of his film story. The Eleven Step Story Structure template can be used as the base of an outline; this can then be expanded to include important events, emotions, plot elements of the story that can be built into each section of the classic story template. An outline is a tool used to keep a writer on track and on story. (See Treatment, which is a polished outline that can be used as a sales tool or as a document to turn into a producer/studio/ executive for approval before the writer goes to script.)

PITCH: The verbal presentation of your film story. A good pitch should be no more than ten minutes, should concentrate on the main character's growth and journey, set up the world and major conflicts of the story, sketch in the opposing and aiding forces and be exciting as you can make it. Be creative, bring in simple visual aids if available, but keep it short. Using the Eleven Step Story Structure as a guide will ensure that the pitch has a solid beginning, middle and end, includes a series of conflict and character change.

PLOT: Plot is the development of events and actions that move a story along.

PLOT TWIST: A sudden turn in the driving force of the film that either opens up or shuts down a story path in an unexpected way.

PREMISE: The story arc the writer is trying to explore with his film story: use the "WHAT IF…." (**TOOTSIE:** What if a chauvinistic actor who doesn't know how to treat women has to go undercover as a woman in order to get a part on a soap opera and find true love?)

PRODUCER: A person whose job entails shepherding a script to finished film.

PROTAGONIST: The main character of the film story who goes on a journey to achieve his goal. The "good guy," the hero or anti-hero. The character with whom the audience should get invested in and be willing to join on an emotional journey. The person with whom an audience is most likely to identify. This *active* character propels the action of the story forward.

PUBLIC DOMAIN: A book, article, or literary piece that is available to the public to freely adapt due to the length of time from its original publish date.

RESOLUTION: The final outcome of the film story, usually revealed at the conclusion. The resolution may include a glimpse of what the future holds. This is the time to tie up loose ends, to explain the previously unexplained.

REVELATION: A character comes to understand life, a person, a situation or himself in a new way.

REVERSAL: A story element that changes the direction of the film. Everything seems to be going well for your character and then quickly shifts to become an adverse situation. Or, conversely, everything seems to be going poorly and suddenly takes an upswing. Reversals will ensure that your story is filled with action and conflict.

RISING ACTION: The tempo of the telling of the film story begins to increase in pace. Most films will increase in pace (use shorter scenes) as they approach the climax and resolution

RUNNER: A series of repeating actions or words that have no plot arc in themselves. A runner can help show time passage, add comic relief, even serve to aid an epiphany. A runner can be "repeated as needed" in a screenplay. Examples: The series of breakfast scenes in **KRAMER VS KRAMER,** the bottle of wine Miles is keeping for a special occasion in **SIDEWAYS.**

SCREENPLAY: The film script. The written work the director, actors and film crews use as a base to create a film.

SCRIPT READER: A person who works at a studio or production company who reads scripts and recommends (or not) them to a Development Executive or Producer. (See Story Analyst and Coverage.)

SEQUENCES: The organization of a series of scenes that form a beginning, middle and end and move the story forward in a timely fashion.

SLUG LINE: The heading in a screenplay that tells the reader where a scene is taking place as well as the time of day. Example: EXT. PINK'S ROADHOUSE —NIGHT.

STEP SHEET: A breakdown, by location, of all the scenes in a story. This is a tool to reveal what's happening, scene by scene, in each act.

STORY ANALYST: A person who works at a studio or production company who reads scripts and recommends (or not) them to a Development Executive or Producer. (See Script Reader and Coverage.)

STORY EDITOR: A person who helps shape and polish stories and script for production. Usually a term used in television

SUBTEXT: The true meaning of a scene or piece of dialogue. What the character doesn't say, but clearly feels or desires or wants to say. A good actor will play the subtext of a scene. A good writer will not want to write "on the nose" (a term that refers to writing exactly what the character is thinking), but construct dialogue so that an actor understands the subtext of a scene.

THEME: The lesson or revelation or truism that the film story explores.. A simple way to figure out a theme is to try fill in the blanks: Without _____ there can be no _____. Examples: Without love there can be no happiness. Without believing in yourself, you can never achieve your goal.

TICKING CLOCK: An element of time imposed on a story to accelerate tension and excitement.

TREATMENT: A document, 8 to 12 pages in length, that relays the film story in prose style, much like a short story style. The treatment focuses on the protagonist's goals and character arc. The theme of the story should be apparent, as well as tone and genre. The most important plot elements should be included. This is not a step sheet or outline of the entire film story, a treatment is, in most cases, considered a sales tool; therefore the task is to highlight the main characters and the broader strokes of the plot that contribute to the character arc.

WGA: Writers Guild of America. The union which represents film and television writers. The union is a source of information for writers; lists of literary agents, legal advice and other business concerns of writers. It strives to build a community and regularly hold conferences for writers.

About the Author

JULE SELBO
PROFESSIONAL BIOGRAPHY

Jule Selbo's feature film **HARD PROMISES** stars Sissy Spacek and William Peterson. She wrote the animated **HUNCHBACK OF NOTRE DAME, PART DEUX,** released in 2002; winner of the BEST PREMIERE DVD award. The film was also nominated in the Best Screenplay category. She is a writer on **CINDERELLA TWO,** a Disney Video release, nominated for a Best DVD PREMIERE award. She has completed two fairytales projects for Disney and a script from her original pitch: "Fairies."

She has recently completed **UGLY** for the Jim Henson Company, co-written with Matthew Jacobs. Her pilot for a new **TIGGER** series has been put into production at Disney: **"SUPER SLEUTHS."** Her live action feature film, **THE GIRL WHO STRUCK OUT BABE RUTH** and the live action musical, **SLEEPING BEAUTY** at ABC Disney Studios are in development. She is a contributor on the animated series, **HEROES** and PBS' **MISADVENTURES OF MAYA AND MIGUEL.**

She has produced and written over 200 hours of television, among her credits: George Lucas' **YOUNG INDIANA JONES CHRONICLES, HERCULES** (Universal) ABC'S **LIFE GOES ON,** CBS'S **TOUCHED BY AN ANGEL,** Aaron Spelling's **MELROSE PLACE,** PBS'S **VOYAGE OF THE MIMI,** FOX'S **SPACE: ABOVE AND BEYOND,** HBO'S **PRISON STORIES: WOMEN ON THE INSIDE** (Cable Ace Award nomination), MTV'S **UNDRESSED,** ABC'S **TIME COP,** NICKELODEON'S **SPORTS THEATRE** as well as **THE FLASH, SINBAD** (Syndicated) **TALES FROM THE DARKSIDE, MONSTERS, SEARCH FOR TOMORROW** (Writer's Guild Award for Outstanding Writing). She was executive-producer and head writer on a MTV series created by Roland Joffe, completing 110 episodes.

More animation work includes Disney's **ANGELA ANACONDA** for Fox Children's Network and Disney's **CLASSIC STORIES.**

Her most recent play, **OBJECTS** was produced Spring 2004 in Santa Ana at the Grand Central Theatre, directed by Larry Peters. Another play,

ISOLATE, received productions in New York (Westbeth Theatre) and Los Angeles (Theatre 6470). Other plays; **NO STRANGER** (Annenberg Center, Philadelphia) **SOULS ON ICE** (NYC), **BOILING POINT** (NYC) **THE WEDDING** (Actors Theatre of Louisville One Act Festival), **DR. FEDDER** (Actors Theatre of Louisville Children's Theatre) **TWO NOT SO TALL WOMEN** (Interact Theatre, Los Angeles).

Her first young adult fiction book **PILGRIM GIRL, DIARY AND RECIPES OF HER FIRST YEAR IN THE NEW WORLD** (co-written with Laura Peters) was published March 2005. Her short stories have appeared in **ALFRED HITCHCOCK MYSTERY MAGAZINE.**

She is a full time professor at California State University in Fullerton, where she teaches Screenwriting. She conducts seminars and classes at UCLA Extension as well as other venues and works as a private script consultant.

Index